THE NEW
GRAPHIC
DESIGNER'S
HANDBOOK

THE NEW
GRAPHIC DESIGNER'S HANDBOOK

Alastair Campbell

RUNNING PRESS
PHILADELPHIA, PENNSYLVANIA

A QUARTO BOOK

First published in the USA as
The Graphic Designer's Handbook in 1983 by
Running Press

Reprinted 1984
Reprinted 1985
Reprinted 1986
Revised 1987, 1988
Reprinted 1989
Reprinted 1991
Second edition 1993

9 8 7 6 5 4 3 2 1
Digit on the right indicates the number of this printing

ISBN 1-56138-286-8 (cloth)

This edition was designed and produced by
Quarto Publishing plc
6 Blundell Street, London N7 9BH

Senior Editor Cathy Meeus
Copy Editors Maggi McCormick, Deirdre Clark
Designer Alastair Campbell
Art Director Moira Clinch
Publishing Director Janet Slingsby
Photographs by Michael Freeman, Peter Hince, Anthony Blake
Illustrations by Alastair Campbell, Edwina Keene, Elaine Keenan,
Abdul Aziz Khan, John Woodcock, Martin Woodford

This book contains examples of computer software and graphic design work.
These examples are included for the purposes of criticism and review.

Film output in Great Britain by The Alphabet Set
Manufactured in Hong Kong by Regent Publishing Services Ltd
Printed in Hong Kong by Leefung Asco Printers Ltd

The author would like to thank the many people who have helped in the
preparation of this book, especially the following: Simon Phillips; Clive Crook;
Roger Pring; Michael Freeman; Peter Hince; Nicholas Dawe of Folio; David
Broad; and in particular Cathy Meeus at Quarto.

This book may be ordered from the publisher.
Please add $2.50 for postage and handling.
But try your bookstore first!
Running Press Book Publishers
125 South Twenty-second Street
Philadelphia, Pennsylvania 19103

Contents

INTRODUCTION

"**W**ho needs a graphic designer? Bill in sales has got a desktop computer, so *he* can design our next catalog." The now familiar cry in this cost-sensitive world. But does that mean that *anyone* with a computer can design, typeset and generate fancy graphics? Hardly. Just as putting a Stradivarius into the hands of Bill in sales won't necessarily enable him to produce beautiful music – or any music at all – so giving him the right tools doesn't mean he'll be able to create successful graphics.

When I wrote the first edition of *The Graphic Designer's Handbook*, the "designer-friendly" desktop computer did not exist, and that edition bore no references to the use of computers as a design tool. Things have certainly changed! For better or worse, it will not be unusual for a computer to be the *only* tool in a design studio. And it was only ten years ago that I wrote the book. In that relatively short time some sections of the graphic arts industries have been all but wiped out.

Take typesetting, for instance. In that industry, old-style craftsmen have been replaced by, or transformed into, a new generation of technicians, many of whose education and training owes more to the microchip than to the esthetics and traditions of typography. Thus the responsibility of preserving the craft of typography now lies almost solely with us – the graphic and typographic designers. While we must respond to innovations positively – after all, the new technology has produced some excellent design tools – at the same time, we must monitor their use so that aesthetic standards are upheld.

Design technology may seem as daunting for contemporary designers as a printing press might have been to a medieval scribe. However, whatever the technology, the fundamental properties of design have not varied over the centuries; the main purpose of any design – and, hence, of any designer – is to communicate its intentions with clarity, flair, and esthetic appeal. Of course, the design task is now far more complex than it was for the scribe, whose only concern were his pens or brushes, paints or inks and the parchments on which his designs were directly created. Today, we designers have a far more complex task. Although our aims remain the same as those of the scribe, the technology involved in achieving them has reached a point of bewildering complexity. At no time in design history have we been required to know and understand as much as we are today. Unlike the medieval scribe, no modern designer can design in isolation, but some designers will inevitably have similar feelings when faced with digital typography to those of the scribe when he was confronted with movable type. Thus, to work effectively as designers, it is essential that we overcome the barriers that have been created, ironically enough, by technological progress. We can achieve this only by a thorough understanding of new technologies so that we can shed the restrictions and inhibitions borne of ignorance, leaving us free to get on with the creative aspects of design.

These days, to fulfill our responsibilities to our profession, we designers must accumulate knowledge from a variety of sources hitherto unrelated to graphic design. The main purpose of this book is to provide such a source. It aims to provide an essential reference guide to both the process of graphic design as well the technology involved in generating an end product. It will provide you with access to information previously only available in lengthy and highly-specialized technical tomes. Thus, this new edition incorporates references to computers in all the appropriate places, and contains a more detailed explanation in the chapter on equipment.

What else does the book offer? In planning it, I decided it should fulfill three basic functions. The text, in general, serves as an introduction to the design process, primarily for the novice designer (a prevalent species these days, with the advent of "desktop publishing") or, indeed, user of design, although I hope that some of the information in it – particularly that on new technology – will serve as a reminder to seasoned professionals that a refresher course in basics can sometimes be useful. At the same time, it is designed to provide instant reference – in the form of tint charts, conversion tables and so on – for the experienced designer. Finally, I believe it can provide an insight into various technical aspects of the design process which readers may not previously have experienced.

The hype surrounding the ease-of-use ethos of the desktop computer – bringing the world of typography and design, and the means to manipulate it, to the fingertips of all – would lead us to believe that the days of the professional graphic designer are numbered. Paradoxically, however, this very availability of high-quality desktop output of typography and design may also bring with it a greater understanding by the layman of the design process as a whole, and of the creative elements of that process in particular. Hopefully then, the designer's role will become increasingly valued for its creative and esthetic contribution to the world we live in.

The more readily information about your tools is available at your fingertips, the easier it will be for you to get on with the work in hand. Don't drown in the sea of technology. And remember that, as yet, there is no substitute for the imagination and individuality of a creative designer – no computer has yet been devised – or ever will be – to take over that job.

Alastair Campbell

1
THE DESIGN BRIEF
The client/Briefing and checklist/Fees/
Schedules/Contracts/Roughs

Whatever its end purpose, all design starts from the same premise. This is that the task of the designer is to fulfill two fundamental considerations—one to the client, the other to the client's market. In every undertaking, these considerations are the most important and upon them rest the design's success or failure.

The client It will be extremely rare for you – the designer – to work without a commission of some kind; and, even if an original concept comes from you, someone else – the client – will eventually pay for the work. Although, in purest terms, the client is ultimately the person who pays the bills and who takes final decisions, he or she may not necessarily be the one who is most informed about how the market is to be reached. This is why advertising agencies, design groups, publishers, and art directors frequently act as marketing advisors and intermediaries.

Briefing This, the first stage in virtually any job, is the moment when its parameters must be established. Certain vital factors such as budgets and schedules will be discussed, but the first consideration for you as the designer is to decide whether you are suitable for the job. Under no circumstances should you overestimate your capabilities, and for this reason it is essential to establish the scope and complexity of any commission during the initial stages of the first briefing.

Briefings differ according to whether you are freelance, or work as a staff designer. As the former, you may be given a greater degree of freedom than as the latter, when you may find that the job specifications have to fit within a predetermined house style. This is particularly so in the case of corporate programs and in publishing. Since freelance designers are often also given a greater degree of financial responsibility than staff designers, it is very important that they are able to inspire the client with confidence at a briefing.

The language designers use must always be tailored to the understanding of everybody present. For instance, if the briefing is with an art director, language can be more specialized than if non-technical people are present. It is a great mistake to try to impress an audience by using highly technical terms, as this can often be intimidating.

While nearly all designers may go into a meeting with their own predetermined ideas, it is unwise to stick to them rigidly – even though they can be useful in forming a basis for discussion. A dogmatic approach may well cost you the commission – you must expect issues to be raised from all sides until some kind of composite picture evolves.

Even if your work is known to the client, it is always a good idea to take examples of previous work to a briefing in order to assist discussion of ideas that may be difficult to explain verbally. This makes it much easier for you to put forward your point of view or to point to particular treatments or techniques.

It is essential to take a notepad for jotting ideas or summarizing facts. Sometimes a calculator and a cassette recorder can be useful when complex technical details need to be worked out or recorded for future reference (use a tape recorder openly – in some places, it is illegal to use it without the knowledge or consent of those others who are present). It is of paramount importance that you remember to ask all the necessary questions about the job before going on to the next stage of the commission. To make sure that nothing is forgotten, prepare, in advance, a checklist of questions covering all eventualities – even if some questions may be irrelevant once the exact nature of the job has been established. Areas of doubt may lead to problems later; it could be embarrassing to have to contact the client after the initial briefing with questions the meeting was arranged to answer.

After all the basic facts are established, you must then decide whether or not to accept the commission. In most circumstances, you will make this decision at the first briefing. However, it may not be possible to give an immediate answer since, before you undertake to do any work, you should give careful thought to every aspect of a job, such as the costing and schedule. It is better to take time considering whether a job is possible before agreeing to take on a commission, rather than risk letting the client down later.

Briefing checklist A list of general questions, such as the following, worked out in advance will provide a basic structure for discussion at the briefing:

Client Make sure you know exactly who this is – and get the spelling of their name right!

Date and time Make a note of when the first meeting takes place – if you are dealing with, say, related topics or products at separate meetings, this will reduce the chances of confusion later.

People present Write down the names of all the people present at the meeting and do not be afraid to ask how any unfamiliar ones are spelled. Just as important, find out what their role is and why they are at the meeting. It may be that the person with whom you will be working most closely did not actually contribute much in the initial meeting.

Job description Agree on a name for the project, or at least give it a working title.

Market It is essential that you understand who the job is aimed at – to some extent the market will dictate the level of design. Establish, for instance, whether the job is to be aimed at a more sophisticated audience ("up-scale"), or a less sophisticated one ("down-scale"), and find out what the age group of the intended readership will be as this can influence design. Clients often already have a fairly clear picture of the type of people – their age-group, tastes, and lifestyle – who make up their market. It is up to you to ask for relevant information so the design can be tailored accordingly: sophisticated diagrams, for example, will not be appropriate for a readership of young children. No matter how well executed, any design should always be produced with a well-defined target audience in mind.

Budget considerations Establish whether a budget has been set –

usually it will have been, but sometimes clients are out of touch with current prices. Always agree to give the client a detailed break-down of all costs, including your own time. It is a good idea to over-estimate slightly when working out the budget so that the client is not presented with an unexpectedly inflated bill when the work is finished. In cases where the budget has already been determined, it is your responsibility to decide how the money should be apportioned within the job, although everybody working on the project should be consulted. Broadly speaking, budgets should make provision for the following:

Design fee This is what you charge the client and the figure should be adhered to strictly, provided the job specification does not change in any way.

Copywriting/text The cost of this can be difficult to work out, but it becomes easier with experience. You should make a rough estimate of how many words will have to be commissioned – writers generally charge per word (in the United States) or per 1,000 words (in the United Kingdom).

Illustration/photography To an extent the intended readership will dictate the degree of sophistication of imagery and therefore expenditure. If pictures have to be bought in from an agency or library, a picture researcher will probably have to be hired and copyright fees may have to be paid.

Printing Designers handling a high volume of work usually have a constant, sometimes unwelcome, stream of printers knocking at their doors offering print quotations. While it may be tempting to ask each and every one of them to provide quotations for a job, three is generally considered adequate. When choosing a printer, cost must be balanced against quality and to this end you should aim to achieve the highest possible standard – and maintain it over-all – at the lowest possible price. Sometimes it is more expedient to ask a printer to quote for all related services such as typesetting and color separations, but today these are usually handled by specialists and you should obtain independent quotations. Many clients and writers now supply copy on computer disk; if you do not use a computer yourself, a typesetter or service bureau will charge you either by the hour or by the page (depending on size) to output it as typeset copy. If they are required to key a job, typesetters usually charge per 1,000 ens or by the number of keystrokes required to complete the job. There will be extra charges for complicated setting – for instance, where words have to be set or run around an irregular shape.

Originators of black-and-white and color images ("origination house" or "color separation house") will want to know not only the quantity, but also the size of each individual image and whether

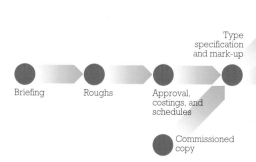

Right: This flow chart shows all the stages of the design process, from the initial briefing to printing and the finished job. The briefing session between designer and client is of paramount importance, since it is there that the concept of the project is discussed and defined. From then, the designer's task is to fulfill the demands of the brief that has been agreed, produce the job on time, and keep within the budget.

Briefing

Roughs

Approval, costings, and schedules

Type specification and mark-up

Commissioned copy

there will be silhouettes or other peculiarities. If a job involves a large quantity of separations, as in an illustrated book, some origination houses can be persuaded to estimate on a flat rate basis – that is, they will give a single price for each separation regardless of size or, alternatively, they may quote a page rate for the job, regardless of how many images there may be on each page.

Although final details may depend on the design solution, the printer will need to be given the following information before a price can be quoted: the run, extent, format, printings (one color = one printing), paper quality, approximate number of halftones, type of binding, and to where the job is to be delivered. The printer will also need to know whether computer disk, final film, or flat artwork will be supplied, or whether the job will require complete page make-up. If the latter is the case, the printer will need much more specific information, such as sample layouts showing the proportion of type to halftone illustrations, ruled lines, and so on. It is usually necessary to obtain confirmation quotations from the printer once a design has been approved by the client.

When obtaining quotations it is important to remember that the fields in which printers work are as varied as those of designers. A large, traditional book printer, for instance, may not be able to turn a rush job around quickly, while a trade printer who does general work of all kinds, though extremely quick, may be very expensive. Also, a small printer (sometimes called a "jobbing printer") might not be able to bind a booklet and would therefore send the job out, thus increasing the cost.

Schedules In virtually all cases your client will tell you when the job should be completed, and you should then give an immediate indication as to whether it can be done in the time. If it seems completely outside the bounds of possibility, you should say so immediately. How much time a job will take to do will vary according to its complexity and your own experience as a designer. Another important factor is how fast you and everyone else involved with the project normally works. Some people enjoy working under pressure, but others do not and this may affect the speed and, sometimes, quality, of the work produced. Of all the elements involved in scheduling, only the more mechanical ones, such as printing, can be forecast with any degree of accuracy, and even these will be prone to a degree of uncertainty.

Contracts During the early stages of a design commission, some kind of written agreement should be drawn up between you and your client. In many cases the confirmation of the commission may not occur until after the presentation of the initial concept of a design idea, since you may be in the increasingly common position of having to "tender" for the job (compete with other designers). The

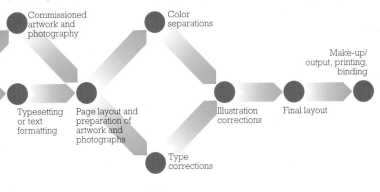

Commissioned artwork and photography

Color separations

Make-up/ output, printing, binding

Typesetting or text formatting

Page layout and preparation of artwork and photographs

Illustration corrections

Final layout

Type corrections

extent of an agreement or contract will normally reflect the complexity of the work commissioned. Small jobs, such as a letterhead or a poster, may need only a letter, whereas jobs such as a complete corporate program will require a proper contract, or memorandum of agreement. Even before a contract is drawn up, a few guidelines should be observed:

Put everything in writing No matter how seemingly insignificant, all points raised at a meeting – whether resolved or not – should be put in writing. This will reduce the chance of any misunderstanding arising in the future.

Agree the fee before starting work It is sometimes difficult, if not impossible, to know exactly how much a job will cost at the outset, but you should give your client an indication of the minimum and maximum requirement before any work is undertaken. In any event, once a final presentation has been made, the fee must be agreed with the client. If possible, try to agree some sort of rejection or cancellation fee at this stage as well. A client may not wish to proceed with a job – or accept a design solution – for any number of reasons, but a job is much less likely to be cancelled or rejected on a whim if such a fee has been agreed in advance. On the other hand, you must not expect your client to accept unsatisfactory work, so, before a rejection fee is paid, expect your client to ask for further solutions. If these are still not accepted, you can only, at very best, expect to be paid for the work you have done to date – and, most probably, your client will resist paying you anything at all.

Costing design time
Costing the time involved in any commission accurately is vitally important. As a rule of thumb, a designer working alone should cost an appropriate hourly rate, based on a notional annual salary, and multiply by 2. If studio space is shared, the minimum multiplier should be 2.5 and, if other people are employed, 3 to 4, since the extra overheads must be taken into account.

Agree schedule of payments The method by which payments are made largely depends on how you conduct your business. If you are working alone, you will have a very clear view of your cash flow and know when you need to be paid. The larger your company or group is, the more the terms of payment need to be controlled.

The complexities and time span of the job will also affect the schedule of payments. The simplest and most common method is to give the client an invoice once the work has been completed. Other methods of payment are merely variations on this. Sometimes you may wish to ask for an advance payment of anything between 10 and 50 percent of your design fee; generally speaking, the larger the job, the larger the advance that you can expect. Sometimes when fairly substantial sums of money are involved, payments are spread over a longer period of time. The criteria for spreading the payments depend to a large extent on the amount of money you will be required to pay out during the course of the job for illustration, photography, and so on. The client will also have to make sure that paying out advances will not cause serious problems with his or her own cash flow. A simple way of achieving an interim payment schedule is for you to agree with your client that you be paid a fixed sum of money at regular intervals, say monthly, over the time span of the job. Most clients, however, prefer payments to be related to specific, tangible moments in the job schedule. For example, the total fee may be split into three equal installments with one-third payable at the beginning of the job or on signature of a contract (as a gesture of faith), one-third on approval of the design, and the final installment once the job is completed.

Roughs Once briefed, the next stage is for you to show your client a preliminary drawing – known as a "rough," "visual," "scamp," or "tissue." This can take a variety of forms – from an outline rough, giving an indication of a basic idea, to a detailed, realistic facsimile of the final thing. Again, the level varies according to the demands of the client or whoever is being given the presentation. A rough for an art director, say, need not necessarily be rendered as fully as one being prepared for a salesperson who has less experience of visualizing final stages.

Although the medium in which the rough is executed must be sympathetic to the style of the design, pencil and felt-tipped pen are usual choices for hand-rendered roughs. The former is better for more detailed work, particularly if typography plays an important part in the design, whereas the latter is ideal for rendering rapid impressions of photographs or artwork. If you use a computer, you will most likely present roughs as laser proofs, or, at least, use laser proofs as an integral part of the rough. If you present laser proof roughs, edit them down to only the relevant ones – a pile of paper with what looks like the same design on each will not impress your client.

One of the purposes of the preliminary rough is to create a talking point – it should never be inflexible. For instance, if the design incorporates pictures, at this stage you do not have to supply the actual transparencies that are going to be used. What is important is to establish what type of images are envisaged. Similarly, in a typographical design, there is no need to choose the exact font to be used, but the rough should certainly show headings, subheadings and the projected area the text type is to occupy.

The designer may wish or may be asked to present two or three alternative versions of these first thoughts, and because this can be extremely time-consuming, the problems of time and cost-effectiveness should be considered yet again. Even if you are not completely satisfied with a piece of work, there is always a point at which you should stop making further changes to it. This is particularly the case when making a preliminary rough, which may well have to be altered several times.

A "finished" rough, on the other hand, must be an accurate facsimile of the final product. Although any images still need not be exact or final, they must give a very good impression of the final artwork or photographs; rough images should therefore be quite elaborate renderings, colored if applicable. It is also sound practice to bring examples of the illustrator's or photographer's work to the approval meeting, so that the client has a clear idea of what style and standard the end product will eventually be. In some cases, especially in advertising, the actual, final artwork or photographs form part of the presentation, even at the risk of rejection by the client.

What is finally presented should obviously be as attractive and professional as possible. In most cases the finished rough should be mounted on black card, protected with an acetate covering and given a black or colored surround. Remember that the client may wish to use it for display purposes and may even want to photograph it. Sometimes, all typesetting – headlines, text, captions, and so on – must be "live," or real, otherwise "dummy," or false, type can be used. If live copy is required the designer must establish an effective liaison with the writer, so that the illustrative treatment reflects the text and is ready when needed. However, even if dummy type is being used, the headings should be live if possible.

2
COMMISSIONING
Words/Photography/Illustration/
Agents/Copyright

There are few design jobs which can be completed entirely by your skills alone, and most involve the added expertise of specialists such as illustrators, photographers, writers, editors, and so on. In many cases, such people may have already been commissioned to work on your job, but more often it will be up to you to enlist the services of any extra necessary professional services that are required.

Words Commissioning words is normally the responsibility of an editor rather than the designer, but sometimes you will be called upon to commission words if they have not already been supplied by your client. In ideal circumstances, you should specify the total number of words required and, if the design is sufficiently advanced, the number of lines and the measure (number of characters per line) to which they should be typed. This is by far the most efficient method, as it means that problems which arise if the copy has to be cut and reset can be avoided. However, it may also impose a degree of rigidity on the design at a relatively early stage.

Sometimes, particularly in book publishing, the text supplied may be "final": in other words, it cannot be changed or cut, and so it is the crucial determining factor in the design. More frequently, the designer asks the person responsible for the words to cut, fill, add, and even rewrite if the need arises.

If a designer is totally responsible for the text, and possibly required to commission a technical specialist, it is a good idea to involve a copy editor to make sure that the final text is of an acceptable standard. Whatever the job, the designer and editor or copywriter must collaborate; neither process can be carried out in isolation. This is especially important if captioning is involved, although this is normally done – particularly in book publishing – at a later stage.

The procedure involved in preparing and editing text varies, depending on how many people are required to read it and what form it takes. The "raw," or first, copy will be read and then submitted for the client's approval. It will then be amended and sent for typesetting. The typeset text should be read initially for literal errors – typos or spelling mistakes – by the typesetter's own readers and then returned to the editor or designer, who will each check it in turn. If you are setting text on your own computer, you must be extra careful in checking it for typos, although if the original copy was supplied on disk, there is less likelihood of errors creeping in.

Photography Photographs used by designers either exist already and are held by picture libraries and museums or must be specially commissioned. If a photograph is to be commissioned, the brief you give to the photographer must be as full as possible, and this may well necessitate the client being present. You should select a photographer specifically for the job in hand since most specialize in particular subject areas such as fashion, food, still life, travel, reportage, and so on. A photographer may also prefer using a particular format, although this will be determined mainly by their chosen subject area – fashion photographers, for instance, tend to use smaller format cameras not only because of their portability, but also because of the copious film use which is usually necessary when photographing people.

Having chosen your photographer, then, your immediate decisions now concern film format (large, medium, or small) – this decision depends on what the subject matter is and how you intend using the pictures – and whether the photographs are to be color, black-and-white, or a selection of both. The type of picture needed should be described as clearly as possible, particularly in terms of atmosphere and style, although you will preempt lengthy discussion if you are already familiar with the photographer's work .

Economic constraints must also be taken into consideration. Photographers normally charge by the day, and it must be ascertained whether the day rate includes expenses, since this can add considerably to the cost. Expenses normally consist of the cost of film and processing, travel costs, hire of models or props, and so on. These ancillary costs become particularly important in special circumstances; for example, if an outdoor location is required, you may also need good weather – something that is not within your control (in such circumstances, "weather" insurance – although expensive – is often prudent). Another important thing to remember is that if a photograph requires a special set to be built in the photographer's studio, a fee will usually be charged – usually, although by no means always, at a reduced day rate – for the time it takes to be built, as it is likely to prevent the photographer from doing other work at the same time.

If models are required for a shoot, be sure that they have signed a "release" form. This waives any claim to the photographs that a model may make at a later date. The photographer will usually make sure that the release is signed, *but always check that it has been.*

The photographer can supply the designer with either prints or transparencies, so you should specify which of these you require. Transparencies are virtually always the *de facto* norm, especially if color separations are to be made for commercial printing purposes. It is normal for more than one shot of the subject to be presented, unless large formats are involved. Having a selection will give you a greater degree of choice and the photographer a reasonable margin of error.

Ownership of the copyright in the photographs *and of the photographs themselves* (ownership of the former does not necessarily mean ownership of the latter, and *vice versa*) must be established in advance. There are many ways in which this system works, including the following:

1 You, on behalf of your client, will buy the copyright and the original work (that is, the physical print or piece of film) in its entirety, including all the shots taken on that assignment whether they are used or not. This is particularly the case when large investments in photographic commissions can be justified only by further use of the photographs. In such cases it is important that any assignment of copyright is made in writing with the signatures of both the client and the photographer. Also make sure that the photographer fully understands what is being agreed. This is particularly important when the photographer is confronted with such daunting, but quite usual (and legitimate), clauses as this:

"In consideration of the total amount to be paid by your company to me on delivery of the work detailed herein, I hereby assign to your company the ownership of the original work and the whole of the copyright and rights in the nature of copyright throughout the world in the said work for the full period of copyright and all renewals and extensions thereof."

If there is nothing in writing to the contrary, ownership of both the copyright and of the original work automatically belong to the photographer.

2 The client, having bought all rights, may agree to the pictures being placed in a photographic library, with the photographer receiving an agreed percentage of the monies the client receives and the library retaining the remainder.

3 The client may require ownership only of rights and pictures of the photographs actually used, with the "overs" (unused pictures) being returned to the photographer. In some cases the client will insist on being informed, and sometimes asked for formal permission, before photographs can be re-used. The client may also insist on an acknowledgement being printed alongside the photograph.

4 The client may be granted use of the photographs for one time only, with any further use being subject to a further fee. In this case, the photographer will retain all rights and ownership.

Existing pictures are usually obtained from a picture library, agency, or museum photography department by a researcher working from a brief prepared by you and, if appropriate, from a text. The brief should specify the total number of pictures, subject areas, and budget limitations; unless specific pictures are required, the selection should be as wide as possible within the subject area. The time taken to obtain pictures must also be considered, particularly if a selection from an international source is required.

It is essential at the earliest possible stage to specify which reproduction rights are needed so that the costs can be taken into account. This normally means specifying exactly in what form, size, and country the photographs will appear, so that reproduction fees, usually payable upon publication, can be calculated. Some museums and galleries charge a rental fee instead of a reproduction fee, so these pictures should be returned as soon as possible. Photographs borrowed from other sources should also be returned as soon as possible after use; otherwise, holding fees, as well as reproduction fees, may be charged. Many sources, particularly museums, sell prints or transparencies as duplicates – that is, prints from either specially commissioned photographs or existing negatives. Although you are not required to return these after use, if you re-use them for a purpose other than that for which they were originally bought, then further permission should be sought.

Whatever the source of the photograph, take care of the original; replacement fees can be extremely high, especially if the picture is a rare one. Transparencies should be carefully checked for any kind of mark as soon as they are received. If there is a mark on a transparency, it is essential to inform the agency or supplier immediately that it was damaged on receipt so that they do not charge you for it. Picture agencies frequently supply duplicate transparencies;

because they are not usually as sharp as the originals, they should also be thoroughly examined for acceptability. Finally, if you handle transparencies frequently, you would be well advised to take out an insurance policy to cover any possible damage or loss.

Illustration Like photographers, most illustrators specialize either in a particular subject area or by having an individual style. You must bear this in mind at the commissioning stage, since the style of the illustration must be sympathetic with the subject it is illustrating. Again, familiarity with the artist's work is highly desirable. You should be wary of asking an illustrator to produce work in a style with which he or she is unfamiliar – the result may not only be a disaster, but may also be very costly.

Fees must be established in advance, and you should give the illustrator the fullest possible brief. You must tell the illustrator whether the illustration is to be reproduced in full-color, specially mixed colors, or black-and-white; the size to which the artwork is to be drawn; whether any overlays are required for mechanical tints; and so on. Cost – always such an important factor (illustration can be far more expensive than photography) – must be balanced against quality. Any substandard work which cannot be improved should be rejected, in which case you may have to pay to the illustrator a rejection fee, although such an eventuality must be established in advance since this could play havoc with your own budgets. It is also vital to establish very clear deadlines for delivery of the material, preferably well in advance of the date at which the work is actually needed, to allow time for approval and possible alterations. Many designers and art directors will threaten cancellation or a reduction of the fee if work is not delivered on time.

The artwork itself is frequently drawn at a larger size than the one at which it will finally print. "Half-up" (actually, one and a half times final print size) or twice up (x 2) is the most commonly used scale for illustration work. Use of this technique can make the printed ver-

---

THE LAW OF COPYRIGHT

For all designers, understanding what copyright means and the regulations covering it is a vital part of the job. The subject is complex and subject to frequent change. Therefore the advice given here should be taken only as a general guide and not as a substitute for professional legal advice. Broadly speaking, copyright is designed to protect original work and stop it from being used or copied without the agreement of the person who originally created it, unless the copyright has been legally relinquished. This must be agreed formally in writing in what lawyers term an "assignment" of copyright. This is irrevocable, as opposed to giving permission to reproduce a copyright work. In the latter case, the user of the work is granted the right to reproduce it under certain terms, conditions and circumstances – and in no others. The artist retains so-called residual copyright. Paintings, sculptures, drawings, engravings, manuscripts, and photographs all enjoy natural copyright protection, with the creator of the work owning the copyright in it from the moment of its creation. This ruling seems simple, but, in fact, the legal position is more complex because of the problem of commissions. Some work is protected by copyright, even if

commissioned, and some is not. Commissioned photographs and portraits – whether painted, drawn, or engraved – are not the artist's copyright but all other work is, unless the artist has relinquished copyright protection. Conversely, an artist's employer owns copyright in any work produced during the period of employment, again unless the rules of copyright are formally varied to the contrary. Copyright in artwork lasts for the artist's lifetime and (in the United States) for 75 years after his or her death, during which time the copyright is owned by the artist's heirs. Copyright in photographs lasts for 75 years from first publication. Unpublished photographs are protected indefinitely.

If work is reproduced without express or implied permission, the user is in breach of copyright and can be sued by the artist.

Copyright exists naturally in all completed work, with the exceptions given here. It also cannot be used to protect an idea, though it does protect rough notes and sketches Though there is no legal requirement to do so, it is sensible to indicate any claims to copyright with a credit line, including name, the copyright symbol and the year of creation.

sion look crisper and tighter; it can also help cut costs at the separation stage because it is cheaper to originate a number of illustrations in proportion. Many illustrators, however, stipulate that their work must be used at the size at which it is drawn, and some may even prefer their work to be enlarged; this is because the style and character of their work may rely upon the artwork being reproduced at the same size or larger.

Some illustrators prefer to provide roughs even before they quote for a job – it can be difficult to estimate the time a drawing may take to do, and in any case the illustrator may not have the same solution in mind as the designer. An advance pencil rough will also guarantee that the brief has been fulfilled and that all the elements required are present. For the final artwork most surfaces are acceptable, although a flexible one is most desirable since, for reproduction purposes, it can be scanned direct (see p111). Otherwise, a photographic transparency may have to be made from the artwork.

You should also establish who owns the illustration, as distinct from who owns the copyright. It is law that unless it is clearly stipulated that the client is buying the artwork, the original remains the property of the illustrator after its initial use, and he or she retains the copyright.

Agents Generally speaking, one of the simplest ways to gain immediate access to a wide variety of photographic or illustrative skills is to consult an agent. Agents often operate in specific fields such as publishing or advertising, or represent photographers or illustrators who specialize in particular subject areas such as natural history. However, many agents will accept work of any kind. Obviously, larger agencies will be able to offer the widest range of services, although smaller agencies, operating with as few as 12 artists, but in more specialized or sophisticated markets, offer an equally valuable service.

One immediate advantage of using agents, apart from the sheer volume of choice, is that they are frequently far more flexible than an artist or photographer when it comes to negotiating fees. A general fear is that by dealing with an agent, an image will inevitably end up costing more than by negotiating directly with its creator. However, agents will claim that this is not the case and that their charges – particularly if they are artists – are able to devote more time to the job in hand if they do not have to worry about fees and finding future work. Nevertheless, there are always exceptions, and if the budget is a major factor, it is nearly always possible to find an artist who will do a job cheaply – but remember that the standard of work may not be quite so high.

Another concern among art directors and designers is that by using agents it is often easy to lose the rapport and creative feedback that is generated by dealing directly with an artist. However, agents are moving toward a less proprietorial attitude, and most will happily allow, and even encourage, a direct working relationship between artist and client.

Agents pay great attention to the territories in which rights are granted. Artists and photographers generally accept that they are paid for work done regardless of where it is seen, whereas an agent may want to charge for specific territorial or multiple rights, although this usually only applies to further use of photographs or artwork. Eliminate the confusion caused by such assumptions by clarifying the rights situation with everyone concerned on the job – including your client – *before* anyone does any work.

3
THE DESIGN PROCESS

Typography/Preparing manuscripts/Proofs/Design/
Grids/Layouts/Preparing photographs and artwork/Color
correction/ Paste-up/Printing/Book production/
Magazine design

In many respects, it is curious that the term "graphic design" is given to a profession in which the time spent on *design* itself represents such a small proportion of the whole job. In practice, you – as designer – will probably act more as a coordinator, with your knowledge incorporating extensive aspects of every ancillary reproduction process from computer typesetting systems to complete magazine or book printing. This knowledge permits you to make esthetic decisions with the maximum amount of flexibility within each technical parameter. Indeed, you must use such esthetic awareness to police the standards so often eroded along the path of technological advancement.

It is important, therefore, that you are totally familiar with every aspect of the design process in order that you can tackle with confidence and assurance the most important part of your involvement in that process – that of design itself.

Typography Among the many basic considerations of typographic design, the two which require perhaps greatest understanding are the varying width of alphabetical characters and of the spaces between them. This understanding is essential in order to achieve the twin aim of esthetic appeal and legibility.

The width of alphabetic characters, or the space allotted to them, depends largely on the equipment used to produce them. For instance, manual typewriters use characters all of the same, or "fixed," widths. Thus, in order to maintain consistent letter spacing, they use exaggeratedly wide serifs on letters such as "i" and "l" (that is, i and l). This gives a string of characters (words) an apparently even appearance by reducing the amount of white space between them. Computer systems, on the other hand, generate characters of almost infinitely variable widths, thus providing the potential for perfect optical spacing between characters which, in turn, permits type designers total freedom when creating typefaces.

The second consideration, that of word spacing, presents a more complex problem mainly due to a convention that was introduced in medieval times. Because they wanted to make facing pages in books symmetrical, scribes insisted that both the left- and right-hand edges of text should be vertically aligned. This could be achieved only by abbreviating words that fell at the ends of lines. This led to the introduction of additional symbols, called contractions, being used to fill the spaces which had been left by abbreviated words or short lines.

Type anatomy Each character in a line of type has its own individual characteristics. The terminology relating to different parts of a typeset character is extensive and a wide range of words are in common usage. Much of the nomenclature and measuring systems of traditional typography remain standard language on computers. Traditional type measurement on a computer derives from the body size of a non-printing piece of metal, and even though computer type has no physical basis, this idea has been extended for measuring computer-generated letterforms – instead of being based on the physical body size of metal type, computer type is based on an imaginary em square.

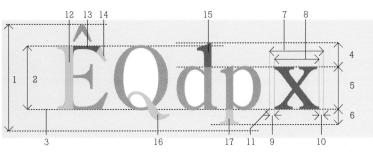

Point sizes For many years, printing was an inexact science. No two printers could agree on a standard system of type measurement, which meant that type cast by one foundry could not be used with type cast by another. It was not until the 18th century that the pioneering French typographer Pierre Fournier successfully proposed a standard typesetting unit called the point. This was developed by another Frenchman, Firmin Didot, into a European standard. Even today, however, the process is not complete, since Britain and the USA base their system on one point measuring 0.01383in. (72 do not quite make an inch), the European equivalent being 0.0148in. The 12 point unit is a pica in the first system and a cicero in the second. The advent of the computer as a typographic tool has introduced a new standard, dividing one inch into exactly 72 parts, making one point equal 0.013889in.

Right The unit system used in typesetting for measurement and counting. Usually 18 units make up an em, the size of the unit varying with the type size. In the word Mot, the M is 18 units wide, the o 10 units wide and the t 6 units wide. The system enables spacing to be finely adjusted.

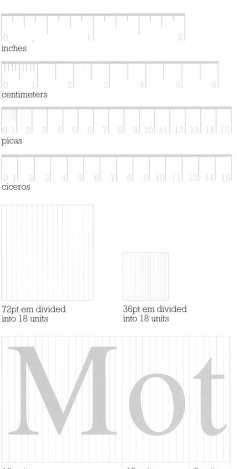

inches

centimeters

picas

ciceros

72pt em divided into 18 units

36pt em divided into 18 units

18 units   10 units   6 units

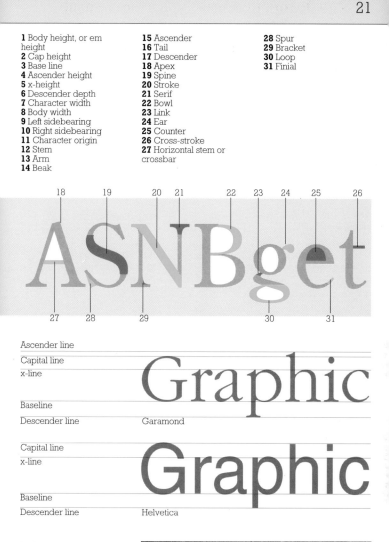

1 Body height, or em height
2 Cap height
3 Base line
4 Ascender height
5 x-height
6 Descender depth
7 Character width
8 Body width
9 Left sidebearing
10 Right sidebearing
11 Character origin
12 Stem
13 Arm
14 Beak

15 Ascender
16 Tail
17 Descender
18 Apex
19 Spine
20 Stroke
21 Serif
22 Bowl
23 Link
24 Ear
25 Counter
26 Cross-stroke
27 Horizontal stem or crossbar

28 Spur
29 Bracket
30 Loop
31 Finial

Ascender line
Capital line
x-line
Baseline
Descender line

Garamond

Capital line
x-line
Baseline
Descender line

Helvetica

Body size and leading

Traditionally, the body of a piece of type determines its point size, although only the face of the type is visible when printed. Thus type is measured from baseline to baseline rather than from highest to lowest extremity of the face. When the space between lines of type is increased, it is known as "leading," the term deriving from the days when strips of lead were placed between lines of type (**right**). Leaded type was specified as the size of type plus the amount of leading – e.g., 10pt type with 2pt leading. On desktop computers, the term "leading" is frequently used, erroneously, to describe the spacing of type from baseline to baseline.

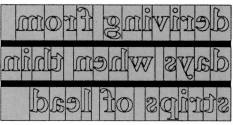

Set solid

Leaded

This convention was sustained by the introduction of movable type, although more by mechanical requirements than by esthetic considerations; in order to take an impression from a group of pieces of type, all the pieces had to be locked together under tension in a metal frame called a form. This meant that all the lines of type, including spaces, had to be the same length – otherwise, all the type would have fallen out of the form as soon as it was lifted. In other words, the whole area between each edge of the form had to be filled with wood or metal – whether it represented type characters or the spaces between characters. The convention of vertically aligning edges of blocks of text was made possible by distributing approximately equal spaces between each of the words along a line. Today, this technique of making sure that all the lines on a page are of the same length is known as "justified" typesetting. Text with even word spacing is usually vertically aligned on the left ("flush," or "ranged," left), with the right-hand margin set ragged ("unjustified"). Computers now permit almost limitless control over how the spaces are apportioned between characters and words in justified setting.

Type measurement Because the earliest type consisted of solid blocks of wood or metal (the "body") upon which the area to be printed ("face") was carved or punched, all measurements historically relate to these three-dimensional objects – the most modern typesetting systems today still use many of these measurements, even though they employ what is, to all intents and purposes, a two-dimensional system of generating type characters.

There are three type measurement systems with which you must be familiar: points, picas, and units – although the adoption of computers by designers as a design tool has meant that inches and millimeters are now also often used. These measurements can be confusing in that the Anglo-American system is different from the European system, even though both use the term "point" (the European point is sometimes also referred to as a "corps"). The art of printing spread swiftly through Europe following its initial development in Germany; so swiftly that the many type foundries that sprung up were casting type that was incompatible with that of another foundry. It was not until the early 18th century that an attempt was made to standardize a system of type measurement. This happened in France, when Pierre Fournier proposed a standard unit of measurement which he called the point. The innovations made by Fournier were developed by another Frenchman, Firmin Didot, to produce a European standard, but neither Britain nor America adopted it, even though their system was based on it.

Anglo-American system This is based on the division of one inch into 72 parts, called points; mathematically, one point should equal 0.013889in. – but, in fact, it equals 0.013837in., meaning that 72 points only make 0.996264in. Twelve points make a pica (or pica em) and measure 0.166in.

European system The European point is 0.0148in. and 12 of these form a unit measuring 0.1776in. This 12-point unit is called a cicero in France and Germany, a riga tipografica (riga) in Italy, and an augustijn (aug) in the Netherlands.

There is no relationship between the Anglo-American point and the Didot point, and neither of them relate to the metric system. Thus typographic measurements in points coexist with European, British, and metric measurements, the latter of which are used in virtually every other allied trade. While it was thought that there would be a gradual move toward the metrification of typographic measurements, the advent of the computer as a design tool has probably established a new international standard of measurement based on the Anglo-American system – except that, on desktop computers one point actually equals 0.0138889in., thus 72 points really *do* equal one inch.

Although some designers refer to a pica em simply as an "em," technically this is incorrect – an em is the square of the body of a piece of type, regardless of its size (so-called because the letter "M" originally occupied the full unit width of a piece of type). A 36-point em, for instance, measures 36 points, not 12.

The most important measurement in controlling line length is that of each character width. This measurement is determined by dividing an em into vertical "slices." These are called "set" points or widths or, more commonly, units. The number of units in an em varies, and it is not uncommon to find character em-widths divided into as many as 15,000 units. Units control not only the width of characters, but also their height and the spaces between them. Although the actual size of the unit varies according to the size of the type, the proportions always remain the same because there are always the same number to the em, regardless of size.

In the design of typefaces, each character is given an amount of space, sometimes called "sidebearings," at each side of the character. The width of a character is the total of its body width and side-bearing, and is known as the character "set-width" or "set," These are measured in relative units, as are the spaces in between each character or word. The set-width of a character controls the amount of space between itself and the next character and can be increased or decreased for special purposes.

Because different fonts vary considerably in their characteristics, the set-widths of characters also vary from typeface to typeface; a condensed typeface, for instance, has a narrow set-width relative to its body size.

Typefaces Much to the bewilderment of many designers, there are several thousand typefaces available today. But this is a relatively recent phenomenon – during the first 400 years of movable type, the form it took depended upon the mechanical limitations of the printing processes of the day, and only in the 19th century did type design even begin to transcend the barriers of craft into art. Even then, typeface designs had to be translated by craftsmen using individual punches to cut the precise form desired. Only in very recent years, with the advent of desktop computers and the ease with which some programs make it possible to generate typefaces, has type design proliferated to its present, seemingly saturated, state.

Type classification The increasingly massive number of type designs has prompted several attempts to establish a universally recognized classification – but without real success. The dominating presence of the computer in type design has further compounded the problem with the introduction of a whole new era of stylized typefaces. Even now, the most widely accepted classification is based on the 1964 classification by the Deutsche Normenaus-schuss, which itself is based on the earlier (1954) classification by Maximilian Vox. This classifies typefaces into nine basic groups, although a tenth – "stylized" – has been added lately to cope loosely with such latter-day oddballs as MICR (magnetic ink characters) and dot-matrix printer fonts. The nine groups roughly trace the historical development of type design:

Graphic Movable type was developed in Germany, and the design of the type reflected the local handwriting, known as Gothic, Black

Letter, or Textura. The letterform itself was written in such a way that curved forms were difficult to reproduce and were thus kept to a minimum, which resulted in a distinctive typeface. This group now includes latter-day "drawn" typefaces such as Cartoon.

Humanist A type design deriving from 15th century minuscule writing, a typical example being Centaur.

Garalde It was the introduction of printing to Italy that led to type design taking on the appearance it has today. Formal documents were handwritten in a style known as Chancery Italic, which is much lighter and more legible than Gothic. These Old Style letterforms are characterized by a left-leaning stress to the vertical axis and a robust triangular serif (a small line used to complete the main stroke of a letter). Bembo, Caslon, Garamond, and Goudy Old Style are classic examples.

Transitional Gradually, type design became more influenced by the refinement of printing processes – and its associated materials such as paper and ink – than by the conventions of handwriting, and printers' type began to assume its own separate identity. Transitional faces are identified by their color – generally lighter than Garalde – and by the emphasis of the curved strokes tending to be vertical rather than diagonal and the serifs more horizontal. Probably the best-known example of a transitional face is that named after its English designer John Baskerville in the mid 18th century.

Didone During the 18th century, developments became more rapid, and in 1798 another style of type emerged. This was the work of an Italian printer named Giambattista Bodoni and became known as the "Modern" style. Bodoni, who was clearly influenced by the then current vogue for classical Greek and Roman artistic styles, gave his name to the typeface which most typified Didone faces, and had maximum contrast between thick and thin strokes, with fine horizontal hairline serifs, while the ascenders (the parts above the body, such as in "b" and "h") and descenders (the parts below the body, as in "g," "p" and "y") are both extended.

Slab serif The Industrial Revolution in the 19th century brought the introduction of mechanical typesetting, which combined with market demand – particularly in advertising – to produce yet more type forms. The advertising requirements at the time were for loud, bold designs that would stand out from their surrounds. This desire was fulfilled by a type design that was bold and black, with serifs carrying as much weight as the rest of the letter. This form became known as "Egyptian," or Slab Serif. Typical examples are Rockwell (in which this book is set) and Clarendon. More exaggerated – and in some cases illegible – forms were called Fat Face.

Lineale The bolder a typeface becomes, the smaller its counters are, until a point is reached when it becomes illegible. Because of the search for ever more striking designs, it was this factor which led to serifs being abandoned altogether. These were called "Sans-serif" types and were initially used for posters, but before long they became used in general printing. This classification is often divided into four sub-categories: Grotesque, Neo-grotesque, Geometric, and Humanist.

Glyphic Typefaces deriving from stone-carved, chiseled forms rather than calligraphic forms. Albertus is a typical example.

Script Typefaces, such as Shelley, that resemble cursive writing.

Using type The evolution of type design does not rest solely on historical precedent, but also on the continuing development of production methods, with typefaces being designed, or redesigned, for specific technological innovations. With the introduction of Lino-

Type characteristics Of the thousands of different typefaces available today, each has its own design characteristics which make it different from other typefaces. These characteristics are classified into broad groups (see Type classification. p.23). The main design elements discussed in those classifications are described on this page. For example, a typeface will either have serifs, or it will not. If the typeface has serifs, they will be bracketed, hairline, or slab.

mode
Serifed face (Times)

mode
Sans-serif face (Helvetica)

mode
Bracketed serif (Times)

mode
Hairline serif, unbracketed (Walbaum)

mode
Slab serif, unbracketed (Rockwell)

x-height A fundamental characteristic of a typeface is the size at which it *appears* when compared with other typefaces of the same physical size.

abc
36pt Bernhard "small appearing"

abc
36pt Goudy

abc
36pt Walbaum "large appearing"

Contrast This is determined by the relative thicknesses of the strokes.

mode
High contrast (Walbaum)

mode
Even contrast (Rockwell)

Stress This is determined by the general direction indicated by the thickest part of curved strokes.

mode
Vertical stress (Walbaum)

mode
Oblique stress (Goudy)

Weight A typeface's weight is determined by the thickness of its main strokes, relative to the stroke thicknesses in other weights of the same design. Many typefaces are available in a full range of weights, from light to ultra bold (sometimes called black), and most have at least a roman (or medium), and a bold version.

mode
Gill Light

mode
Gill Light Italic

mode
Gill Sans

mode
Gill Sans Italic

mode
Gill Bold

mode
Gill Bold Italic

mode
Gill Extra Bold

mode
Gill Ultra Bold

mode
Schneidler Light

mode
Schneidler Light Italic

mode
Schneidler Roman

mode
Schneidler Roman Italic

mode
Schneidler Medium

mode
Schneidler Medium Italic

mode
Schneidler Bold

mode
Schneidler Black

Small capitals These are capitals designed for use with lower case letters, and are thus the same x-height. Small caps scaled optically from standard capitals produce a lighter weight than lower case letters.

Designed SMALL CAPS

Reduced SMALL CAPS

Ligatures When two or more characters are joined and set as a single unit, they are called ligatures. They should not be used on smaller sizes when tracking (letterspacing) is tight, as overall spacing may become uneven.

fi ffi fl ffl ff

fi ffi fl ffl ff

Kerning When the spacing between specified pairs of characters is deliberately reduced it is called kerning – as distinct from "tracking," which describes the spacing between a string of characters. The term derives from the days of metal type, when part of a type character was designed to overhang the body of the adjacent letter. The overhanging part was called the "kern." When used carefully, kerning can greatly improve letterspacing, and becomes particularly important on larger type sizes.

f — Kern
— Body

VAULT VAULT

AT	AY	AV	AW	Ay	Av	Aw
FA	TO	TA	Ta	Te	To	Ti
Tr	Tu	Ty	Tw	Ts	Tc	LT
LY	LV	LW	Ly	PA	VA	Va
Ve	Vo	Vi	Vr	Vu	Vy	RT
RV	RW	RY	Ry	WA	Wa	We
Wo	Wi	Wr	Wu	Wy	YA	Ya
Ye	Yo	Yi	Yp	Yq	Yu	Tv

Numerals Traditionally, fonts were often cast with options for numerals both as aligning and non-aligning choices. Nowadays, however, this is a less common option.

1 2 3 4 5 6 7 8 9 0

Non-aligning numerals

1 2 3 4 5 6 7 8 9 0

Aligning numerals

Fractions These come either as "true" fractions, in which the fraction is designed as a single character, or "piece" fractions, where a fraction is built (**below**) from three pieces – a numerator (**1**), separator (**2**), and denominator (**3**).

1/8 1/4 1/3 3/8 1/2 5/8 2/3 3/4 7/8

True fractions

1/8 1/4 1/3 3/8 1/2 5/8 2/3 3/4 7/8

Piece fractions

1/32 3/32 5/32 3/16 5/16 7/16

True fractions

1/32 3/32 5/32 3/16 5/16 7/16

Piece fractions

1
2
3

type and Monotype at the beginning of the 20th century – the first mechanical typesetting machines – existing typefaces were remodeled and adapted to the characteristics of the two systems. Linotype produced each complete line as a single piece of metal, whereas Monotype produced individual characters and spaces from which a line was formed.

An important factor in type selection is the paper and printing process to be used. Earlier typefaces were designed to be printed by letterpress on handmade, cartridge, or other uncoated papers. Thus, when printed on modern, smooth papers, they can often appear fragile and light. It is also the case that Didone faces, such as Bodoni and Walbaum, look more mellow and robust if printed by letterpress on uncoated paper. Similarly, typesetting equipment can alter the appearance of a typeface – laser-generated fonts on bromide paper, for example, generally appear lighter than the equivalent metal face printed with ink.

Drop-out type – that is, white type on a black or colored background – usually demands a heavier typeface, since faces with fine lines as an integral part of the design such as a Didone face or a light weight of type, are susceptible to the erosion of the image by surplus ink, and parts of the letters may disappear as a result. Gravure printing can have the same detrimental effect upon the same range of typefaces.

Besides such practical considerations, type selection is influenced by esthetic demands. For example, Lineale, or Sans-serif, faces, being simple, uncluttered and unpretentious, are sometimes more suitable for technical literature. They are also used extensively for children's books, with the design of the letterforms such as the ''a'' and ''g'' more closely resembling today's handwriting. Serifed faces are more suitable for text matter in books, particularly novels, and are also used by the majority of newspapers.

Tables, indexes, and bibliographies requiring complex typography, are best suited to a typeface with a wide choice of weights and italic, such as Garamond or Bembo, while Times offers a particularly comprehensive range of symbols for setting mathematical formulae. Color and leading are the two other most important considerations when selecting typefaces. When set as text, each typeface produces its own tonal value, which is referred to by typographers as ''color.'' This color is influenced by the amount of space between each line, called ''leading'' – a name which derives from the days of hand setting, when strips of metal, known as ''leads,'' were used to space the lines farther apart. The term leading is still in common usage even in computer typesetting.

Some typefaces are known as ''large appearing,'' that is, when the overall height of the body of the lower-case letterform (the ''x-height'') is large in comparison with its ascenders and descenders. Conversely, typefaces with small x-heights and large ascenders and descenders are known as ''small appearing.''

Preparing a manuscript All copy, however it is to be typeset, first has to be prepared before it can be entered (''input'') into a typesetting system. It is difficult, if not impossible, to establish a clear typographic structure if the text is not typewritten or supplied as laser proofs from a computer. It usually helps if the copy is typed with the same number of characters per line as the eventual typeset form. The copy should be typed with double line spacing and ample margins on both left and right for editorial comments and corrections, and typesetting instructions. The tendency these days is for copy to be entered directly onto a word-processing system or

Rules These are a useful compositional device. They can be used to help visual organization by providing form and structure; they can also provide a sense of character for what may otherwise be monotonous, straight type. In common with line spacing, rules are defined in points or fractions of a point. Some also have names – a ¼ point rule is usually referred to as a hairline rule, while a ½ point rule is a fine rule. Lengths are normally specified in picas. Computer applications offer a wide variety of rule styles at virtually any size. When using rules, there are two important points to remember: first, specify the spacing required below them; second, check proofs carefully for breaks and jaggedness where you have specified continuous rules.

0.25pt	0.0882mm
0.3pt	0.1058mm
0.4pt	0.1411mm
0.5pt	0.1764mm
0.6pt	0.2117mm
0.7pt	0.2469mm
0.8pt	0.2822mm
0.9pt	0.3175mm
1.0pt	0.3528mm
1.25pt	0.4410mm
1.5pt	0.5292mm
1.75pt	0.6174mm
2.0pt	0.7055mm
2.25pt	0.7937mm
2.5pt	0.8819mm
2.75pt	0.9701mm
3.0pt	1.0583mm
3.25pt	1.1465mm
3.5pt	1.2347mm
3.75pt	1.3229mm
4.0pt	1.4111mm

0.25pt	2.0pt		2.5pt
0.3pt	2.25pt		3.0pt
0.4pt	2.5pt		3.5pt
0.5pt	2.75pt		4.0pt
0.6pt	3.0pt		4.5pt
0.7pt	3.25pt		5.0pt
0.8pt	3.5pt		5.5pt
0.9pt	3.75pt		6.0pt
1.0pt	4.0pt		6.5pt
1.25pt	4.25pt		7.0pt
1.5pt	4.5pt		2.5pt
1.75pt	4.75pt		3.0pt
2.0pt	5.0pt		3.5pt
2.25pt	5.25pt		4.0pt
2.5pt	5.5pt		4.5pt
2.75pt	5.75pt		5.0pt
3.0pt	6.0pt		5.5pt
3.25pt	6.25pt		6.0pt
3.5pt	6.5pt		6.5pt
3.75pt	6.75pt		7.0pt
4.0pt	7.0pt		7.0pt

desktop computer system – some of which are compatible with typesetting machines and may even be the same machines being used by the typesetter, such is the sophistication of computers today. At least, data can usually be easily transferred from one machine to another, usually by means of a "diskette," or "floppy disk." Apart from the obvious advantage of saving on keying time, this method enables near-final corrections to be made even before the copy emerges as typeset text in any form. In the absence of a computer, retyping part of the manuscript to the desired line length can also serve to confirm the typographic structure of your layout and will allow you to make an accurate estimate of the number of lines, and thus pages, that a typeset manuscript will take up. At some stage, whether at the same time or after the text face has been determined – although, most likely, before you even started the job – stylistic decisions must be taken on such things as size and position of headings, subheadings, crossheadings, references, footnotes, and so on, even though additional copy-editing may be needed later. This normally means that, particularly in jobs involving large amounts of text such as books and manuals, you must read the text before such decisions can be taken. Ideally, however, you will have been able to predetermine the typographic structure so that text can be written accordingly, especially where visual impact may be just as important as the content of the words themselves.

Casting-off Estimating the number of characters and lines that a piece of typed copy will occupy in its typeset form is called "copy-casting," or "casting-off." This is an important process for the design of any printed matter.

If you use a computer, working out the number of words required to fill a space, or *vice versa*, is a relatively easy affair; nevertheless, you will, at some stage, be required to estimate a word count or fit manually.

Without a computer, the methods by which the length of a manuscript can be calculated are at best only approximations – with such a plethora of seemingly identical typefaces available (albeit with different names) you can never be absolutely sure which version will be used by your typesetter. It is advisable, then, when you are casting-off, to round up any calculations and even to allow a margin of error – about 5 or 10 percent – in your calculations. This allowance should take into account the complexity of the manuscript and the number of words per line once it is set in type, but bear in mind that short lines, hyphenated words, or exaggerated white spaces due to words being carried over to the next line will further complicate the estimate.

If the manuscript is typed on a fixed-spacing typewriter or on a word-processor using a fixed-space font, casting it off is made much easier because there are always the same number of characters per line, which you can measure and count with a ruler or type-scale (the latter is sometimes called a "depth" scale). If the manuscript is typed on a machine with a variable character width, you must count the characters manually. Special manuscript paper can also be extremely useful as it is printed with pica measures on it, making casting-off much easier.

First, an approximation must be made of an average line, each word space counting as a single character, and you can achieve this by counting the number of characters in, say, five lines and then dividing the number of characters by five (the number of lines counted). This will give you a fairly accurate average line count, which you then multiply by the total number of lines of manuscript.

Again, you can measure this by using a depth scale rather than by counting each individual line to give the total number of characters involved. This figure can also be useful when you are estimating the cost of typesetting.

The next thing to establish is the amount of space the typeset manuscript will fill, which will vary according to the typeface you choose. Normally, this is where cost considerations must be made; it will be rare that you be required to increase the amount of space text may occupy, particularly in book work. More often, your task will be to balance readability with fitting the text into a predetermined number of pages.

To calculate the space required for the copy, you will need to refer to a sample alphabet, in the appropriate type size, provided by either the typesetter or the font vendor. If at all possible, refer to a sample produced on the exact equipment which will be used for the job, since the line length of the same typeface produced by different foundries may vary – as may the various attributes (such as kerning) applied by the typesetter.

Some type foundries (although, alas, a diminishing number) produce special tables covering their complete range of typefaces that make it easier to calculate text lengths. These can be presented in different forms; some will give the number of lower-case letters per line for each face and size over a given length, while others may be given reference numbers which, when used in conjunction with a special copycasting table, will give the number of characters per line. Others may give the number of characters per pica for every size of every typeface.

Some type specimen sheets include a sample text set in a variety of different leadings and measures, as well as a complete type synopsis. These sheets are worth collecting since through them you can assess the appearance of different typefaces without having samples set.

Marking up copy Once a manuscript has left the editor's hands, you will be required to mark on it a set of instructions so that the compositor or computer operator can "format" it for typesetting. First, supply a master style sheet of instructions specifying the fonts required and the general style of the typography. This should always be attached to the manuscript for permanent reference. On the manuscript itself, clearly indicate the exact words, lines, headings, or paragraphs to be capitalized, italicized, set in a bold face, small capitals, or a different size. There may come a point when these instructions become too dense to follow clearly, and in such cases it is better to use a coding system based on numerals or letters and keyed to the master style sheet.

Always remember that there may be more than one operator keying-in the copy and that a completely separate team – either within the typesetting company or entirely outside – will be responsible for the page make-up. For this reason, you are advised to confine the type mark-up to the manuscript, and the layout instructions, such as the position of the text on the page, to the layouts.

Inputting text If you use a computer, your first consideration is how to avoid spending your working life keying-in text. Fortunately, technology has advanced to such an extent that such fears are – in the most part – groundless. It may still be necessary to do some manual keying, such as taking in corrections and typing headings, but it is now possible to input text in a variety of ways:

OCR scanning Much of the text you receive will come as typewritten manuscript, or "hard" copy. If it is a small amount of text consisting of, say, 200 words (a nominal maximum, depending on how fast you can type), it's not really a problem just keying it in yourself. Otherwise, you can input text into a computer by scanning it (on a desktop scanner) and, by using one of the many "optical character recognition" (OCR) applications that are available, convert it into editable form. The error rate using OCR applications is generally very low, provided that the original copy is relatively clean. Most OCR applications provide a means of automatically "flagging" suspect words which the scanner may not have been able to "read," making it fairly easy to check scanned text for errors.

Text on disk If possible, persuade your client to supply text on disk, since this is the most efficient way of inputting it. Although compatibility between computers made by different manufacturers used to create problems when transferring files from one to the other, this is no longer the case. Providing that you have appropriate software, your computer will probably be able to "read" a disk (so long as it is the right size – and even that is now less of a problem than it used to be since most service bureaus offer a disk conversion service).

Text by modem If you and your client both use modems, you can take in text instantly (called "uploading"). A modem is also useful for returning files for correction purposes, although this may be inappropriate since you may, because of file transfer requirements between some computers or modems, be forced to use a file format which causes typesetting attributes to be lost.

If you have no other means of inputting text, you may have to bite the bullet and key it in – or at least, pay a service bureau to key it in. There are also, as an alternative to service bureaus, many people offering freelance typing services at a reasonable price.

Proofs The first proof (or piece of typeset copy) provided by the typesetter is known as a galley proof. This is sometimes the last chance to get everything right, so you should scrutinize it with meticulous care. In the first instance, this examination may be done by the typesetter's own reader, who will check it against the manuscript and mark any errors in red. While the client also marks typesetting errors in red, all other corrections or alterations should be marked in a different color – this guarantees that typesetters do not charge for their own errors.

Next, the author or editor, or both, will be required to read the galley proof, even though, in principle, all editorial alterations and corrections should have already been incorporated into the manuscript. The editor or proofreader will need to check the text for typesetting aberrations such as "widows" (single words set on a line at the end of a paragraph), and so on, and to make adjustments to ensure the text fits the space allowed on the layout. The designer should also check it for more esthetic inconsistencies or anomalies such as wrong fonts, erratic word spacing, or "rivers," which are white lines running down a column of text caused by the coincidence of word spaces on consecutive lines falling adjacent to each other.

It should be possible at this stage, with straightforward text, to return the corrected galleys to the typesetter for final galleys – which will be used as "camera-ready" art – or for making into page film. However, it is quite usual for typesetters to supply second – and sometimes third and even fourth – proofs before final approval is given. The number of galleys supplied depends, of course, as much upon the schedule as on the need to achieve perfection or upon the complexity of the job – although with very complicated setting, such as timetables or mathematical formulae, it may be necessary to go to many proofs.

If you supplied galleys in the form of laser proofs from your own computer, you may be required to take in corrections yourself although, if you received text on disk in the first place, you would not expect to find many corrections. In ideal circumstances, corrections are made by your client's office directly onto the disk you supplied with the galleys.

Design The style, or design, represented on a surface is a process of constant decision-making that evolves from an initial concept. Whereas the finished, printed item may represent what appears to be a single and whole solution, it can only materialize as the result of making a constant string of decisions, usually spread over a protracted period of time. Even the most fastidious and accurate roughs will be subject to change during the evolution of a job.

Before any copy is sent for typesetting, you will first be required to determine the context into which the job fits – and whether the design is purely typographic or whether illustrations will also be involved. You will need to determine the types of heading involved and to find a satisfactory way of displaying any required emphasis in the text, whether it be single words or complete paragraphs. There are several ways of achieving this; methods include capitalization, a change of size or weight, a change of font, addition of color, use of space or indentation, or any combination of these, although, of course, overemphasis may be counterproductive.

Naturally, the layout of text is determined by the number of lines that will fit within a page, and this in turn is affected by the combina-

Proof correction marks Proofs that are being checked should have corrections marked up in the margin as well as in the text. This is because the printer always looks down the margin to see where the corrections occur. Typesetting errors should be marked in red; other alterations in a different color.

Instruction to printer	Textual mark	Marginal mark
Correction is concluded	None	
Leave unchanged	typeface groups	STET
Remove unwanted marks	typeface groups	✕
Push down risen spacing material	typeface groups	lower
Refer to appropriate authority	typeface groups	?
Insert new matter	groups	typeface
Insert additional matter	type groups	A
Delete	typeface groups	
Delete and close up	typeface grooups	
Substitute character or parf of one or more words	tipeface groops	
Wrong fount, replace with correct fount	typeface groups	wf/fix
Correct damaged characters	typeface groups	✕

Instruction to printer	Textual mark	Marginal mark
Set in or change to italics	typeface groups (underlined)	_ital_
Set in or change to capitals	typeface groups (double underline)	cap
Set in or change to small capitals	typeface groups (double underline)	sc
Capitals for initials small caps for rest of word	typeface groups (triple underline)	cap + sc
Set in or change to bold type	typeface groups (wavy underline)	bf
Set in or change to bold italic type	typeface groups (wavy underline)	bf + ital
Change capitals to lower case	typeFACE groups	lc
Change small capitals to lower case	typeFACE groups	lc
Change italic to roman	_typeface_ groups (circled)	rom
Invert type	typeface groups	⦃
Insert ligature	filmsetter	n̂
Substitute separate letters for ligature	filmsetter	fi
Insert full point	typeface groups ⊙	⌒ ⊙
Insert colon	typeface groups	⌒ ⦂
Insert semi-colon	typeface groups	⌒ ⨟
Insert comma	typeface groups	⌒ ⋀
Insert quotation marks	typeface groups	⌒ ⸌/⸍
Insert double quotation marks	typeface groups	⌒ ⸌⸌/⸍⸍
Substitute character in superior position	typeface groups	sup
Substitute character in inferior position	typeface groups	sub
Insert apostrophe	typeface groups	⌒ ⸍
Insert ellipsis	typeface groups ...	⌒ ᴐ000
Insert leader dots	...typeface groups	⌒ 000ᴐ
Substitute or insert hyphen	typeface groups	⌒ =
Insert rule	typeface groups	⌒ (2pt rule)
Insert oblique	typeface groups	⌒ ≠
Start new paragraph	are called set points. The dimension of	⌒ ¶
No fresh paragraph, run on	are called set points. The dimension of	⌒ (no ¶)

Instruction to printer	Textual mark	Marginal mark
Transpose characters or word	groups typeface	tr.
Transpose characters (2)	tpeyface groups	tr.
Transpose lines	The dimensions of are called set points.	tr.
Transpose lines (2)	The dimension of are called set points.	tr.
Center type	typeface groups	center
Indent 1 em	typeface groups	indent 1em
Delete indent	typeface groups	flush left
Set line justified	typeface groups ‖	Justify
Set column justified	‖	Justify col.
Move matter to right	typeface groups ⌐	⌐
Move matter to left	⌐typeface groups	⌐
Take over to next line	typeface groups	break
Take back to previous line	typeface groups	move up
Raise matter	typeface groups	⌐
Lower matter	typeface groups	⌐
Correct vertical alignment	‖ typeface groups	‖
Correct horizontal alignment	typeface groups	Align
Close up space	type face groups	⌒
Insert space between words	typeface groups	#
Reduce space between words	typeface groups reduce #	reduce #
Reduce or insert space between letters	t y p e f a c e groups	⌒ #
Make space appear equal	typeface groups	equal #
Close up to normal line spacing	typeface groups	normal spacing
Insert space between paragraphs	are called set points. The dimension of	#
Reduce space between paragraphs	are called set points. The dimension of	reduce #
Insert parentheses or square brackets	typeface groups	{ { or [ ]
Figure or abbreviation to be spelt out in full	12 point twelve pt.	sp. out
Move matter to position indicated	are called The set points. dimensional	tr.

tion of type size and leading. The intended size, for instance, may be difficult to read when set solid (without space between lines), so additional line spacing may be required. This will result in a reduced number of lines on each page, which, in turn, will mean that more pages in which to fit the text may be required. It is also important to make allowances both esthetically and practically for the blank spaces that may appear as the result of editorial or typographical constraints, such as subheadings and paragraphing, since, in addition to the possibility of appearing ugly, such spaces will inevitably increase the number of lines of text.

When illustrations are to be included in a design, the problems are multiplied. Illustrations are usually accompanied by a caption, which ought to be as close as possible to it. Conversely, the captions for a group of illustrations on a page may be placed together, in which case the pictures to which they refer must be clearly identified (there are a number of ways of doing this; the most common is to use "directionals" such as "above" or "top left," or alternatively to use numbers; another method is to use graphic devices, or "ornaments," but care should be taken when using these because the result can easily look messy or ambiguous). Illustrations should also be placed as near as possible to the relevant passage of main text, whether captions are used or not. It is also important, when incorporating illustrations, to achieve a degree of consistency in the layout so that illustrations are balanced not only with each other, but also with the text, and from page to page.

Grids Almost all jobs that involve the integration of pictures with type should be designed on a purpose-made plan, or grid. The exceptions are those of the "one-off" variety – those which involve few words or illustrations such as record covers and book jackets as long as they do not fit into a series.

The purpose of a grid is two-fold; first, it guarantees consistency, whether the job is a single broadsheet, whether it requires page turns, or if it forms the basis of a series design such as product labels of a chain store. Second, it serves as a reference for all those involved in the various stages of production.

The grid should show all the features common to all pages, such as column widths, text and illustration areas, positions of headings and folios (page numbers), trim size, folds, gutters, column depths, margins, and so on. It is important that this information is as complete as possible, since other designers, illustrators, photographers, editors, and printers will all be working from it. The grid, however, should never be regarded as a straitjacket; if an idea or situation demands it, the rules you laid down can occasionally be ignored.

Printed grids are common in large jobs – books and magazines, for example (even though most magazines are laid out electronically these days) – and their use helps to minimize the amount of time required to prepare layouts; it also helps to reduce any errors that might occur if each page were to be drawn up individually.

It is always a good idea to prepare a version of the grid on transparent material (although make sure that it is dimensionally stable – plastic drafting film is generally suitable), as this can then be used to check that originated proofs are the right size and that each double-page spread has been made up correctly. This is done by simply laying the grid over a proof.

If the grid is to be printed, it is advisable to have two versions supplied – one on semi-transparent layout paper and the other on thin board. The former can be used for tracing illustrations and for making rough layouts – even if you use a computer to prepare final layouts. However, it should not be used for checking the size of illustration proofs, as layout paper is dimensionally unstable. The latter is for more accurate paste-up purposes, such as mechanicals (camera-ready text paste-ups for photographically converting into page film). Grids are best printed in pale blue ink since it is not sensitive to the emulsions used in photographic reproduction. Always remember to check the grid itself for accuracy, as soon as it is returned from the printer, since inaccurately printed grids, however slight the error, cannot be used.

Electronic grids If you use a computer, a grid is even more important, since most page make-up applications require you to set one up – albeit a simple one – for even a single-page job. On the other hand, a grid for a long document can become quite complex – particularly if it is laden with typographic styles and graphic devices. Fortunately, however, most page make-up applications provide the facility for generating "master pages" which enable you to define such things as page margins, text columns, automatic page numbering, tints, and repeated items such as rules and running headings. Some applications allow you to set up a number of master pages – for accommodating such things as a different number, or width, of text columns – which you can then apply to any page. It is also usually possible to set up, within master pages, "style sheets" for every possible variation of text style in your design and assigning each one a keyboard command of its own.

Layouts Having progressed through the preparatory stages of your

Grids These are an essential part of the design process, particularly for jobs which run into many pages, such as a brochure or book. Their use aids the positional accuracy of repetitive items, such as running headings, text columns, folio numbers, and so on. They also help to minimize the amount of time required to prepare layouts, and to reduce the errors which might otherwise occur if every double page was to be drawn up separately. The basic grid should include all the essential elements around which the designer must work, the column depths and type widths and text and illustration areas to margins, and the positions of folios. When all this information is combined in permanent form, it serves as reference both for the designer and the various craftsmen involved in the production. Grids take two forms: where computers are concerned, most page make-up applications require you to construct a grid in the form of "master pages," and this can be printed out if necessary; with conventional page make-up, grids are generally printed onto semi-transparent layout paper or onto cardboard.

295 × 222 mm

commission, you can begin the task of assembling all the different elements – photographs, artwork, text and so on, in preparation for eventual printing.

This is done by generating "layouts" – literally, laying out the various elements together on a page. This serves two purposes; first, you can manipulate the images and type until you achieve a satisfactory result – both esthetically and practically. Second, it enables other people to carry out their part of the job, such as editors or authors who, once they know how much space is allocated and the position relative to the picture, can write captions.

Layouts can also be useful for the various people involved in production, such as typesetters – especially if complicated setting is required – and origination houses, who may require them for reference when making color separations. Although layouts take the form of a working "blueprint," which may contain much technical information, in many cases, particularly small jobs of a one-off nature, the layout may simply be a photocopy or duplicate of a presentation visual. All relevant instructions – for example, to artists and the origination house – can be added to the photocopy.

Layouts should contain as much information as possible. Headings should be written in (or drawn as a facsimile of the relevant typeface, so that the length can be assessed); areas of text and captions should be accurately indicated with their exact number of lines; and illustrations drawn in to show how and where they are to be positioned (with a code number that matches that on the

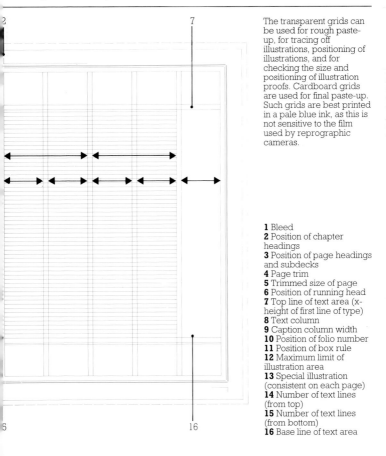

The transparent grids can be used for rough paste-up, for tracing off illustrations, positioning of illustrations, and for checking the size and positioning of illustration proofs. Cardboard grids are used for final paste-up. Such grids are best printed in a pale blue ink, as this is not sensitive to the film used by reprographic cameras.

1 Bleed
2 Position of chapter headings
3 Position of page headings and subdecks
4 Page trim
5 Trimmed size of page
6 Position of running head
7 Top line of text area (x-height of first line of type)
8 Text column
9 Caption column width
10 Position of folio number
11 Position of box rule
12 Maximum limit of illustration area
13 Special illustration (consistent on each page)
14 Number of text lines (from top)
15 Number of text lines (from bottom)
16 Base line of text area

artwork, photograph, or transparency, whether it is to appear in full color, black-and-white, or other colors, and to whom any credit is to be given). You should number the pages and indicate whether they are to print in four-color or otherwise. Always photocopy the layouts before you send them out, and keep a set of copies for your own reference.

Layouts are frequently made before the illustrations and, less often, photographs, are commissioned. For this reason, layouts involving artwork should be drawn to a high level of accuracy, since the artist will need to know the exact dimensions of an illustration, especially if it is to occupy a free shape (one that has a loosely defined perimeter). If the illustration is to contain specific information – say, of a technical nature such as maps, charts, and diagrams – the layout must be fully worked out – even to the extent of writing in any labeling (annotation) or call-outs, so that the artist has a precise visual guide to what is required.

Electronic layouts If you lay out your design work on a computer, you can output layouts in the form of laser proofs. These layouts do not need to display a great deal of technical information since most elements appear as they will when the job is finally printed. However, if you do, typical information on these layouts will be instructions to an editor to add or cut copy or instructions to a color separator concerning images for reproduction. If you intend using a service bureau to output bromide or final film, you will need to supply a laser proof of the files to be output.

If your computer is connected ("networked") to others, as they frequently are in editorial environments, it may not be necessary to produce laser-printed layouts at all, since most of the other people involved will be working directly onto your layouts.

Selecting and preparing photographs The way you select and use photographs is mainly determined by the requirements of the job in hand. For instance, a photograph for an advertisement may have been shot by referring to an accurate layout produced by you, in which case selection will be restricted to mostly technical considerations such as exposure, sharpness, and color. The photographer should always supply more than one alternative. On the other hand, photograph selection for an illustrated book may be from stock material supplied by picture libraries, which may range from the excellent to the barely discernible, in which case the overall effect of a design will depend as much on esthetic judgments as on technical ones.

Photographs exist in two forms: either as flat prints – color or black-and-white – or as transparencies ("slides," if they are 35mm format), which are always in color. Although color prints can be made to a very high quality, they are considered less suitable than transparencies for reproduction purposes. This is because light has to be reflected from a print, thereby losing its strength (it starts to become gray), whereas light passes directly through a transparency, thus retaining its full strength and consequently, optimum color saturation (the degree to which white, gray, or black is eliminated).

Photographers, to be on the safe side, usually supply bracketed shots – that is, photographs of the same subject, but shot using a variety of slightly different exposures and camera angles. It is important, therefore, to know which density will reproduce best, though the only real guide to this is experience. Generally, however, the picture that looks best invariably reproduces to a better standard, simply because the best-looking picture is most likely to be the one at the correct exposure – the exposure that is at the right level of density for reproduction. For instance, a red object photographed on a white background will give an exaggeratedly bright (fully saturated), and perhaps desirable, red if it is slightly underexposed, but the background will reproduce as an undesirable gray. On the other hand, a slightly overexposed shot may give a perfect white background with a slightly washed-out red subject.

Color transparencies should be viewed on a color-corrected light box, that is, a light box that has had its light source balanced to give the correct type of light (color temperature) required for viewing color film.

Many photographers, particularly in situations where color is of paramount importance such as the reproduction of fine art, will include in the transparency some sort of color scale. This will be outside the usable area of the transparency. This scale, called color control patches, gives highly accurate reproductions of each of the three layers of film emulsion – cyan, magenta, and yellow. In addition, there are patches of black and combinations of the three emulsion colors. These patches indicate any bias there may be in a transparency, either as a result of the lighting conditions in which the picture was taken or because of natural fading of the transparency over a period of time. Apart from being useful during the processing of the film, color control patches are helpful to color origination houses when making separations.

Sometimes, you may be faced with the problem of having to produce a colorful result, but only having black-and-white photographs to use – particularly common when the subject is of an historical nature. One way around this is to use, from the black-and-white original, combinations of colors from the four-color process to produce duotones, tritones, three, two and one-color tints, and so on. If you have a computer, the variations you can achieve are limitless. However, even if you don't use a computer, a color origination house can achieve virtually the same results. Using the four process colors naturally means that the combinations of colors you choose must fall within the limits of the process.

Although not immediately apparent, good reproduction of black-and-white photographs can be difficult to achieve, so you must take care when selecting a suitable original. In reproduction, the image is broken into tiny "halftone" dots (see p102), so solid blacks lose their density, whereas lighter tones suffer from loss of detail and whites become gray. This means that the ideal black-and-white original is one that has maximum contrast from black to white and yet retains all the detail and subtle shades of the middle tones – a result that is difficult to achieve in practice. However, the increasing sophistication of desktop scanners has given computer users hitherto unprecedented control over the quality of black-and-white – if not color – halftone reproduction.

You should carefully check photographs and transparencies with a magnifying glass both for sharpness and for blemishes such as scratches. Damaged pictures frequently need retouching, which is normally done by a specialized studio (although, if you are scanning the pictures yourself, it is a fairly simple matter to retouch photographs digitally – particularly if they are black-and-white). Retouching can be taken to greater extremes if you consider portions of the photograph to be undesirable or if you require alterations or substitutions – in fact, using image manipulation software on a computer, the creative opportunities for designers are huge.

Sizing pictures The first step when marking up pictures for

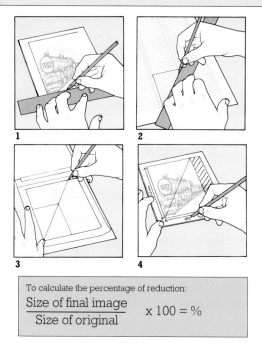

1

2

3

4

Sizing pictures Picture fit must be specified before an image can be sent for separation. This involves first squaring up the picture area on a transparent overlay (**1**). Then take the overlay and use it to draw a diagonal line on the layout across the area the picture is intended to fill (**2**). This shows how much of the picture area can be fitted into the allocated space (**3**). Mark the dimensions on the overlay, plus, if appropriate, the area to be cropped, which should be indicated by shading (**4**). If the picture is to be enlarged or reduced, calculate the percentage enlargement or reduction. Same size is 100 percent. Thus, a reduction in size from 6 inches to 4 inches square would mean a percentage reduction of 66 percent.

To calculate the percentage of reduction:

$$\frac{\text{Size of final image}}{\text{Size of original}} \times 100 = \%$$

reproduction is to determine which portion of the original, if any, needs to be "cropped" (excluded from the printed image), although, of course, you will already have a rough impression of this from the initial layout. You can achieve this by a procedure known as "scaling": first the picture area of the original is traced to square it up on a transparent overlay. Then the tracing is placed on top of the corresponding picture area on the layout, with one corner of each matching. Next, a diagonal line is drawn from this corner to the opposite corner of the picture area on the layout, the line being extended to meet an edge of the area of the original. Where the diagonal line meets this edge is the corner of the final image, the remainder being cropped. You should attach the tracing, with the area to be cropped clearly marked, to the original picture, and the dimensions of the image as it will finally appear should also be added.

The next step is to calculate the reduction – or enlargement – percentage. This is because the dimension controls of reproduction scanners are calibrated in percentages, rather than sizes. However, it is still necessary to indicate linear dimensions because the edges of the image at its final size will require cleaning up, or "masking." Same-size reproduction is 100%, while pictures to be reduced in size are less than 100% and those to be enlarged are greater. For instance, a reduction in size from 6 inches to 4 inches would mean a reduction of 66%, while an enlargement from 4 inches to 6 inches gives an enlargement of 150%. You only need one dimension each of the final size and of the original size, although of the same axis, to make this calculation. The mathematical formula for calculating the enlargement or reduction percentage is: size of final image ÷ size of original x 100. Knowing the percentage of reduction or enlargement is also useful in that it is possible to group pictures of the same, or very similar, ratio together, thus saving money because they can be scanned at the same time.

You should also specify on the overlay whether the image is to be squared up, silhouetted (cut out), or cut into another image. A squared-up image sits on a page with its edges square, while a silhouette picture is one that has a free shape, its background having been removed. With transparencies that are to be silhouetted, it is best to select those in which a subject with a fairly simple outline is set against a white or pale background; otherwise, the resulting image may have dark or messy edges. With black-and-white pictures, unwanted areas should be painted out – on a copy of the original – with opaque white paint. "Cut into" means that a picture overlaps, or sits completely within, another. You should give the origination house very clear instructions, specifying which picture is to be cut into which, plus a layout showing their positions, with all the dimensions marked.

Other essential information to include on the picture overlay is a code number. Each picture in a job should have its number recorded on the layouts. This is just in case the origination house has any queries about a specific picture or needs to be given any special instructions, such as whether it is to appear as a duotone, or if a color original is to be reproduced as a black-and-white (not unreasonably, origination houses always assume that if a color original is supplied, then color separation is required; and similarly, if black-and-white is supplied, it is to appear as a black-and-white).

Pictures and computers Generally speaking, most designers do not scan in color pictures with color separation in mind, and pictures are almost always scanned in as a guide for position only (FPO). Indeed, it is arguable that it is not advisable to scan in images at all, given the huge amount of disk space they occupy. However, a scanned image (even at low resolution) does allow you to indicate very precise crops to your printer or origination house and is worth doing for this purpose alone if you have the facility. Scanning images also allows you to make very precise text runarounds. As for the problem of disk space, a simple way around

Silhouetting Cutting out an unwanted background is a frequently used design technique. This is much easier to accomplish with pictures with a light background, since the image area can be more clearly defined than with a dark one. In this instance (**above**), it is important to shade out the areas that are not to reproduce, and to define the outline of the figure. Dimensions should be clearly marked on the overlay.

Scanning Scanned images demand large amounts of disk storage space, the amount occupied increasing with image size, pixel depth (the number of bits assigned to each pixel), and scan resolution. The chart (**below**) is based on images scanned at 300dpi, and the file sizes are approximate. The problem of file size can be partially alleviated by using file compression software or a special file compression card fitted inside the computer.

Bits per pixel (pixel depth)	1	4	6	8	24
Colors or gray shades	1 (b/w line)	16 grays	64 grays	256 grays or colors	16.7 million colors
File size of 4 x 5in. image (102 x 127mm)	300K	900K	1.3Mb	1.7Mb	5.2Mb
File size of 8 x 10in. image (203 x 254mm)	900K	3.5Mb	5.2Mb	6.9Mb	21Mb

Line art, 72dpi, 1-bit

Line art, 300dpi, 1-bit

Line art, 800dpi, 1-bit

Halftone, 72dpi, 8-bit

Halftone, 300dpi, 8-bit

Halftone, conventional

this is to keep the picture files on your hard disk only until you are ready to output your job to film – print out sets of laser proofs that include the images, for your reference as well as for the origination house, but delete them from the document before outputting on an imagesetter.

If you intend using scanned images for reproduction, such as line art, halftones, or color illustrations, you must not only leave them in the document file, but include the original picture files with the document file so that it can be output correctly by the imagesetter.

Preparing artwork If artwork to be reproduced is "flat" (i.e. with no additional overlays to be incorporated) and in four-color, the marking-up procedure is the same as that for transparencies. Complications arise, however, if other elements are to be incorporated into the final image. These elements appear on the artwork in the form of overlays of drafting film taped over the base artwork. Registration marks must be added to show how each overlay fits together with the base artwork. Any type is pasted in position and any lines drawn onto the film. Each separate overlay fulfils a different function; a map, for instance, with a base drawn in four-color may have the following overlays:

1 Type and other line work to appear in black.
2 Type and other line work to reverse out of color.
3 Type and line work to appear in cyan.
4 Type and line work to appear in magenta.
5 Areas to appear as cyan tint.
6 Areas to appear as magenta tint.

A map is an extreme example in that there could be almost any number of overlays, each one representing a different combination of line printings and almost limitless tint combinations. It is most common to have one overlay only on a four-color piece of artwork, which is normally used for type.

Black-and-white artwork can be made to appear in four-color by the use of mechanical tints which are laid by the printer or origination house. These can be selected from a process color tint chart (see p119–125) or alternatively, they can be specified as combinations of specially mixed "spot" colors.

Areas to print as tints can be prepared in one of two ways. The first is to use one overlay with key lines defining each area to be tinted – in other words, only one overlay is required to show all the various colors. The second is to use a different overlay for each combination of tints, although this can get very cumbersome if many colors are used. The former, therefore, is more convenient, but can be more expensive since it involves a considerable amount of hand-work (as opposed to photographic) by the lithographic planners – the people who lay tints in an origination house.

If artwork has been generated on a computer, tints can be applied within the application in which the artwork was created, and will automatically be separated into the desired colors when output to film through an imagesetter. All you need supply with your layouts is the original illustration file.

Color correction Depending on how you supplied the original material, proofs can be returned by the origination house for color correction in one of two forms: the illustrations will either be proofed in the exact position that they will be in when finally printed (whether they are combined with text or not), or they will be proofed – at the correct size – in random order, called "scatter" proofs, which are much cheaper to produce than proofs in position, as a greater number can be included on a proofing plate.

An alternative to conventional "wet" proofing (press proofing using ink and paper) is the use of a "dry-proof" method such as Cromalin or Matchprint, although this process requires separated film, making it cumbersome and expensive. A cheaper alternative is proofing from a dye-sublimation printer, which can be linked directly to a desktop computer and which does not require separated film. Both dry-proof and dye-sublimation proofs are accurate for color values, but the disadvantage of both methods is that neither will reveal "dot gain," where the size of halftone dots increases either during the transfer of the image from film to printing plate, or because of the effect of inking. Thus, for high-quality reproduction, it may be necessary to see wet proofs as well as dry proofs.

When making color corrections, your most crucial task is to check the color closely against the original. If there is a discrepancy, ask the origination house to correct it. In order to know the extent to which color can be corrected, it is important that you understand how color separation works (see Color reproduction, p105). For example, any increase or reduction in the amount of color is achieved not by altering the amount of ink on the plate, but by enlarging or reducing the size of the halftone dots on the separation film. A color is strengthened by reducing ("etching") the dot size on the negative film which, in turn, means that the dots are larger when converted to positive film. To weaken a color, dots are etched on the positive film. However, sometimes a proofed image has too much or too little of one color, which can only be accurately corrected by adjusting the proportions of one or two of the other colors. To increase the amount of magenta, say, it may be necessary to reduce the amount of cyan and possibly yellow.

With the increasing dominance of computers in color reproduction, it is now cheaper for origination houses to implement color corrections electronically, simply outputting new film for each corrected image. In conventional color reproduction, there was a limit to which a dot size could be altered without having to reoriginate the subject. This limit was usually about 5%, although it was sometimes be possible to achieve a 10% variation. Because the dots were etched by a hand process (ferrocyanide applied with a brush), there came a point when exaggerated corrections began to show on the proof – either as uneven patches or with defined edges to the etched portion. The use of computers in color correction avoids such aberrations.

To gauge whether a wet proof has been correctly inked on the proofing press, check the color control bar ("codet") on the edge of the proof sheet (see p114).

Proofs should also be checked for screen clash ("moiré" – common with electronically generated color separations), register, blemishes, scratches, acid stains, and broken screens. Use a magnifying glass to see whether the screen is damaged. If it has been, it may be necessary to "remake" the subject, although highly skilled retouchers can sometimes work wonders. A subject that is out of register (strictly speaking, called "out of fit" – the term "out of register" is usually used to describe a sheet in which *none* of the images on a plate are in register) is one that has two or more colors appearing "out of sync" with the others, although the edges of the illustration are clean and in perfect register with each other. If the edges are also out of register, then the film has merely been incorrectly stripped together for proofing purposes and can easily be adjusted. This is less likely to have occurred if the proof was electronically generated.

Finally, it is vital to check that the images are reproduced at the correct size, and that they are the right way around and not reversed. If the latter happens, the picture has to be "flipped," or "flopped." This is not just a simple case of turning the separated film upside down; a new piece of film has to be made so that the emulsion is on the correct side of the film, since the emulsion, whether on negative or positive film, has to come into contact with the surface of the printing plate.

When marking corrections on proofs, it is best to be as explicit as possible. If you do not know how to achieve the desired end result, tell the origination house what effect is required – they will know what needs to be done. Color correction symbols are particularly useful if there is a language barrier – for example, if the origination house is abroad.

Paste-up The conventional method of assembling proofs of type and pictures together on a page is called paste-up. This term usually refers to the final state of camera-ready art ("mechanicals") as given to the origination house or printer, but it is preceded by a preliminary "rough" paste-up, in which galley proofs and picture proofs or position guides are assembled together on layout sheets so that everything can be checked for size and fit before the final paste-up begins. If you use a computer, these stages are normally eliminated altogether, since the equivalent of a rough paste-up is produced in the form of laser proofs with everything in position, the next stage being to produce final film. However, it is not uncommon for bromide prints to be output from computers, via imagesetters, and these are subsequently used for mechanicals.

Final paste-up takes two forms, depending on what the typesetter or printer is contracted to supply. If it is the typesetter's job to carry out page make-up, you will need to supply an accurate paste-up consisting of final galley proofs and picture positions, clearly indicating, on the same piece of board, everything that is to appear in print – body text, captions, headlines, folios, and rules – marked up for any special requirements such as color and the thicknesses and length of rules. Accuracy is obviously extremely important as this paste-up will accompany the typesetter's text film output to the origination house.

If the typesetter is providing text in bromide galley form (called "repro"), you will need to have this pasted up so that it can be placed directly under the camera and photographed to produce final text film. This is called "camera-ready" paste-up (or art), or, more commonly, "mechanicals." With this method, only type and rules should appear on the mechanical, since if illustrations were incorporated onto the same surface, they would have to be masked out for final film to be made. You should mark any areas to print as a tint clearly on a tracing paper overlay – which also serves as a protective covering – along with any type or rules that are to print in a different color. Typesetting galleys used for camera-ready art are generally called "repro" (short for reproduction pulls), but more specifically bromides or PMTs. Repro should not lift or curl at the corners, so it must be securely stuck with an adhesive that is reliable, but one that permits you to remove or reposition it without damage. There are several brands of adhesive wax and rubber solutions suitable for this purpose. Small pieces of repro – such as individual words – can be secured with double-sided adhesive tape, but it is difficult to remove.

Printing Unless final film was generated by a computer, the next stage is for the text film to be matched to the illustration film. This will normally be done by the origination house or printer, depending on how film is supplied or who has been contracted to do the job. The origination house, for example, may have made film separations in page position and will then receive either page film from the typesetter or camera-ready art from you. The process of assembling film in page position is usually called "stripping," although it is more correctly known as "planning." Each page is stripped into the position (called "imposing" or "imposition") in which it will finally print, onto a much larger support film. This will eventually be photographically converted by way of a contact print into a single, flat piece of final film.

Before the final film is made, a single-color, photographic proof is made from the stripped together, imposed, film. This proof is called variously "blues," "dyeline," or "ozalid" (brown line or blue line) proofs. Text and illustration can now be seen in the positions that they will be printed. This is the last stage at which any corrections can reasonably be made. In some cases, especially in commercial work, pages are proofed after the ozalid stage from the final print-ing plates ("machine proofs"). Once the printing ("machine") plates have been made, making corrections is a costly process.

The main purpose of the blues is to serve as a positional check for the designer, since illustrations can easily be repositioned even at this stage as they are individually taped to the carrier film. Tex-tual changes can also be made, although the printer will have to cut up the film manually to position new type – or reposition old. The blue should also be checked to make sure that the film is free from marks and that no broken type needs to be repaired. Blues of four-color jobs will usually only consist of film of the black "printer" (the piece of film that is to print black) plus illustration film of one – or occasionally two – of the other colors.

After the return of the blues, final, "clean" film is produced and used to make plates. Any machine proofs after the ozalid stage are checked to see that each piece of color film has been correctly assembled, the alterations carried out, and that the film has not been damaged prior to platemaking.

Ideally, when printing starts, you should be present to view the illustrations, particularly if color is involved. Even at this stage, color can be minimally corrected through "manual" (actually, these days, inking is controlled by a computer) alteration of the inking process. This is done by regulating the ducts which control the amount of ink passing from the ink reservoirs onto the rollers and thence the plates. Color can only be corrected in strips parallel to the direction the sheets of paper come off the machine, and great care must be exercised to make sure that, by adjusting the color on one section of the sheet, the balance of color in another part is not upset, espe-cially where two halves of the same illustration appear in opposite corners of the sheet (see Imposition, p136). Sometimes, an individ-ual image can be very slightly altered – for instance, by adding packing behind the printing plate, thus increasing the amount of ink reaching the paper by making a heavier impression.

In all cases, the printer will be on hand to offer advice, although once the running sheets have been adjusted and pasted, more for-mal approval will be required, usually in the form of your signature on the printed sheet. This is quite normal, and while it absolves the printer from any recriminations by a dissatisfied customer, it puts all the responsibility firmly and squarely on your shoulders. An added burden for you is that any decision about whether color needs adjusting must be made almost instantly; presses print extremely quickly and stopping one is very expensive.

Book production The production of a book depends on what kind it is and how it is to be printed. For instance, producing a book that consists entirely of text – such as a novel – is relatively simple. How-ever, the moment pictures are introduced, the procedure becomes much more complicated. The most difficult type of book to produce is probably an illustrated reference book, but there are quite a few procedures that are applicable to all book production. One of these is at the earliest stage, where, as opposed to the rough, the design concept is normally presented in the form of a dummy book, or "bulking" dummy – a blank book is ordered from the printer to show its proposed size, bulk (the thickness determined by the num-ber of pages and the quality of paper), and binding. Inside, a num-ber of dummy pages are pasted, and these can either be "live" (with real type and artwork), make-believe, or a mixture of the two – real pictures with dummy text (or *vice versa*), for instance. In any case, these pages should show the style and level of the projected content, such as the proportion of illustration to text.

Depending on the scale of the project, presentation spreads (two pages together) are sometimes made by preparing flat sheets mounted on board and protected by transparent acetate film to accompany the bulking dummy. Again, they can be dummy, live, or a mixture.

A book can be the most complex job a designer has to put together – especially if it contains a large number of pages or if it involves distribution of full-color, two-color, and black-and-white pages – so it must be carefully planned in advance. This is done by drawing up a "flat plan," showing the chapter breakdown, number of pages devoted to the end matter and preliminary pages, where color pages fall, and so on. The most complex flat plans are called "flow charts," and these serve as a visual contents list, giving an idea of what will appear on every page of the book. These consist of pages drawn in miniature, showing text and illustration on every page, and they are often used more for sales purposes than for editorial input, although they can be very useful as a conceptual guide for both designers and editors.

Binding and budgetary considerations also have to be taken into account, especially when planning the color distribution. If a book is to be bound in 16-page sections, the designer has to work in multiples of 16. That is, each block of 16 pages must be consistent within itself – either four-color throughout ("four backed four"), or four-color spreads alternating with two- or one-color spreads ("four backed two," "four backed one"). It may be the case that, while a book is to be bound in 16s, it will be printed on sheets of 32 pages – 16 on one side and 16 on the other ("16 to view") – in which case each block of 16 pages of one treatment must be matched by an identical block of 16 elsewhere in the book. It does not matter if those blocks are not consecutive since the sheets can be cut ("slit") after they are printed. It is possible to divide a 16-page section in two – say eight pages of four-color followed by eight pages of one-color. In this instance, the printer uses a procedure known as "work and turn," whereby both sides of the 16 pages appear on one plate, which is used to print both sides of the sheet, thus printing two copies on one sheet.

Book jackets The design of a book jacket is often thought by the publisher to be more important than the inside of the book, because, more often than not, it is the cover that is deemed to sell the book. Thus the cover not only has to convey the book's quality and content instantly to the prospective buyer, but it also has to project this information boldly from the midst of a vast array of books, many or all of which may be on the same subject. The selection of jacket designs is usually made by several people, usually representatives of the sales, marketing, editorial, and management departments of a publishing house. In many instances the final decision will be a compromise, since a combination of opinions tends to rule out intuitive judgments. For this reason, it would be a mistake for you to consider a book jacket merely as a design exercise. It is not. Certainly, a designer always starts with the premise that the solution that looks esthetically pleasing is the one most likely to appeal to the prospective buyer, but what may appeal to you may not appeal to the market at which the book is directed, and *vice versa*.

Market research is rarely, if ever, carried out on a book or book

1

	Sheet
1 2 3 4 5 6 7 8 9 10 11 12 13 14 15 16	A
17 18 19 20 21 22 23 24 25 26 27 28 29 30 31 32	A
33 34 35 36 37 38 39 40 41 42 43 44 45 46 47 48	B
49 50 51 52 53 54 55 56 57 58 59 60 61 62 63 64	B
65 66 67 68 69 70 71 72 73 74 75 76 77 78 79 80	C
81 82 83 84 85 86 87 88 89 90 91 92 93 94 95 96	C
97 98 99 100 101 102 103 104 105 106 107 108 109 110 111 112	D
113 114 115 116 117 118 119 120 121 122 123 124 125 126 127 128	D

2

	Sheet
1 2 3 4 5 6 7 8 9 10 11 12 13 14 15 16	A
17 18 19 20 21 22 23 24 25 26 27 28 29 30 31 32	B
33 34 35 36 37 38 39 40 41 42 43 44 45 46 47 48	B
49 50 51 52 53 54 55 56 57 58 59 60 61 62 63 64	C
65 66 67 68 69 70 71 72 73 74 75 76 77 78 79 80	C
81 82 83 84 85 86 87 88 89 90 91 92 93 94 95 96	A
97 98 99 100 101 102 103 104 105 106 107 108 109 110 111 112	D
113 114 115 116 117 118 119 120 121 122 123 124 125 126 127 128	D

3

One color   Two colors   Four colors

	Sheet
1 2 3 4 5 6 7 8 9 10 11 12 13 14 15 16	A
17 18 19 20 21 22 23 24 25 26 27 28 29 30 31 32	B
33 34 35 36 37 38 39 40 41 42 43 44 45 46 47 48	A
49 50 51 52 53 54 55 56 57 58 59 60 61 62 63 64	C
65 66 67 68 69 70 71 72 73 74 75 76 77 78 79 80	C
81 82 83 84 85 86 87 88 89 90 91 92 93 94 95 96	B
97 98 99 100 101 102 103 104 105 106 107 108 109 110 111 112	D
113 114 115 116 117 118 119 120 121 122 123 124 125 126 127 128	D

4

1	2	3	4	5	6	7	8	9	10	11	12	13	14	15	16	17	18	19	20	21	22	23	24
25	26	27	28	29	30	31	32	33	34	35	36	37	38	39	40	41	42	43	44	45	46	47	48
49	50	51	52	53	54	55	56	57	58	59	60	61	62	63	64	65	66	67	68	69	70	71	72
73	74	75	76	77	78	79	80	81	82	83	84	85	86	87	88	89	90	91	92	93	94	95	96
97	98	99	100	101	102	103	104	105	106	107	108	109	110	111	112	113	114	115	116	117	118	119	120
121	122	123	124	125	126	127	128	129	130	131	132	133	134	135	136	137	138	139	140	141	142	143	144
145	146	147	148	149	150	151	152	153	154	155	156	157	158	159	160	161	162	163	164	165	166	167	168
169	170	171	172	173	174	175	176	177	178	179	180	181	182	183	184	185	186	187	188	189	190	191	192

Wraps   Inserts   Wraps

5

1	2	3	4	5	6	7	8	9	10	11	12	13	14	15	16	17	18	19	20	21	22	23	24
25	26	27	28	29	30	31	32	33	34	35	36	37	38	39	40	41	42	43	44	45	46	47	48
		49	50	51	52	53	54	55	56					57	58	59	60	61	62	63	64		
65	66	67	68	69	70	71	72	73	74	75	76	77	78	79	80	81	82	83	84	85	86	87	88
		89	90	91	92	93	94	95	96					97	98	99	100	101	102	103	104		
		105	106	107	108	109	110	111	112					113	114	115	116	117	118	119	120		
121	122	123	124	125	126	127	128	129	130	131	132	133	134	135	136	137	138	139	140	141	142	143	144
		145	146	147	148	149	150	151	152					153	154	155	156	157	158	159	160		

Flat plans These are essential for working out the fall of color pages whenever a large job is to be printed in more than one color. The plan ensures that the right colors are on the correct side of a sheet so that the sheet only requires two passes through the press (one for each side) when a multi-color press is used. The first three examples show a 128-page job, using four sheets of paper with 32 pages printing on each sheet. The pages are arranged in 16-page strips, since they will be bound in 16-page sections, or signatures.

When planning the color fall on a book specified to print with 64 pages of four-color and 64 pages of single-color, the simplest method is to arrange the color so that one side of the sheet prints in four-color and the other in one color. The result is that every alternate double page spread is in four-color (**1**). The distribution can be varied by, say, arranging four colors to be printed in two blocks of 16 pages – 32 pages in each block – to make up the 64 pages available. These 32-page blocks can be located anywhere in the job, provided that each 16-page section matches up with another 16-page section so that 32 pages always print complete (**2**).

Another possible variation is 48 pages of four-color, 32 pages of two-color and 48 pages of one-color, remembering, again, to work in matching 16-page sections (**3**). The basic determining factor is the number of pages on each side of the sheet and the binding requirements.

"Wraps" and "inserts" are used when illustration is less evenly distributed than in the other examples shown here. Wraps literally "wrap" around the outside of a folded section, while inserts are placed in the center fold of a section. Here (**5**), a 160-page job is printing as 128 pages of single color, and the separate insert of 32 pages of four-color can be wrapped around, or inserted into, each section in blocks of four pages. Wraps and inserts are inserted when the sheets are folded and gathered, prior to binding.

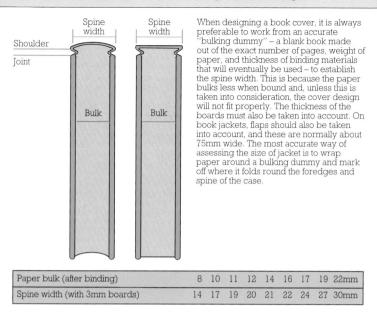

When designing a book cover, it is always preferable to work from an accurate "bulking dummy" – a blank book made out of the exact number of pages, weight of paper, and thickness of binding materials that will eventually be used – to establish the spine width. This is because the paper bulks less when bound and, unless this is taken into consideration, the cover design will not fit properly. The thickness of the boards must also be taken into account. On book jackets, flaps should also be taken into account, and these are normally about 75mm wide. The most accurate way of assessing the size of jacket is to wrap paper around a bulking dummy and mark off where it folds round the foredges and spine of the case.

| Paper bulk (after binding) | | | | 8 | 10 | 11 | 12 | 14 | 16 | 17 | 19 | 22mm |
| Spine width (with 3mm boards) | | | | 14 | 17 | 19 | 20 | 21 | 22 | 24 | 27 | 30mm |

jacket prior to its publication, and any reasons a publisher may have for preferring one jacket design over another is very often based on precedent – if particular types of jacket have worked for a particular audience in the past, then further designs on that subject are likely to fall within known parameters. These precedents will often extend to such things as preference for one color over another, and even these preferences will vary from publisher to publisher – for instance, one may have had considerable success with predominantly black jackets, while another may not.

Individual taste is another important factor in book jacket design, whether it is based on precedent or not. A designer who is familiar with the likes and dislikes of the personalities involved in decision-making is more likely to find a design accepted.

As with most design jobs, the level to which a rough jacket design is drawn depends largely on the criteria for making final decisions – an in-house designer, for instance, may only have to satisfy an art director, in which case a fairly rudimentary visual, showing the intent rather than the final effect, will suffice. In any other circumstances, however, the only way to put across the total impact of a design is to present a full-scale mock-up, complete with actual photographs or illustrations and type, covered with self-adhesive film laminate to give the impression of proper lamination and wrapped around a bulking dummy.

Magazine design Editorial procedures in magazine production roughly parallel those of book production, although on a more labor-intensive scale, depending on the frequency of the publication. Magazines are put together as a result of constant discussion between the editor, art editor, and picture editor, as well as various feature editors and staff writers. The largest single influence on the number of editorial pages available is that of the number of advertisements sold in any one issue, since most magazines rely on advertising for their profit.

Having decided what is to go into an issue, the pictures are obtained first, since most magazine features cannot be laid out without the pictures. Two or three main features will then be assembled as layouts, and any of them which are disliked are discarded at this stage. More features are prepared than are actually needed for a single issue just in case any are rejected. Those that are acceptable may be held over for a subsequent issue. Magazines usually rely heavily on picture libraries for main features such as sporting events and also for back-up material. Many articles will require specially commissioned photography. If this is to be done in a studio, the designer should try to be present at the shoot.

The method used for printing a magazine is a major factor in determining its design limitations, as is, of course, the market at which the magazine is aimed. If, for instance, a magazine is printed by offset lithography, roughly the same principles and limitations apply as those of book production. On the other hand, magazines printed by gravure require special considerations; design for gravure-printed magazines needs to be much bolder than for litho, not least because everything – including type – is screened. This means that more delicate designs may start to break up or even disappear entirely. Also, subtle detail in pictures is much more difficult to control in gravure printing; while very deep blacks can be achieved, any detail in dark areas will disappear. Even the degree of blackness in a picture can be somewhat variable – the result is just as likely to be very thin as it is to be very black. These technical limitations thus affect the size at which a picture can be satisfactorily reproduced, whereas an image to be reproduced by litho can retain a certain amount of detail at sizes of one inch or even less. Two or three inches is probably the smallest size that gravure can handle before the readability of an image becomes difficult. It is interesting that although the results achieved by gravure-printed magazines can be somewhat unpredictable, postage stamps – which require the highest standards of technical reproduction – are also printed by the gravure process, but at much slower speeds and on equipment that can produce much greater fidelity.

The reasons for using one printing method as opposed to the other rests solely with the quantity of magazines to be printed. While the quality of offset litho is much higher than that of gravure, litho plates will generally only print up to about 100,000 copies before the image quality becomes unacceptable and the plates need to be remade, whereas gravure cylinders can print an almost limitless number. Some weekly magazines may be printing up to four or five million copies.

Speed is another important factor when deciding which printing process to use – gravure machines run at much faster speeds than web-offset litho machines. It is becoming increasingly common for magazines to be printed by a mixture of gravure and litho, the latter often being used for regional inserts. This enables advertisers to aim at selective, localized markets, without having to pay the considerably higher rates for national coverage.

Nearly all magazines are now produced on computers, from copywriting right up to the print stage, involving people in a wide variety of disciplines: designers, copywriters, editors, page make-up operators, color separators, and so on. Although this has led to a radical change in the way that magazines are put together, the basic process remains the same as when they are put together traditionally. Having obtained the material for a feature, the designer sets about making a rough scheme of the layout. The pictures are scanned for position only straight from the transparency (conventionally, they are sized up and printed on black-and-white document paper). Text is entered directly by trained operators or copywriters, formatted, and then laid out (conventionally, areas of type are indicated by using cut up text from previously printed issues, so that everyone working on the magazine knows exactly where the type is going to be and how much is required). Copy-editing takes place directly onto the laid-out pages as opposed to marking galley proofs (although this still occurs on occasion).

Color images are normally sent down to the printer about six weeks before the magazine is due to appear; the deadline for monochrome pictures is about four weeks before publication. It is possible for last-minute features – on a current topical theme, for instance – to be put together within two or three hours and sent to the printer as late as one week before publication, but if it can be avoided, it rarely happens, due to cost of printers' overtime.

The fall of color pages throughout a magazine is determined by the printer in consultation with the production editor, but it is never so rigid that the designer is not permitted to make last-minute changes, provided, of course, that this does not affect the location of advertisements – the main criterion in deciding color imposition.

In non-computerized operations, one or two days after the color has been sent off, the text copy is marked up and headlines are specified. These are then typeset, assembled, by the printer, in position with the color pictures and returned as black-and-white photoprinted page proofs. At this stage the position of color pictures cannot be changed, but alterations can be made to the type. Correction marks are then made on the proofs and sent back to the printer, who makes the corrections and returns them. These latest proofs are called "as to press," and it is extremely difficult to make any changes at all at this stage. Many of these stages and constraints are eliminated when computers are used, since each of these tasks will already have been carried out on screen.

The as-to-press proofs are returned to the printer who then makes color proofs of the pages – but without any type appearing unless it is to be in color. These color proofs do not contain any monochrome pictures either – the next time they are seen is on "running" copies (the actual printed copies of the magazine).

The proofs are then color corrected, and when all the corrections have been done, the gravure cylinders are put onto machine and printing begins. Once the magazine is being run (printed), it is very difficult to make last-minute color adjustments – not because of technical difficulties, but because any adjustment may affect the color of an advertisement. Since it is the advertisers who provide the financial backing for producing most magazines, they must be satisfied with the quality of their advertisements. If they are unhappy with results, advertisers simply will not pay the bills, even though they already have had the opportunity to reject any unsatisfactory proofs.

4
PHOTOGRAPHY AND DESIGN

Photography for reproduction/Black-and-white film/
Color film/Film speeds/Film formats/Digital imaging/
Lenses/Shutter speeds/Lighting/Studio effects/
Prints from transparencies

After typography, photography is perhaps the next most important and widely used element in graphic design, and the revolu-
tionary technological changes affecting the former are now having
a profound effect on the latter. However, technological progress has
been slow to take a firm grip, not just because of the immense technical difficulties in replacing film as a highly portable and relatively
stable medium capable of producing high quality results, but also
because of the resistance of many professional photographers to
switch to a medium which does not offer *them* the versatility they
have been used to, despite what it may offer you, as a designer, or
other reprographic processes along the course of a job. The
change, then, from one medium to another is most likely to occur as
a result of demands made by the increasing number of computer-
based graphic designers – provided that the quality offered by new
technologies makes the grade. In the meantime – and for some
time yet – film will remain the preferred medium, and to this end
Kodak has provided a halfway house between film and digital photography with its "PhotoCD" system.

Your involvement with photography will depend entirely on the
requirements of the job in hand. For instance, although a photographer will often be working from detailed layouts produced by you,
your presence will generally be required at the shooting session.
This is necessary because instant decisions may be needed concerning changes if circumstances prevent the subject – for whatever reason – from behaving the way you expected it to. In such
cases, the designer controls the compromises needed to convert
the initial concept to the finished picture.

On the other hand, and at the other extreme, is when your job will
simply be one of selecting pictures from a mass of stock material,
such as that offered by a picture library. This frequently involves
considerable compromise when the layout must be manipulated to
fit the picture, taking into account that uncommissioned photography can range from the superb to the unacceptable – although in
the case of the latter, you probably wouldn't be using it.

For design purposes, photographs are used either to provide an
illustrated record or to add to or enhance an editorial or promotional concept – photographs are only rarely used for their own
sake. Success is achieved in the first case by the photographer's
skill in recording a sharply-defined, evenly-lit, and correctly
exposed image – if that's what you require. Second, success

depends upon close communication between photographer and designer and, in particular, upon the designer's understanding of the way in which photography and photographic reproduction work.

Photography for reproduction Among the many qualities that photographs to be used in design work should have, the most important is what is termed the "reproduction ratio." In theory, a photographic original can be enlarged to a huge extent and yet remain intelligible – for instance, on a movie screen a 35mm format is enlarged by more than 30,000%. In the context of a printed page, however, the same original would begin to look blurred and weak in color at an enlargement of only 1000%. The typical enlargement ratio for a 35mm transparency ranges between 100% (same size) and 1500%. At an enlargement of 1000%, a 35mm transparency would cover this entire double-page spread, while a 4 x 5in. would require 247% enlargement, and an 8 x 10in. would be slightly larger than same size at 112%. Since the grain size of film of a particular type and speed is the same regardless of format, larger sizes of transparency produce a clearer definition when reproduced.

Black-and-white film General-purpose black-and-white camera films are panchromatic; they react to all colors in the visible spectrum, though not to quite the same degree in each case. Although this wide range of sensitivity is generally considered desirable, in certain cases the use of filters may be necessary in order to distinguish certain colors more clearly from the surrounding colors, or even to eliminate one completely. A yellow filter, for instance, will enhance the appearance of white clouds in a clear blue sky by reducing the amount of blue light reaching the film. Consequently, the sky area appears darker on the resulting print, producing a greater contrast with the white clouds. Alternatively, colored stains on a document can be weakened or eliminated in a photographic copy by the use of a suitable filter, such as a filter of the same color as the stain.

Color film Reversal ("slide," or "transparency") and negative films both contain three layers of light-sensitive emulsion – a blue-sensitive layer forming a yellow dye, green-sensitive forming magenta, and red-sensitive forming cyan. Most colors, with the exception of fluorescent ones, can be produced by combinations of the final processed dye layers. It is important that the correct type of color film is used for the conditions in which the shot is being taken, such as "daylight" and "artificial" light types.

All reversal film types are fundamentally the same, but substantive varieties such as Ektachrome can be processed by the user. Non-substantive films such as Kodachrome – which is usually sold process-paid – require special treatment and so they have to be returned to the manufacturer for processing.

The capabilities of the two types of film are more or less the same, except that, because it cannot be specially developed, non-substantive film is of no use if circumstances dictate that the film must be uprated ("pushed") to a faster speed. This can, however, be achieved with substantive films during the developing process, although it is not altogether desirable since pushed film will result in a loss of picture quality with increased graininess and contrast, as well as degraded color rendering.

Because the manufacture of reversal color film is such an exacting process, the reaction of films from different production batches to the same subject may not be identical. For this reason, film boxes are stamped with the batch code and expiry date so that films required for the same shooting session can be matched together.

Negative color film is generally used only to produce prints for presentation purposes such as in dummy packs or books. Negative duplicating film is used to make master originals in the mass-production of transparencies for audio-visual use.

Film speeds The speed of a particular film depends on the size of the grains of silver in their chemical structure – the larger the grains, the faster the film. One of the fundamental rules with either black-and-white or color film is that an increase in film speed inevitably leads to a loss of quality in the final image, although modern film technology is reducing the differences between quality of films of different speeds. The speed of a particular film can usually be recognized by the rating given to it by the American Standards Association, thus the term "ASA." German "DIN" (Deutsche Industrie Norm) is also used, but both this and ASA are being gradually replaced by ISO (International Standards Organization). Camera films generally range in speed from 32 ASA to 1250 ASA, although this upper limit can be extended to about 3000 ASA by forced development.

Color

Panchromatic film

Orthochromatic film

Black-and-white film and color All designers should have a basic understanding of the nature of black-and-white film and how it works when faced with the problem of recording color subjects. When black-and-white film is used, there are anomalies in the way the various types of film react to color. When compared to the sensitivity of the human eye, for instance,

most black-and-white film reacts most strongly to the blue end of the red/green/blue (RGB) color spectrum, whereas the eye is most sensitive to green.

"Orthochromatic" films, although theoretically producing an accurate record of all colors ("ortho" meaning "correct"), do not respond at all well to red colors, while modern "panchromatic" films are sensitive to the full range of

visible spectrum colors. This point is illustrated (above), where the response to color of orthochromatic and panchromatic black-and-white films is clearly demonstrated. Panchromatic films are generally used more widely by photographers than are orthographic films, which tend to be used by the reprographics industries.

Black-and-white film	Speed (ASA)	Type	35mm	Roll	Sheet	Comments
Normal contrast						
Agfapan HPX	25	P	●			
Ilford Pan F	50	P	●			
Kodak Panatomic-X	32	P	●	●		
Agfapan 100	100	P	●	●	●	
Ilford FP4	125	P	●	●	●	
Kodak Plus-X	125	P	●	●	●	
Fuji Neopan	400	P	●	●		
Fuji Neopan	1600	P	●			
Ilford HP5	400	P	●	●	●	
Ilford XP2	var	P	●			Final image in dye
Kodak Tri-X	400	P	●	●		
Kodak Recording 2475	1000	P	●			
Kodak T-Max	3200	P	●	●		
Kodak Prof Copy	25	O			●	Available U.S. only
Kodak Gravure Pos	20	O			●	
High contrast						
Kodalith type 3	12	O	●		●	35mm bulk rolls
Kodalith Pan	40	P			●	
Specials						
Agfacontour		O			●	Special effects
Agfa Dia-direct	100	P	●			Reversal slide film

var = variable; O = orthochromatic; P = panchromatic

Grade 0

Grade 1

Grade 2

Grade 3

Grade 4

Grade 5

The chart (**top**) details some major black-and-white film types. No less important than film to the quality of a black-and-white photograph is the type of paper it is printed on, and, when ordering a print, it is vital to specify the paper to be used, since each grade of paper has its own characteristics. The prints (**above**) show the effects of printing on Grade 0 paper through to Grade 5.0 is very flat or soft, and is intended for use with high-contrast negatives, while 5, on the other hand, is very hard and is used with soft negatives. While hard grades make full use of the paper's tonal range, they produce harsh images, with no detail at either end of the scale.

Filters Any designer commissioning black-and-white photography should be aware of the importance of filters and the way they can affect color subjects. The scene (**right**), shown in color, was photographed again in black-and-white to demonstrate the effect that filters can have on the end result (**below**).

No filter

Yellow filter

Blue filter

Red filter

When photographing certain colors in black-and-white, a filter must be used to distinguish a subject from its background. In color (**right**), the tomato contrasts clearly with the lettuce, but red and green produce roughly the same shade of gray when shot with panchromatic film (see p.55), so in black-and-white there would be little distinction. A red filter, however (**below left**), allows red light to pass, blocking green light. Thus, the tomato prints lighter and the lettuce darker. With a green filter (**below right**), this is reversed.

The choice of film speed is influenced not only by the amount of light available, but also by the subject, the context and degree of enlargement in reproduction, and the chosen format. In addition, some purely mechanical factors must be taken into consideration, such as the distance from the camera the subject comes into, and goes out of, focus. The limits within which the portion of the photograph remains in focus is called depth of field, and this can be regulated by the size of aperture in the camera lens through which the light passes. The smaller the aperture ("stop," shown on the lens control as an "f" number), the greater the depth of field.

If a greater depth of field is required, the lens aperture can be stopped down (on 35mm cameras the lens f-numbers normally range from f1.2, the largest, to f32, the smallest, depending on its focal length), but because the same amount of light must reach the film in order to make a perfect exposure, the camera shutter must be set at a slower speed. At slower speeds, subject or camera movement, or both, may degrade the image. Alternatively, a faster film can be used, thus permitting a faster shutter speed, but the resulting increase in grain size may prove unacceptable.

Changing to a lens of shorter focal length such as a 28mm (wide-angle) lens will give a greater depth of field than a standard 50mm lens set at the same aperture, but it will also reduce the size of the subject within the film frame. Moving closer to the subject with a wide-angle lens to make it large enough may result in an undesirable exaggerated perspective because of the change in viewpoint. A smaller lens aperture would be possible if the subject could be lit with brighter lighting, but this may be difficult to achieve except in a large studio. Similar, and generally more complex, problems usually face the photographer in all but the simplest commissions.

Film formats Apart from jobs which require the photographer to have mobility – travel and reportage photography for instance, where the norm is 35mm – the choice of format is usually a compromise between cost and definition. The larger the format, the more expensive photography becomes – in terms of equipment, film, processing, lighting, and studio space required, and sometimes the photographer's fees. However, it is important to remember that, to achieve the highest quality, the format must match the printed application wherever possible.

35mm The most widely used format is the 35mm system, especially the single-lens reflex, which produces a frame size of 24 x 36mm. This system is far more flexible than any other and is often used in preference to the others even when considerable enlargement is required. The photographer is thus able to work at high speed if necessary, and because a wide range of film emulsion is available at a relatively low cost, a high degree of experimentation and intensive subject coverage is possible. The motor-drive of the 35mm camera – firing the shutter and moving the film forward at up to five frames per second – means that a photographer can snatch the opportunity of a completely fortuitous shot with comparative ease without having to judge the right moment.

Finished transparencies must be handled with great care so that they are prevented from being damaged. Individual frames, whether mounted or unmounted, should be sealed in transparent sleeves. The mounts themselves should be of a type which permits easy removal of the transparency, as the scanning method of color separation requires that transparencies be removed from their mounts. Glass mounts, intended for projection only, are unsuitable since they break easily and could well damage the transparency.

The 120 system Cameras using 120 and 220 roll film fall into three groups: the twin-lens reflex types such as Mamiyaflex and Rollei and the single-lens reflex such as the Hasselblad. Both these types produce 2¼ x 2¼in. (60 x 60mm) images, but the advantages of this square format are not fully realized in reproduction since most designs seem to call for rectangular shapes. This is where the third group of the 120 system – the single-lens reflex such as the large format Pentax – comes into its own. Two frame sizes are produced. The first, the so-called "ideal format," measures 1¾ x 2¼in. (45 x 60mm), and the other, larger size is 2¼ x 2¾in. (60 x 70mm).

Larger formats Because studio conditions can be controlled with powerful lighting equipment and cameras can be mounted in fixed positions, large film formats are used so that the highest standards of reproduction can be achieved. Of the several available, three formats are particularly popular: 4 x 5in., 5 x 7in., and 8 x 10in.

The film is supplied in packs of single sheets – hence the name

35mm	2¼in. square	5 x 4in.

561%   367%   159%

640%   556%   254%

1200%   737%   333%

Effect of enlargement A good deal of design work requires the enlargement of photographs, so you should take into account the effect that this will have on the qualities of the original pictures. The greater the enlargement, the more detail that will be lost and the more "grainy" the printed image. The strips (**above**) show the same image photographed on different film formats – 35mm, 2¼in. square and 5 x 4in. – and the effect on the subject of varying degrees of enlargement. It is clear that the larger the original format, the greater the clarity and detail when the image is enlarged.

Color film Although photographers sometimes argue that there is little difference between the results produced by different color films, these enlargements clearly show the difference. This knowledge is particularly important to the designer, who will be frequently asking for original prints and transparencies to be enlarged. The Kodachrome 25 transparency remains clear and sharp, and there is virtually no graininess. The colors are well-saturated, with the reds and yellows being particularly true to life. The Ektachrome 400 transparency is flatter and more grainy by comparison, with poorer color saturation. This is partly due to its extra speed. In addition, it is very slightly bluer overall. The test strips on the facing page show the color qualities of various reversal (slide) films. The two Kodachrome examples differ from the others in that the color dyes are added during processing. This reduces graininess. In general, the basic rule is the faster the film, the more grainy the result.

Ektachrome 400

Kodachrome 25

Kodachrome 25

Kodachrome 64

Ektachrome 200

Ektachrome 64

Agfa RS50 plus

Ektachrome 400

Fujichrome 100

Agfa RS100 plus

Fujichrome 400

Fujichrome 1600

''sheet-film'' – which is loaded into a double-sided, light-tight holder as required. This holder, or ''dark slide,'' displaces the camera's focusing screen when the desired composition has been made, and a movable sheath is slid back ready for the film to be exposed to the light when the camera shutter is opened. A Polaroid film holder can also be fitted to allow a preview of the finished photograph. The photographer will normally have one sheet of film processed before the final shot is taken or, alternatively, two or three sheets of different exposures will be processed before the set is dismantled.

Cameras using large film formats are very versatile, and image shapes can be manipulated by using the built-in movements of lens and film planes. Use of these formats also allows a scale drawing of the required design on tracing paper to be taped directly onto the focusing screen as a final compositional check.

Digital imaging In electronic digital camera systems, film is replaced by an ''imager'' – typically a ''CCD (charge-coupled device) array'' – and a means of storing the ''captured'' data, usually either in the camera's ''memory,'' or on a storage medium such as magnetic disks similar to those used by computers. The resolution of an image depends upon the density of the CCD array, measured in pixels. Typically, a 35mm frame may have as many as 1.3 million pixels (1,024 x 1,280), using Kodak's Professional Digital Camera System. The Canon ION Still Video Camera generates images of a lower resolution (795 x 596 pixels), as this system is intended for use with screen display equipment – either on a regular television set or on a computer screen.

Digital conversion of film images to a computer storage medium is possible using Kodak's Photo CD system, where processed slides or negatives are recorded digitally onto a compact disc. The advantages of this system are that it permits viewing on a standard television screen (with a special player, that allows panning and zooming), manipulation on a desktop computer, and prints which can be made from the CD. Each Photo CD image is stored at different levels of resolution, from 128 x 192 pixels to 2,048 x 3,072.

The advantages of digital imaging to the computer-based graphic designer is immediate, allowing prints or slides to be made, pictures to be instantly cropped, sized, or otherwise manipulated directly on screen, and even direct color separations to be made.

Lenses The ''normal'' lens for any particular format is that which is the nearest to normal human vision. A photographic image is totally unlike one perceived by the eye – not surprisingly since a camera only has one lens – but people have two eyes thus enabling surroundings to be perceived in three dimensions as opposed to the two dimensions of a photograph. The overall ''angle of view'' of the human eye is about 180°, far wider than the 45° of the normal lens, but the eye's area of focus is comparatively small.

Any deviation from the normal lens will begin to distort or alter perspective – close-up shooting with a wide-angle lens distorts the features of the face, for instance, while a long-focus lens will compress perspective. This compression is an illusion, since the image presented by a long-focus lens is simply a magnification of a portion of the same subject as seen by a normal lens from exactly the same viewpoint. The distortion is less if a wide-angle shot is reproduced large, or if a telephoto shot is reproduced small.

The magnifying property of a lens is described by its focal length. In the 35mm format, a 50mm or 55mm lens is normal, 28mm format or less is wide-angle, and 90mm, 135mm, or more is long-

¹/₃₀ sec. f4 = +3 stops

¹/₃₀ sec. f16 = −1 stops

¹/₃₀ sec. f5.6 = +2 stops

¹/₃₀ sec. f22 = −2 stops

¹/₃₀ sec. f8 = +1 stop

¹/₆₀ sec. f22 = −3 stops

¹/₃₀ sec. f11 = through-the-lens reading

¹/₁₂₅ sec. f22 = −4 stops

Under- and over-exposure It is important, when directing photography, to understand that color film inevitably reacts to different quantities of light, and that there are strict exposure latitudes within which an optimum result can be achieved.

The examples (above) show how a strip of Kodachrome 64 produced very different results when the exposure was deliberately varied from the "through-the-lens" meter reading of ¹/₃₀ second at f11 (**bottom left**). As the number of f-stops was increased from +1 to +3, the picture changed noticeably. An extra f-stop made the sky less intense and gave it a slight green tinge. Two stops bleached large areas of highlights to white, while three stops produced a totally over-exposed result. There are virtually no hues, while almost all detail is lost.

The shots in the right-hand column show the effects of decreasing exposure from −1 stop (**top**) to −4 stops (**bottom**). As the exposure is progressively reduced, the more features disappear from the shadow areas. From the designer's point of view, very slight under-exposure is usually preferable to over-exposure since, although the choice is subjective, under-exposure generally gives a better chance of more fully saturated colors.

focus. With larger formats these figures increase – 80mm is normal for $2\frac{1}{4}$ x $2\frac{1}{4}$, 150mm for 4 x 5in. and so on. Variable focal length ("zoom") lenses can replace a number of fixed focal-length lenses in the 35mm format, but, because they usually contain a large number of lens elements, contrast and definition may be substantially reduced. They have the added disadvantages of smaller apertures and greater bulk.

There are a variety of specialist lenses at each end of the focal-length scale. For instance, ultra-wide-angle lenses for 35mm cameras – such as 20mm or less – produce increasing degrees of linear distortion, whereas the fish-eye lens with curvilinear ("barrel") distortion, produces a circular image of everything in front of the camera and even slightly behind it. More compact long-focus lenses, such as telephoto lenses, are shorter and mirror lenses even more so. The latter have only limited application since they have no conventional diaphragm, so exposure can only be controlled by changing the shutter speed of the camera. Pictures produced by mirror lenses can be recognized by the circular "doughnut" form out-of-focus highlights in the background. Generally, all longer and heavier lenses need to be supported on a tripod to avoid camera shake.

When extreme close-up work is required, the camera lens must be moved farther from the film plane than the ordinary focusing mechanism allows; and special focusing mounts, extension tubes,

A view camera can be used to manipulate the shape and sharpness of an image. Here, the vertical tilt of the film back means the sides of the front surface do not appear parallel.

By tilting the lens panel back, the shape of the cube stays the same, but the distribution of sharpness alters. Here the panel is almost vertical.

or bellows allow magnification of up to about three times life-size. "Macro" lenses have a specially long range of focusing movement and will magnify without any accessories. Extra care must be taken when lighting close-up subjects, since the lens itself may get in the way and cast a shadow on the subject. Some lenses have been developed to overcome this problem, such as the specialist medical Nikkor which has a built-in ring flash which gives shadowless frontal illumination.

Shutter speeds The photographer's usual aim is to keep exposure time as short as possible since exposures longer than 1/30 second, on a hand-held camera, will almost certainly allow time for the camera or even subject to move. The safest lower limit for acceptable sharpness on a hand-held camera is probably 1/125th second, depending on the focal length of the lens.

Slow shutter speeds can be an effective way of describing speed in an otherwise static medium. By focusing on a speeding car, for instance – provided that the camera is traveling at the same relative "speed" as the subject – a slow shutter speed will produce a background blur of horizontal lines, while the car itself will remain sharp.

The fastest shutter speeds on conventional cameras are usually 1/1000 second, sometimes 1/2000 second, and even 1/4000 second, and movement at these speeds becomes frozen in a picture. Speeds even faster than this that enable you to capture still more

Swinging the camera back to the left means the sharpest focus runs diagonally. The cube's shape is distorted and its position altered slightly.

Swinging the lens panel to the left does not affect the cube's shape, but alters the plane of the sharpest focus to the diagonal running from near left.

| Top lighting/spot | Top lighting/diffuser | ¾ lighting/spot | ¾ lighting/diffuser |

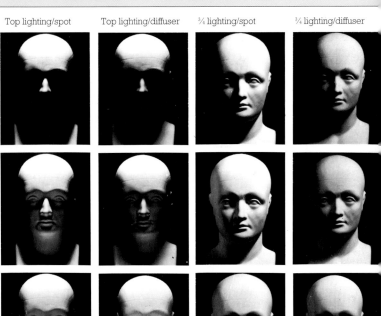

rapidly-moving subjects, such as a drop of falling liquid, can be achieved by electronic flash exposures. In this case, the duration of the flash is shorter than the fastest shutter speed on the camera.

Lighting The way in which a subject is lit, as well as the amount of light reaching the film, is the most important variable in successful photography. The eye responds automatically to changes in lighting, quality, color, and direction, whereas camera film does not. To record every detail of a subject, it must be lit in a way that eliminates shadow areas, thus exposing the detail. In natural, daylight conditions, lighting can still be controlled to a certain extent. For example, details in deep shadows, cast by direct sun, can be retained to a limited extent by using diffusers and reflectors to reduce the contrast.

Artificial lighting primarily sets out to imitate natural light, and, for this reason, the basis of most set-ups is typified by a single diffused high-intensity light. Additional fill-in lights, diffusers, reflectors, and even mirrors are required to retain enough detail in areas of shadow cast by the main light. Care has to be taken, however, when using a group of lights, because shadows cast by more than one can quite easily destroy the unity of the picture. Many of these basic "rules"

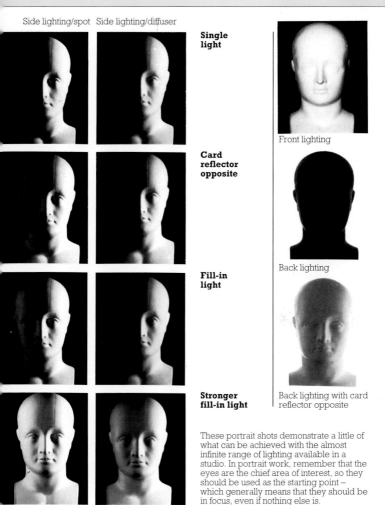

Side lighting/spot   Side lighting/diffuser

Single light

Card reflector opposite

Fill-in light

Stronger fill-in light

Front lighting

Back lighting

Back lighting with card reflector opposite

These portrait shots demonstrate a little of what can be achieved with the almost infinite range of lighting available in a studio. In portrait work, remember that the eyes are the chief area of interest, so they should be used as the starting point – which generally means that they should be in focus, even if nothing else is.

can be broken in order to achieve visual effect and drama – for instance, a shot may be deliberately lit with high contrast to emphasize one small area.

There are two types of artificial photographic light source – continuous tungsten and electronic flash. The first group includes the basic "photoflood" – a more powerful version of the household tungsten lamp – spotlights (more or less the same as those used in the theater), and quartz-iodine lamps.

But the most widely used source is electronic flash, comprising a single (or more) control console which can power up to eight studio flash units, or " heads." Some types of flash unit are self-contained, providing their own charge.

It is impossible to observe the effect of lighting during a test firing of the flash because of its speed and intensity. Instead, each head is equipped with a continuous "modeling" light, usually in the center of the tube itself, so that an approximation of the final result can be seen. Flash light can be controlled by setting individual flash heads to give much lower charges than their rated output. A variety of attachments similar to those used on other lights will also modify their effect.

The "correct" exposure of a flash-lit subject is determined by the use of a special meter. Most such meters give a direct indication of the precise f-stop to be used. On static subjects a cumulative exposure can be made by firing the heads repeatedly, with the shutter remaining open until the total exposure reaches the required level. To light large areas, several heads are required. These are often assembled into a large mobile housing faced with diffusing gauze, the whole assembly being called, whimsically, a "fish-fryer." These units are used extensively to simulate natural daytime lighting conditions on table-sized sets. Even larger sets can be lit with an assembly called a "swimming pool."

There are flashes for special applications, such as the ring flash – developed for medical use – where the flash encircles the camera lens and gives shadowless results at close range. A ring flash is also quite effective at portrait range if the subject is placed close to a flat background, creating an intense rim-shadow. Since all these devices operate at very high voltages and generate considerable heat, safety is of paramount importance in their use.

Studio effects Reality can be subjected to much trickery in the studio by the use of optical camera techniques, filtration, the use of scale models as substitutes for the real subject, illusory backgrounds, and a wide variety of effects borrowed from stage and film techniques. The demand for such photography has somewhat diminished, since it is now simpler to achieve similar, if not better, results by manipulating the digitized image on a computer.

The basic item required for studio photography is a background "sweep" – a wide roll of paper placed behind, and often under, the subject. This can be up to 12ft. (3.6m) wide and in any of up to 40 different colors. A neutral colored background may be required for smaller-scale work, such as with glassware, where objects can be placed on a light box or even a glass-faced fish-fryer, giving uniform, soft, shadow-free lighting. A refinement of this technique can be used to create an impression that an object is floating in space. This is achieved by placing the subject on a sheet of transparent glass or acrylic, taking care that potentially reflective equipment, including the camera, is carefully masked in order to avoid spoiling the illusion. An object can also be "suspended" by attaching a black rod to the back of the subject, with the other end of the rod being attached to the background immediately behind so that it is unseen.

Many other situations – for example, evoking "characterful" settings such as those required in food photography, can be achieved by the extensive use of props, with kitchen sets invariably being built in the studio. Entire room sets can also be built, complete with carpets, doors, and windows, any naturalistic effect – such as a view through a window – being created by the addition of foliage and the projection of scenes onto a screen beyond the window. Projection can be from the front or rear.

A back-up of special equipment is used on subjects to rectify flaws or to enhance effects in the studio. An aerosol of dulling spray, for instance, will deaden strong highlights or reflections, while oil or glycerin will restore the glaze to food covered by an unappetizing film caused by cooling. Another useful hint is to use a mist sprayer of plain water to revive a tired lettuce or enhance water droplets on a cooled glass of liquid. A fizzy drink can be enlivened with a burst of carbon-dioxide gas.

Precise photography may often exaggerate flaws in badly made objects, and for this reason manufactured subjects must be carefully

Original image

Studio and darkroom effects have always provided graphic designers with the means of achieving a myriad of dramatic graphic imagery. Traditionally, this was done by using optical camera techniques, filtration, the use of scale models as substitutes for the real subject, illusory backgrounds, and a wide variety of effects adapted from stage and film techniques. However, it is now possible to apply such effects – often time-consuming and costly to achieve photographically – in a matter of seconds on a desktop computer. A tiny selection of the hundreds of commercially available effects – called "filters" – are shown here.

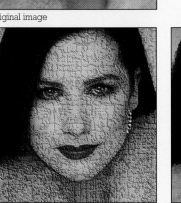

Craquelure

Crystallized

Graphic pen

Pointillized

Spherized

Windblasted

Digital film recording
Although there are cameras which record images digitally, most professional photographers still choose film as their preferred medium. However, the Eastman Kodak Company has developed a method whereby photographers can have their conventional film images digitally transferred to compact disc – this being a popular medium for the distribution of data between computers. This format, called "Photo CD," enables designers to select high-resolution images from a "contact sheet" (**above**) and place them directly into a computer page layout application, from which final, separated film can then be output.

chosen or examined before they are photographed – cardboard packs, for instance, should be carefully folded from flat blanks taken from the production line, and labels stuck onto bottles should not be creased or have glue around the edges.

Prints from transparencies There are two distinct methods by which color prints can be made from transparencies. In the first, an intermediate copy negative ("interneg") is made by a contact print produced from the original transparency. This negative is used to produce what is called a "C-type" print. The second is a direct process, called an "R-type" print, in which the original transparency is projected directly onto printing paper.

With the direct process, prints tend to give a contrasting result, and if the original itself shows excessive contrast, the end result may prove unacceptable. Modifications can be made to a print by using the conventional black-and-white printing techniques of "dodging" and "burning-in," and employing these techniques with colored filters extends the range of controls further. Special papers can be used to make black-and-white prints from both transparency and negative originals. With black-and-white prints for reproduction, it is important that the highest possible quality of print is attained, because detail can be lost and the image degraded by the halftone process.

5
DESIGN EQUIPMENT
Pencils/Pens/Fiber and felt-tipped pens/Inks/
Airbrushes/Photocopying/Computers/
Hardware/Software

All graphic designers need a wide choice of the best possible quality of equipment to enable them to work to the deadlines and to the high standards demanded today. This equipment ranges from tools which have changed little since their invention to those which have been incorporated into the latest technology. For example, while wooden pencils of today are little different to those used in the 18th century, the techniques and effects they produce can now be achieved electronically on a computer. While such dramatic changes are, in the most part, welcome, it is sad that many traditional implements are disappearing from the shelves of art supply stores – indeed, it is increasingly likely that a great deal of, say, airbrush art is being rendered by artists who have never actually held an airbrush. But that is not to deride the supplanting of one tool by another – even though the mechanical version usually possesses a great deal more esthetic charm than its electronic counterpart – after all, technological progress is for our benefit, isn't it? Since it is quite possible that designers who use computers may never come into contact with the tools that their computers are emulating, the more important ones are discussed in this chapter – along with computers themselves.

Conventionally, your basic equipment should include a good drawing board, good light, suitable measuring equipment – an inch and millimeter scale, a type scale, and a steel straight-edge are essential – triangles (the adjustable kind are the most versatile), drawing equipment including a stylo-tipped fountain pen with a variety of different width nibs, and a basic selection of brushes.

Drawing pencils As many as 19 grades of pencil are available, ranging from the softest – 9B, EE, EB, 6B to B, HB – through F, which is of medium hardness, and from H to 9H – the hardest. Carbon pencils are available in degrees ranging from HH to BB. There are three degrees of black Conte pencils – No. 1 medium (HB), No. 2 soft (B) and No. 3 extra soft (BB). "Clutch" pencils consist of a holder made of plastic or metal, or both, inside which is a sleeve that holds and protects the leads, which are available in a wide variety of softnesses and widths, the smallest of which is 0.2mm.

Colored pencils Three main types of colored pencil are widely available. First, those with thick, comparatively soft leads are both waterproof and lightproof, and can be bought in a wide variety of colors. They do not smudge or erase easily, nor do they need to be fixed. Second, the Verithin variety has, as the name implies, a thin,

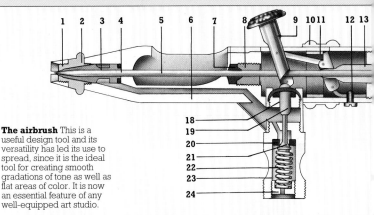

1 2 3 4 5 6 7 8 9 10 11 12 13

18
19
20
21
22
23
24

The airbrush This is a
useful design tool and its
versatility has led its use to
spread, since it is the ideal
tool for creating smooth
gradations of tone as well as
flat areas of color. It is now
an essential feature of any
well-equipped art studio.

When selecting an
airbrush, the most
important factor to take into
account is the type of work
it will be expected to do.
There is a wide range of
models on the market,
from the simplest, which
can do little more than
color surfaces quickly and
apparently evenly, to
extremely complex
versions. Some airbrushes,
for instance, can produce
lettering as fine as six-point
type if required. If an
airbrush is to be used for
detailed graphic work, it is
a false economy to select a
cheaper model; if, on the
other hand, the airbrush is
to be used primarily for
spraying large areas of
color or for simple stencil
patterns, an elaborate
version is an unnecessary
expense. Whichever the
model, accuracy and
evenness of spray depend
on two main factors. These
are the principles of
internal or external
atomization – the former is
more sophisticated than
the latter – and whether the
lever controlling the spray
is single- or double-action.
The Super 63 Aerograph
(**1**), the Sprite Aerograph
(**2**), the Badger 100 (**3**), the
Paasche VI (**4**), the
Paasche VL (**5**), the Thayer
and Chandler A (**6**), the
Olympos (Iwata) I00A (**7**),
the Olympos (Iwata) SPA
(**8**), and the Thayer and
Chandler C (**9**), all have
independent double-
actions. The Conopois F
(**10**), the Humbrol 1(**11**),
and the Grafo 11B (**12**),
have fixed needles and
double-action. The
Paasche Turbo AB (**13**)
allows the medium-to-air
ratio to be altered by the
artist.

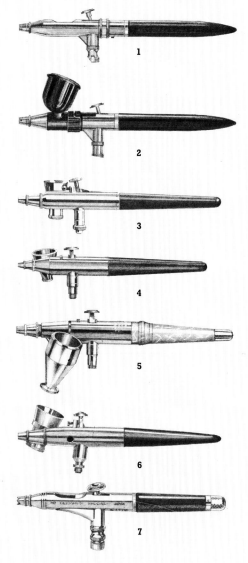

1

2

3

4

5

6

7

The model shown here in cross-section is the Aerograph Super 63. Its features include (**1**) air cap guard; (**2**) air cap; (**3**) nozzle; (**4**) nozzle washer; (**5**) fluid needle; (**6**) model body assembly; (**7**) needle gland washer; (**8**) needle packing gland; (**9**) lever assembly; (**10**) cam ring; (**11**) cam; (**12**) fixing screw; (**13**) square piece; (**14**) needle spring; (**15**) needle spring box; (**16**) needle locking nut; (**17**) handle; (**18**) diaphragm nut; (**19**) diaphragm assembly; (**20**) air valve washer; (**21**) air valve stem; (**22**) air valve spring; (**23**) air valve box; (**24**) air valve spring retainer.

When removing the air cap from an airbrush, always remove the needle first. If this simple precaution is ignored, there is the risk that needle and air cap will both be damaged.

1. Unscrew the handle and loosen the nut locking the needle in position. Take the needle out about 1in (25mm)

2. Unscrew the air cap and remove the nozzle carefully.

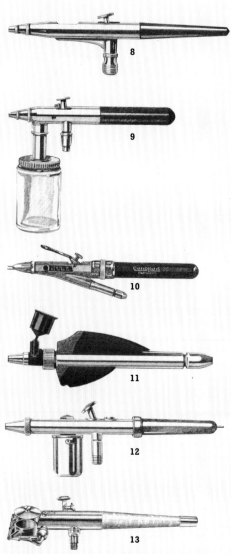

non-crumbling lead, which is useful for fine detail work. The third group are those which are water-soluble. Used with water to produce washes of color, they are something of a cross between pencils and watercolors, and are made by various manufacturers with either thick or thin leads and in ranges of up to about 36 colors.

Pens Stylo-tipped fountain pens are the most useful for design purposes, not only because of the wide range of available widths, but also because they draw a line of consistent and unvarying width. Osmiroid drawing pens – now adapted to take black non-clogging waterproof drawing ink – are extremely useful. They range from those with broad italic nibs to ones with fine, flexible copperplate nibs. Reservoir pens are popular among some illustrators, their chief attraction being that they can be used with waterproof drawing inks of any type, for which there is a wide selection of colors.

Fiber- and felt-tipped marker pens These are now produced in a vast choice of types, mostly with a large selection of colors. Their main virtue is that they produce a dependable, flowing, and consistent line, while their width sensitivity makes working with them similar to drawing with the tip of a brush. Many are made for specific uses, such as drawing on film for overhead projection. They are also available in water-soluble and spirit-based permanent varieties, as well as in an almost daunting selection of tip thicknesses.

Inks Artists' drawing inks are waterproof and dry to a glossy film. They are available in an impressive variety of colors. The range of black drawing inks, sometimes called India ink, is similarly impressive. Bottles of ink should always be shaken before use, since the pigment tends to settle at the bottom of the bottle if it is left unused for some time. Ink may evaporate slightly in summer while it is open during a day's work, with the result that the color becomes deeper and the ink thicker; the addition of just a small amount of distilled water (not a heavy dilution) will thin it again and create an easier flow.

Airbrushes There are two types of airbrush mechanisms – single-action lever and double-action lever. Single-action is the simplest form of airbrush, in which the only way of altering the pattern of spray is to increase or decrease the distance between the brush and the surface being sprayed. Although simple to maintain, this type of airbrush is only suitable for general background work.

By contrast, the double-action brush is essential for the precision and detail required in much technical illustration. Its main advantage is that it gives the user the ability to control the proportions of paint to air; as the lever is depressed, air, not paint, is released through the brush, and only when it is pulled backward does paint meet the airstream – the farther back, the greater the amount of paint released. There is a wide selection of airbrushes on the market today, and choice of a suitable instrument will depend upon what it is to be used for.

The Aerograph Super 63 A-504 is a double-action lever model, giving precision control suitable for most types of work. The Super 63 E-504 is similar to the A-504, but has a coarser nozzle and a larger reservoir, allowing a greater area to be covered in a shorter time.

The Paasche AB is capable of producing the finest hairline thickness or dots, and so it is ideally suited to freehand drawing and photographic retouching. The Paasche H1 and H3 types are single-action control lever brushes with separate controls which can be pre-adjusted for color and air. The air caps and color nozzles are interchangeable to provide a range from fine line to broad spray.

The Paasche V1 and VLS3 are both double-action, the former suitable for fine work and the latter for medium rendering, and both being good for vignetting. Each has a micrometer line adjuster giving rapid setting from very fine to broad. The Paasche air eraser holds an abrasive instead of paint which can erase ink and paint without streaking or smudging. It can also be used for blending highlights and shadows.

An airbrush should be treated with the utmost care. It should be thoroughly cleaned after use because dried paint, for example, may distort the shape of the air cap or even damage the nozzle, thus affecting the quality of spray. Dried paint can even render an airbrush ineffective if it gets into the works.

The air supply to an airbrush should be maintained at an average pressure of 30 pounds per square inch (2 kilograms per square centimeter) and is available in a variety of sources – in an aerosol can, a refillable canister like that used by underwater divers, by a foot pump (hard work), or by an electric compressor. The last is the most efficient method, because the air is supplied at a much more constant pressure.

Photocopying Some kind of reprographic equipment, whether it be a simple photocopier, a photomechanical transfer (PMT) machine, or a color laser copier, is a useful design tool.

The most useful photocopying machine for the designer is one that will produce prints of the largest possible size, but will also give percentage reduction copies when required. The ideal studio photocopier is a color laser copier, such as the Canon CLC, with which you can not only make color photocopies, but also link it to a desktop computer, with which it can be used as an input scanner and for outputting color laser proofs.

Failing a color photocopier, black-and-white photocopies can be colored using the Omnichrom process, whereby areas of color – supplied on a film carrier – are bonded by heat to the black toner on a photocopy.

Photographic copying equipment – as distinct from photocopiers – using transparent or paper negatives, produces high-quality prints which can be used as successfully for reproduction as the original artwork, and can be made at any size within its maximum format.

One of the most popular systems, the PMT machine, produces an excellent quality of reproduction, is cheaper to use than conventional photographic systems, and some types do not require a darkroom for processing. A large variety of different screens is available, and halftones can be produced that, although not as fine as those made by conventional or electronic reproduction methods, are quite adequate for low-budget work or for reference prints.

Computers
The means of engaging in graphic design and producing the results in a form directly suitable for high-end printing is known as "desktop publishing" or, increasingly commonly, "desktop design" – probably because, as far as designers are concerned, the term "desktop publishing" has attracted somewhat derogatory connotations inasmuch that it is used as a catch-all description of anyone who uses a desktop computer, whether or not they are graphic designers. There are hundreds of models of computers on the market, and many of them of them have desktop publishing capabilities to some degree. But at the core of the desktop publishing revolution was the way in which the user enters instructions into the computer, and the way in which the computer, in turn, displays those

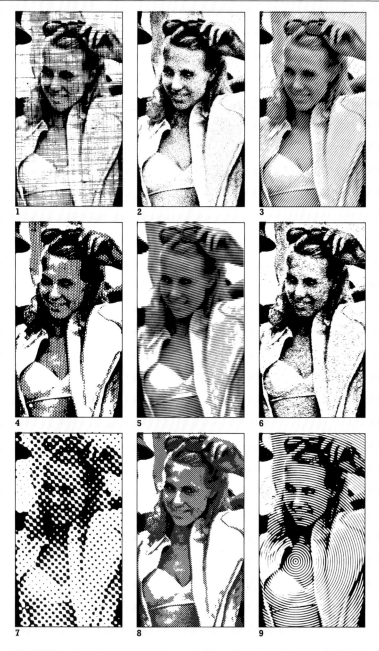

The PMT machine Vertical cameras, or PMT (photo- mechanical transfer) machines, are extremely versatile process cameras. They can convert black to white and vice versa, convert color to black-and-white and reverse left to right. The machines can also be used to apply a wide variety of screen effects to tone originals. The examples (**above**) show some of the various types. These include denim (**1**), dot (**7**), concentric circle (**9**), random dot (**2**), straight line (**3**), weave plus highlight mask (**4**), wavy line (**5**), fine mezzo (**6**), and cross screen posterized (**8**). All produce striking effects. Other advantages of PMT machines include their ability to convert artwork and lettering into instant transfers, or autotypes, of any color. They can also be used to produce cels. In this technique artwork is printed onto clear film, so that it can be maneuvered easily on a layout. Although many computer applications can mimic the effects produced by a PMT camera, it is still a necessary item of design equipment, particularly where large artwork, presentations, and display work are concerned.

instructions – the so-called "user interface." All computers, by virtue of the fact that they must be given instructions, interface with their users. But the real change was the way in which the interface of the new computers began to imitate a desktop, using graphic symbols and a "pointer" controlled by a "mouse." This idea was developed at Xerox Corporation's Palo Alto Research Center (PARC). It became known as a "graphical user interface" (GUI), and Apple Computer Inc. adopted it and developed it further (after an abortive attempt with an earlier model) to use with their Macintosh computer. Hence desktop publishing was born. The Macintosh uses graphics for its interface, which means that the concept of graphic display can be utilized to a prodigious degree.

There are other computer "platforms" (the system which a computer uses in order to operate, see "The operating system," below) which utilize a GUI – the introduction of Microsoft Corp's Windows program has given the world of IBM-compatible personal computers ("PCs") a GUI which is very similar to that used on the Macintosh. The NeXT computer, the brain-child of Steve Jobs, who was one of the founders of Apple, also uses a GUI. But the Macintosh computer had come first, and it has established a stronghold in the graphic arts industries. However, although the support for graphics software on the Macintosh was once unparalleled, virtually everything written for professional graphics use on the Macintosh is now available for Windows. Despite that, and the fact that there are many more PCs in general use than Macintosh or NeXT computers, the Macintosh has still become the *de facto* standard at the high end of the various graphics arts industries.

The benefits of using a computer are numerous: it enables you to transform ideas more speedily into a finished state, and it gives you the opportunity to enhance and control the execution of all those tasks that have hitherto either been difficult to control, laborious, time-consuming, or costly.

However, getting to grips with the way computers work and how you can operate efficiently with one is no mean task. Understanding a few basics will help:

Bits and bytes A computer has some similarities to the brain. Both consist of millions of tiny circuits and switches which are all connected and must be moved into a position that helps to form a circuit, or "path," before anything happens. In a computer, a set of instructions in the form of a code is given to direct the switches to turn "on" or "off." These instructions are given to the computer via an electric circuit, which is either complete (on) or broken (off). The state of the circuit is represented by a 1 (positive, or on) and a 0 (negative, or off), called "binary digits," or "bits," each of which signify something or nothing, black or white, etc. However, one bit all alone doesn't really contain any information, and only by combining several bits together is a computer able to do meaningful work. Two bits, for instance, can give four instructions – 0 and 1 can be configured to give four separate on/off instructions: 00, 11, 10 and 01. To enable you to enter words into the computer, and to provide the means by which your computer can show you what it's doing in a way that you can understand, all characters are represented by a code. This requires more than two hundred separate pieces of information. Thus each character (a total of 256) is represented by a unique 8-bit "code number." Each group of eight bits is called a "byte."

The operating system The prewritten set of coded instructions that enables you to use the computer is a program known as the

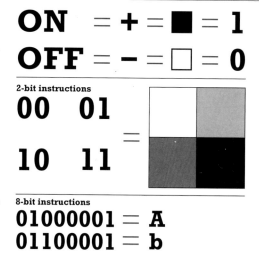

Binary code A computer carries out instructions by responding to an electric circuit, which is either complete or broken (on or off). The state of the circuit is represented by a 1 (positive, or on) and a 0 (negative, or off), called bits (short for binary digits), each of which signify something or nothing, black or white, etc. (**above right**). Two bits can be written in four different combinations and can thus only give four instructions, such as four shades of gray (**right**). Eight bits can be written in 256 different combinations, each representing a single character (**below right**). 24 bits can give 16.7 million combinations.

ON = + = ■ = 1

OFF = – = □ = 0

2-bit instructions

00   01

10   11

8-bit instructions

01000001 = **A**

01100001 = **b**

operating system (or system software). This is loaded into the computer from a "floppy disk" (see p.82). Without these instructions, nothing would happen when you switch the computer on. A second type of coded information represents the work you actually do on the computer: "data" code, or just "data" which appears as plain text if you are typing something, or as lines or shapes if you are drawing.

Applications To create and produce anything on the computer, you need, in addition to the operating system, another set of program instructions, which have been specially written to perform specific tasks and to enable you to do the things you want to do. Such programs are called "application software," "application programs," or just "applications." When you open an application, it is as though you are opening a drawing pad and a box of tools and arranging it on the top of your desk. You can write, draw, paint, or do anything that application is meant for. Most of your work will be done while you are "in" an application.

Files A file is a collection of data that has been given a name so that it can be used or stored in your computer. There are four main groups of files: system files, application files, document files, and folders.

System files These make up a computer's operating system and contain any files that you may have added to upgrade or enhance the system, such as fonts.

Application files These are files that belong to an application, including the application itself. Many larger applications have several files, and some of them may be kept in a special place. As finding somewhere suitable to put all the separate files belonging to an application can be confusing, many applications are supplied with an additional application called an "installer." This puts all the files, such as "Help," "Data," "Preferences," and "Defaults" in appropriate places.

Documents When you create or modify a file with an application, such as a page layout or a letter, it is called a document. The first time you "write" ("save") that item to disk, you must give it a name and put it in an appropriate place.

Folders Folders are places to keep data files, not actually data files themselves. Everything on your computer can be organized by putting documents and applications inside folders.

Memory Just as you record your memories for future reference by writing them down – in a diary, say – so a computer must be able to transfer data from temporary memory to storage of a more permanent kind so that you can recall it when you need it. The computer uses two kinds of memory – one temporary, the other permanent. Temporary memory is called "random access memory," "RAM," or sometimes just "memory." This uses special microchips within the computer. Permanent memory is generally called "storage," for which hard or floppy disks are usually used. There is a third kind of memory called "read-only memory," or "ROM," which contains software, usually part of the operating system software, embedded in a microchip. The information in ROM is always available and, unlike RAM (below), is not erased when you switch your computer off.

RAM Just as your memories are lost forever when you die, so "random access memory" (RAM) is wiped when you switch off the computer. This is because RAM needs power (in the form of an electric current) to retain the information stored within it. When you open an application, you are effectively copying part of it, from the place where it is stored, into RAM. While you are using an application you are working in RAM, and what you do on screen has no permanence until you store or "save" it somewhere. This is, therefore, the most unstable aspect of using a computer, and it is essential to get into the habit of saving your work at frequent intervals.

Storage To save your work permanently, you copy it from RAM to a storage medium such as a "hard disk" or a "floppy disk." Unlike RAM, which you cannot actually "see," storage media are represented on the computer's "desktop." You can usually attach several hard disks to your computer.

Hardware
The microprocessor This chip, the central processing unit ("CPU"), is the "brain" of the computer. A line of computer models produced by one manufacturer will usually use CPUs of the same "series" – for example, Apple Macintosh computers are equipped with CPUs of the Motorola 68000 series (68030, 68040, and so on). Additional chips can be added to the "motherboard" of some computers, enabling you to take advantage of such things as "virtual memory," whereby the computer uses hard disk space for additional RAM.

Speed Of all the things to consider when buying a computer for professional use, speed is one of the most important. A computer's speed determines such things as the time it takes for the screen to redraw or how frequently the CPU needs to access RAM. The speed is dictated by the frequency with which a quartz crystal inside the computer pulsates and is measured in megahertz (MHz) (one MHz representing one million cycles, or instructions, per second), and is referred to as "clock-speed." However, advances in computer technology mean that some modern computers with a seemingly slow clock-speed actually run more quickly than older models with a faster clock-speed.

Your requirement for speed depends upon the kind of design work you intend to use the computer for; this determines the type of application you will be using (the speeds of different applications vary, even if they are performing similar tasks).

If you think you may need even greater speed than the fastest computer can provide, you will need an "accelerator board."

Memory capacity RAM is less of a problem than it once was, not

A basic computer set-up
This illustration shows the hardware you will need in order to get the most out of computerized graphic design. Of course, you could operate without, say, a scanner or a removable hard drive, but only at cost to your efficiency.

1 The computer This contains the "brain" of the system: the central processing unit. In addition to containing a floppy disk drive, the computer also usually houses a hard disk for storing your work as data files. Many computers come with a "CD-ROM" (compact disc, read-only memory) drive fitted as standard since much software and fonts are distributed on CD-ROM discs. You will need a computer with plenty of "random access memory" (RAM) – around 8Mb, although 5Mb may be sufficient to start with. RAM chips can be added as your need for RAM grows. The speed at which your computer is able to process data is important – complex page layouts may take a long time to "redraw" on screen, which can be very frustrating if you are often switching between pages. In time, you may want to add extra devices, such as a modem for connecting to telephone lines, so make sure your computer has enough space for additional expansion cards.

2 Keyboard Many of your instructions to the computer will be input via the mouse, but the keyboard provides an opportunity for many shortcuts.

3 Mouse The means by which you "draw" on screen and perform many other important functions.

4 Monitor The means for displaying your work. There are many permutations of choice, such as screen size, resolution, color, "bit-depth," and more. A large screen is desirable for most work. 8-bit color will suffice unless you intend working extensively with scanned images, in which case you may find you need a 24-bit monitor.

5 Printer Some kind of laser printer is essential for proofing purposes. Most printers have a resolution of around 300dpi, compared with 2450dpi or more on a high-resolution imagesetter, so you will still need to sample work on an imagesetter, as laser-printed proofs will not display the subtleties you will need to make esthetic decisions. A PostScript printer is essential.

6 Scanner You will find a scanner useful even if you intend using conventional methods of origination. You may, for instance, want to scan images for positional guides, or scan rough designs. A scanner resolution of 300dpi is sufficient for most purposes, but if you intend scanning anything for reproduction you may need higher resolution.

7 Backup device Don't think, even for a moment, that nothing will go wrong – it will, so you will need some kind of device, such as an external hard disk or a tape streamer.

8 Removable hard disk drive You will find removable media necessary for transporting large files, especially to service bureaus. A removable drive is also useful as a backup device and is often used as a primary means of storage.

9 CD-ROM drive If your computer does not have one built-in, you will find it increasingly necessary to possess a CD-ROM drive.

Essential software

Whichever field of graphic design you work in, you will need software which provides you with creative versatility and optimum professional standards. In addition to the system software to make the hardware work, you will need applications for:

Page make-up for laying out pages. A good page make-up application will also possess extensive word-processing features, although you may require a separate word-processing application to read certain types of files.

Drawing to create artwork which you may wish to incorporate into your layouts. Most drawing applications possess limited page make-up features.

Image-editing for creative work with scanned or "painted" images. Image-editing applications also offer powerful features for pre-press work, such as color separation and color correction.

Type manipulation to enable you to design and manipulate fonts and other graphic elements, such as logos, that you may wish to incorporate into a font. Good drawing applications also allow a certain amount of font manipulation.

Fonts As many as give you the same creative freedom as hitherto. Many font publishers offer their entire range of fonts on a single CD-ROM disc, from which you can "unlock" fonts as you need them by buying a code from the publisher.

System management utilities for enhancing the performance of both your computer and your applications. Among the most important are:

Font management for arranging menus and handling large numbers of fonts.

ATM (Adobe Type Manager) for making fonts look smooth on screen.

Backup for protecting your work.

Disk utilities for managing your disk.

only because additional RAM chips are now both inexpensive and easy to install, but also because many computers are able to use virtual memory. However, virtual memory is much slower than installed, or "real" RAM, so if possible, have as much real RAM installed as you think you'll need – about 8Mb (megabytes) is usually enough, although greater amounts of RAM may be necessary for image manipulation or for image-intensive documents – or for very memory-intensive operations such as those undertaken by some CAD (computer-aided design) and multimedia applications. System files, large color monitors, and fonts all use up RAM.

Magnetic storage media There are four basic kinds of media used to store data magnetically; all are made of a metal, glass, or plastic underlayer coated with iron oxide particles. When data is recorded (or "written"), these particles are magnetized and aligned in one of two directions ("north" or "south") by the disk drive's "read/write heads," this polarity corresponding to either a 1 or a 0 according to the data being written (see "bits and bytes," p.77).

Floppy disks, or diskettes, are the most basic of all forms of storage, magnetic or otherwise, and most computers come with an internal floppy disk drive. Floppy disks are made up of a single, circular platter of magnetically coated flexible plastic (thus the term "floppy") housed in a rigid plastic case. To use a floppy, you insert it into the slot on the front of the computer, which is the entrance to the drive mechanism.

Floppy disks are usually 3½in. (90mm) in diameter and hold about 1.44Mb of data. Floppy disks are used primarily for software installation, transferring documents between non-networked computers, limited backups, and for transporting files to service bureaus.

Hard disks The majority of computers have the facility for an internal hard disk (drive), if not the drive itself. They may also be attached externally. Typically, the hard disk will have a capacity of 40Mb, 80Mb, 160Mb, or 400Mb; internal hard disk drives with a far greater capacity are available. Hard disks work in a similar way to floppy disks. The main differences are that the disk substrate is rigid; the disk itself may actually consist of several disks (each one called a "platter") stacked one on top of another with a space in between for access by the read/write heads; and the disk is housed permanently within a sealed, dustproof unit.

Removable hard disks Because floppy disks have a limited capacity and hard disk drives are inconvenient to move around, external drives which have removable hard disks are popular. None of the various brands of removable hard disk drives use media that is interchangeable, but all consist of a rigid hard disk housed in a plastic cartridge. Storage capacities of removable hard disks range from about 40Mb to 80Mb, which makes them ideal for transporting large files such as scanned images. Removable hard disks are gradually being replaced by erasable optical ("EO") discs (see below), which are smaller and hold more.

Tape drives Much the same as audio and video tapes, these consist of a reel of magnetic tape housed in a removable cartridge. Unlike disks, on which data can be accessed from any random point on the disk, data on a tape can only be accessed as the tape runs from one reel to the other. This makes them slow in comparison to disks, and they are thus used only for backing up hard disks.

Optical storage media Generally optical media is used for high-volume data storage. An optical disc is similar to an audio compact disc (CD); data is stored by means of tiny pits burned into the disc's surface, the size of which determines a 1 or a 0. Erasing data that had been written in this way used to present problems, and optical storage used to be available only in a form in which the data was either factory-written and could only be read ("CD-ROM," meaning "compact disc read-only memory"), or which could have data written to it only once ("WORM," meaning "write once, read many").

Because they are compact, capacious and cheap to manufacture, CD-ROMs are now widely used for marketing mass reference data such as encyclopedias and educational titles, and most type foundries now supply their complete font library on CD-ROMs. Because of the ability to store digitized, compressed movie sequences and audio data, optical media are particularly important in multimedia and music activities, with most drives providing standard hi-fi output jacks. CD-ROM drives are increasingly becoming a standard built-in part of many models of computer.

Other increasingly important optical media include magneto-optical ("MO"), or "erasable optical" ("EO"), drives – they are similar to CD-ROMs, but can be repeatedly written to, as well as read from. This means they are not limited like the unalterable CD-ROM, but they are much more expensive. Faster, less expensive, but also less capacious EO drives using $3\frac{1}{2}$in. (90mm) discs are also now widely available.

Connections The bewildering selection of "ports," or connector sockets at the back of a computer, and "slots" inside, can be difficult to figure out. Typical ports and slots include the following:

SCSI (small computer system interface) port This port, pronounced "skuzzy," is used for connecting peripheral devices such as external disk drives and scanners. Several devices can usually be "daisy-chained" together, using a single port.

Serial port This port is generally used to connect the computer to printers, modems, or to a network.

Sound, or audio, port This provides a sound-out port to an amplifier or headset.

External disk drive port This connects an external floppy disk drive.

Video port The port used to connect a monitor to a computer that features an "on-board" video facility.

Expansion slot This is a socket found inside many computers, in which you can plug a battery of features and enhancements, such as video cards for connecting a monitor, accelerator cards for enhancing performance, fax cards for connecting to telecommunications lines, cards for connecting to video camera input, etc.

Microphone input port For voice recording.

Cache connector A connection for adding a memory "cache" card to enhance performance.

Monitors A computer monitor works much like a regular television set, in which a screen coated with light-sensitive phosphor, inside a cathode ray tube (CRT), is bombarded by a stream of electrons. The phosphor glows briefly, creating an image. There are several important things to know about monitors:

Resolution The screen image is represented on screen by dots, or "pixels" – the more pixels there are per inch, the smaller they are and the better the resolution of the screen, thus the sharper the image. Most high-resolution monitors have 72 dots per inch (dpi) or more.

Size Monitor sizes are always described in inches, measured diagonally from corner to corner, but this can be misleading when it

Monitor resolution

Computer monitors, although similar to television screens in that they utilize cathode ray tubes, display images at much higher levels of definition, or "resolution," than televisions. Typical monitors have a resolution of between 72 (there are 72 points to an inch – no coincidence) and 87 dots, or pixels, per inch. Despite this high resolution, small sizes of type can be difficult to read on screen (**right**), thus most applications incorporate a "zoom" feature so that you can work with type at any size by enlarging it on screen.

Lorem ipsum dolor sit amet, consectetuer adipiscing elit, sed diam nonummy nibh

7pt Univers

Lorem ipsum dolor sit amet, consectetuer adipiscing elit, sed diam nonummy nibh euismod tincidunt ut

7pt Garamond

Lorem ipsum dolor sit amet,

12pt Univers

Lorem ipsum dolor sit amet,

12pt Garamond

Lor

36pt Univers

Lore

36pt Garamond

1 Monochrome (black and white) monitors, which use 1-bit instructions, simulate shades of grays by "dithering" black and white pixels (arranging them in patterns).

2 Grayscale monitors use 8-bit instructions to produce 256 shades of gray

3 Color monitors can be either 8-bit or 24-bit. 8-bit color monitors produce 256 different colors.

4 24-bit color monitors assign eight bits to each of the RGB colors, producing up to 16.7 million colors.

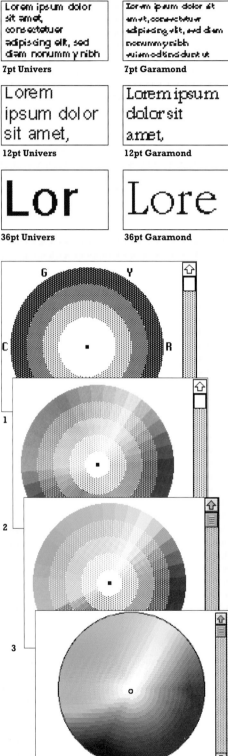

comes to establishing the true dimensions of the total image area of a computer monitor. For example, a 19in. (483mm) screen shows a potential image area of an adequate $11\frac{1}{2}$ x $15\frac{1}{4}$in. (292 x 388mm); but when switched on, it may display only $10\frac{3}{4}$ x $13\frac{5}{8}$in. (273 x 344mm). To establish the usable image area of a monitor, divide each of the horizontal and vertical pixel counts by the resolution – thus a screen described as 19in. (483mm), with a horizontal pixel count of 1,024, a vertical pixel count of 808, and a resolution of 75dpi will produce an image area of $10\frac{3}{4}$ x $13\frac{5}{8}$in (273 x 344mm). For most design work, a 13in (330mm) monitor is quite adequate, but if you work extensively with page layouts where you need to see a two-page spread, you will need a larger screen.

Color Monitors are either monochrome, "grayscale," or color. Monochrome monitors display pixels as either black or white, with no intermediate grays. Grayscale monitors, on the other hand, are able to display pixels in a range of grays, the exact number depending on the "pixel depth" of the monitor, but typically providing 256 grays. Color monitors operate on much the same principle as grayscale monitors, but instead of the pixels being different shades of gray, they are different colors. Pixel depth is important on color monitors – it will generally be either eight bits or 24 bits per pixel – or perhaps more. The difference is startling – 8-bits produces a mere 256 colors whereas 24-bits produces more than 16 million!

Refresh rate This is a background, but nonetheless important, consideration when choosing a monitor. Refresh rate, measured in hertz (Hz), refers to the number of times that the electron beam "rakes" the screen from top to bottom. The slower the refresh rate, the more likely the screen is to flicker. Do not confuse refresh rate with screen "redraw," since the latter refers to the time it takes for the screen image to redraw itself after you make a change.

Laser printers To see what your work looks like before producing high-quality output, you will need a printer – and this almost certainly means a "laser" printer. Screen quality, although supposedly "WYSIWYG" (pronounced "wizzywig," an acronym for "what you see is what you get"), does not render an image with the accuracy that you need to assess the finer subtleties of a design. Even a proof printed on a laser printer will not produce the subtleties of the output from a high resolution imagesetter, and you should never rely on laser printer output to make typographic judgments – always have a sample run out on an imagesetter.

Page description languages When you "send" a page design to a printer, it is intercepted by a kind of "mini" computer called a "controller." The controller uses a program to "interpret" the computer code describing your design, which it then "translates" into a language that the printer "engine" can use to re-create your design on paper. This language is known as a "page description language" (PDL). PostScript is one such language and is licensed by Adobe Systems Inc. to various manufacturers of laser printers who use it with their printers' own, internally-built controllers. It was the introduction of PostScript which contributed to the widespread acceptance of the computer as a professional design tool.

Printer resolution Like monitor screens, printers use bitmaps (see p.90) for creating images, thus outline fonts and object-oriented images must be converted to bitmaps by the controller before they can be printed. Because bitmaps are made up of dots, the more dots per inch (dpi) that a printer can handle, the finer the resolution, or quality, of the printed image. However, resolution of laser printers is not such a major consideration, since the majority output images at only 300–600dpi, compared with the 1270–2540dpi output of imagesetters.

Color printers You should think of buying a color printer only if a large percentage of your work involves color presentations. If not, the cost will probably be much higher than you need, and although the quality is improving all the time, it cannot be used for any other design purpose at the moment. Use a service bureau instead. If you decide to invest in a color printer, consider one that combines color copying, scanning (even from transparencies), and printing all in one unit, such as Canon's CLC laser copier.

Scanners Graphic designers use scanners mainly for four operations: scanning in line artwork for position or for reproduction; scanning in images to be used as positional guides (particularly useful for cutout images); inputting text copy by means of optical character recognition (OCR) software; and scanning images for subsequent manipulation with special effects. You may also find, if you have a suitable scanner, that you can scan in black-and-white continuous tone originals to produce halftones to an acceptable reproduction standard.

A scanner may be monochrome, grayscale, or color; it may be flatbed, sheetfed, handheld, overhead, a video digitizer, or a transparency scanner. Each type is designed for a specific purpose, but few combine all of those purposes.

Scanners employ a light-sensitive scanning head, called a "charge-coupled device" (CCD), which generates an electric charge in response to the various intensities of light being reflected from an original. A 1-bit scan will respond to the tones on both sides of a mid-tone threshold, reducing the image to pixels which are either on or off – black or white, thus producing a line image. An 8-bit scan offers 256 combinations of 1s and 0s per pixel, thus being capable of 256 grays or colors.

Resolution The quality of a scanned image depends upon the resolution of the scanner – the more dots per inch, the sharper the result. However, the final appearance of an image is dictated by the quality of output. Images for halftone reproduction are normally scanned at twice the resolution of the halftone screen ruling. High resolution scanning is important for line artwork, since an image scanned at, say, 300dpi may display a noticeable lack of smoothness when output at 2540dpi on an imagesetter.

File sizes Scanned images require large amounts of both RAM and disk storage space; an 8 x 10in. image scanned with 256 gray levels at a low, but typical, resolution of 300dpi will eat up around 7Mb of both disk and RAM space. This rises to more than 20Mb if you scan with 24-bit color.

Hand-held scanners These small, plastic devices are the most basic type of scanner. As you drag them across an original by hand, the scan head "sucks" up the image as it goes. They are cheap, small and portable, but useful only for rough reference scans and some OCR text scanning.

Flatbed scanners These work much like photocopiers: you place the original face down on a glass screen and a scan head then passes across the original. Flatbed scanners are probably the most useful for design purposes, being easy to use, capable of scanning line artwork reasonably faithfully, and are also good for grayscale scanning and OCR work.

Sheetfed, or edge-feed, scanners These are similar to flatbed scanners, but the original is passed under a stationary scan head.

Sheetfed scanners are used primarily for high-volume work.

Overhead scanners usually consist of a scanning camera mounted above a copy board on which the original is placed. These scanners can be used to scan transparencies (by placing a lightbox on the copy board), three-dimensional originals, and, sometimes, large originals.

Slide scanners These are scanning cameras housed inside a box. The slide original is placed between the scan head and a light source. The more expensive slide scanners can provide quality approaching that of conventional professional color separation, but to get such results, you need considerable experience.

Drum scanners Of all desktop scanners, these most closely resemble the high-end repro scanners of professional color origination houses. A light source – a laser beam – is used to capture the image from the original, which is attached to a spinning glass drum.

Digitizing tablets These devices enable you to draw on screen as you would on paper – if your application offers the appropriate drawing tools and will respond to the features offered by the tablet. A tablet consists of a rectangular pad (the tablet) on which you draw with a stylus, a pen-like device which may or may not be attached to your computer. The most sophisticated tablets are those that feature a pressure-sensitive stylus, enabling you to simulate the marks that a pen or brush would make if you pressed harder on paper.

Software

Virtually every activity involving graphic design has a piece of software specially written to help you do it on a computer. Setting aside those uses where the computer plays an integral part in the end-product – such as presentation graphics and multimedia – a computer really comes into its own in the preparation of design for reproduction.

Page make-up applications Also called "page layout" or "desktop publishing" applications, these are the real work-horses of computerized graphic design.

All such applications at the professional end of the scale allow you to enter text either directly or by importing it from another application. They allow you to make fine typographic adjustments (some to within .001 pt) to kerning, tracking, and scaling and provide a limited selection of drawing tools, enabling you to create boxes, circles and ellipses, rules and, in some cases, polygons and freeform shapes. Most incorporate a facility to lay percentage tints either as spot or process colors, which can then be output into separated film.

As with much other specialist software, there is often little to choose between the most popular applications: **PageMaker** (Aldus Corp.) and **QuarkXPress** (Quark Inc.). The problem of choice is made more difficult because the products are constantly upgraded, overtaking each other in turn.

The important factors to bear in mind when choosing a page make-up application include the degree of accuracy with which you can specify the positions of pictures and blocks of text; the ability to adjust aspects of typography such as kerning, and the ease with which you can edit or rotate text. The maximum number of pages you can create in a document varies considerably and, depending on their complexity, can slow down the application quite dramatically. You will also need to consider the following: file-importing features, both of text and pictures; color separation features – although all applications will provide separations of colors and tints created within the application, not all will separate imported picture files without additional software; compatibility with imagesetting hardware; and finally, the extent to which additional features are available, either from the developer or from third parties.

Drawing applications Just as you sometimes need to create illustration artwork when preparing conventional pasteup, so you may need a facility for doing the same on a computer. The obvious answer may be to buy a fully integrated application that includes drawing tools, but such a program will not provide the power and flexibility of separate page make-up and drawing applications.

Drawing applications are "object-oriented" programs (the shape and characteristics of a drawn line are stored as data in a single point, or "vector"), as distinct from painting and image-manipulation applications (see facing page) that produce "bitmapped" images. Object-oriented applications allow lines, shapes, and text to be altered and edited at any time, whereas bitmapped shapes must be erased and then redrawn or edited by a painstaking process of turning pixels on and off.

The quality of line illustrations created in an object-oriented drawing application is determined wholly by the resolution of the

output device. In bitmapped images, the input resolution determines the output quality.

Drawing applications generally offer a full range of PANTONE colors which can be output as spot color film or fully separated film for four-color process printing. Accurate screen rendering of PANTONE colors is impossible to achieve, and colors should always be checked against a sample from PANTONE's color specifier.

Drawing programs are extremely versatile and can be used for a wide variety of purposes, such as technical illustration, diagrams and charts, maps and all manner of graphic decoration, as well as for general purpose illustration. Being object-oriented, drawing applications also allow you to alter and manipulate outline fonts, thus providing an invaluable aid to logo design and also the means for extensive typographic variations.

Leading drawing applications are **Canvas** (Deneba Software, Inc.), **FreeHand** (Aldus Corp.), **Illustrator** (Adobe Systems, Inc.), and **MacDraw Pro** (Claris Corp.).

Painting and image-editing Applications that enable you to paint and manipulate images on a computer require you to have a large capacity hard disk, since the graphic files produced by these

Page make-up on a computer A typical professional page make-up application allows all the elements of layout to be combined so that it can be output as color-separated film. The illustration (**left**) is of QuarkXPress and shows a few of its features, many of which can also be found in other applications. A pasteboard (**1**) is where you can play around with ideas, outside the page area. To enter text, you first create boxes (**2**), or frames, which can be linked together in any order, so that text flows automatically from one to the other. The File menu (**3**) allows you to create, open, save, and print documents. The Edit menu (**4**) allows you to edit colors, style sheets (consistently used styles for fonts, leading, indents, etc., which can be applied by a single keystroke), and hyphenation and justification parameters. The Edit Color feature enables you to define process, spot, or PANTONE colors. The Style menu (**5**) is where you select such things as typeface, type size, leading, scaling, kerning, etc. The Item menu (**6**) allows you to apply specific measurements to such items as text and picture boxes, rules, runarounds, etc. The Page menu (**7**) enables you to add, move, or delete pages within a document, and to set automatic page numbering. The View menu (**8**) is where you choose the size at which your document appears on your monitor while you work on it, and also enables you to display such things as guides or floating palettes. Utilities (**9**) are facilities for checking spelling, making hyphenation exceptions, identifying fonts and pictures used within a document, and editing tracking and kerning values. In QuarkXPress, this is also where extra features, called Quark-XTensions, appear (**10**). There are a variety of "floating palettes," which you can choose to position anywhere on the screen; the Toolbox (**11**) is where you select various tools which enable you to undertake tasks such as creating, modifying, and moving boxes, drawing rules and shapes, and linking text; the Measurements palette (**12**) and Style Sheets palette (**13**) duplicates some of the commands in the Style and Item menus; the Document Layout palette (**14**) allows you to rearrange the pages in your document; the Library palette (**15**) enables you to store frequently used items; the Value Converter (**16**) is a useful feature for making instant conversions of measurements. The Colors palette (**17**) allows you to instantly apply colors to any item, and the Trap Information palette (**18**) is where you modify trapping values.

Bitmapped graphics
Paint applications make marks by switching pixels on and off. When a shape is created (**1**), the pixels used to render the shape replace any existing pixels, thus when the shape is moved it leaves a white space (**2**).

Object-oriented drawing applications, on the other hand, store information about a drawn line at each end of the line or at points along its length. This means that only the data for a section of line need be stored, as distinct from the need of a bitmapped graphic to store data relating to each individual pixel. A line can be edited by selecting it and making alterations as necessary – changes affecting only the data relating to that line (**3**, **4**), not any other element of the illustration.

1

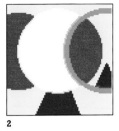

2

3

4

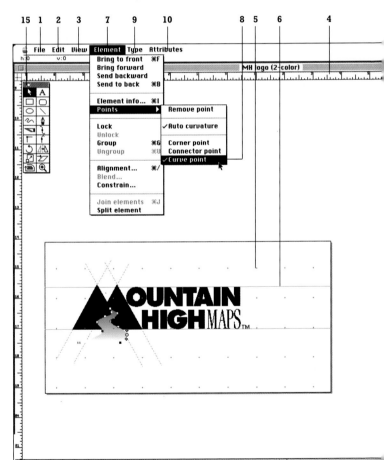

applications can be huge. A 24-bit color card on your monitor is more or less essential for professional work. A lot of installed RAM is also required. To simulate the way you would normally work with a pencil or paintbrush, you should also equip yourself with a digitizing tablet that has a pressure-sensitive stylus.

All painting software packages offer adjustable airbrush tools, which in most cases allow you to control the opacity of paint. Most possess limited image-editing tools, allowing you to blur or sharpen a scanned image, and some allow you to draw Bézier curves. Although all paint applications produce images as bitmaps, some also feature object-oriented drawing tools or at least object-oriented text capabilities. Some applications permit you to make direct process color separations and, sometimes to adjust halftone screen resolution (although this is not a serious problem since you can always save the file in a format that can be separated by another application). Some also enable you to simulate traditional artists' media such as pencil, charcoal, pastel, watercolor, and oil paint – you can even control, via a pressure-sensitive pen, the "wetness" of the "paint" loaded onto a "brush" and the rate at which it "dries."

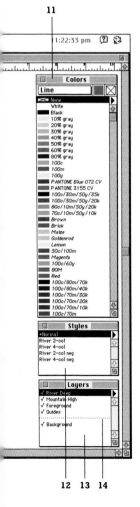

11

12 13 14

Drawing on a computer

Typically, a drawing application (**left**, from FreeHand) provides a File and Edit menu (**1**, **2**) for opening, closing, saving, copying, pasting, etc. In the View menu (**3**) you can select various display options, such as floating palettes, magnification of the page view, rulers (**4**), grid (**5**), guides (**6**), and "snapping," which enables accurate drawing by attracting an element to the nearest point, guide, or grid.

The Element menu (**7**) enables you to modify the different elements of your drawing, such as which part is on top of another, add and delete points to a line (**8**), blend elements to give a graded effect (opposite), and join together or split apart separate elements.

The Type menu (**9**) allows you to attribute typographic styles and also to convert letterforms to "paths" (see below). In the Attributes menu (**10**), you can set the style, color, and thickness of lines, the style and color of filled elements, and specify halftone screen requirements. Drawing applications offer a choice of color selection – either process, spot, or one of several proprietary color systems – and each has its own way of enabling you to specify colors. FreeHand displays colors on a floating palette (**11**), from which you can copy and edit existing colors or

define new ones. Color "libraries," which enable you to store frequently used colors (such as the corporate colors of one of your clients), are also a feature of some drawing applications.

A Style palette (**12**) enables you to define frequently used styles, such as lines and fills, and apply them to different elements of your drawing. The Layers palette (**13**) enables you to assign elements of a drawing to different layers, so that you can work on one element without affecting another – you can, if desired, "hide" other elements. Elements on background layers (below the dotted line, **14**) appear dimmed and do not print.

The Toolbox (**15**), as well as offering several drawing tools, also offers tools that enable you to rotate, reflect, scale, skew, and trace elements. Because object-oriented applications employ mathematically defined lines, or paths, which allow accurate manipulation of a shape by utilizing handles which project from a point on a curve (sometimes referred to as "Bézier" curves), fonts, which use the same method of describing a line, can be manipulated within a drawing application.

Paint applications providing features for professional use include **Painter** (Fractal Design Corp.), **PixelPaint Professional** (SuperMac Software), and **Studio/32** (Electronic Arts), .

Image-editing (or retouching) applications offer, as well as comprehensive sets of paint tools, extensive editing tools for use with directly scanned images. They also support files that come from, or can be used directly by, some high-resolution color scanners. The leading image-editing applications are **Photoshop** (Adobe Systems, Inc.) and **ColorStudio** (Letraset).

Special effects In addition to drawing and painting applications that allow you to emulate conventional methods of preparing illustration, there are other image creation applications that utilize computer technology even more fully: three-dimensional modeling (3D) and "rendering" (applying a texture to a surface or shape).

Although many 3D applications, aimed primarily at professional architects, product designers, and designers who work in CAD (computer-aided design), are complex and expensive, some cheaper and simpler applications offer some useful features – the ability to create fully-rotatable 3D letterforms from fonts, for instance. Many 3D applications also provide animation capabilities

Image-editing and painting on a computer
These applications use "bitmaps" to render images, unlike drawing applications, which are "object-oriented" (see p.90). Although most of these applications have a bias either toward editing images, such as photo-graphs, or to creating painted illustrations, many combine features that do both. Some, such as PhotoShop, are extremely powerful, and to get full use out of them, you will need to have considerable experience of pre-press activities. Even without this experience, most computer-using graphic designers will find an image-editing application useful for the effects they can render, and also for manipulating images (**right**).

The illustration (**left**) shows a PhotoShop screen. Among its menus are: File (**1**), where you select and use a scanner, and where you can apply printing attributes – such as frequency, angle, and shape of halftone screens – to an image; Edit (**2**), which contains sophisticated controls for copying and pasting selected parts of the image; Mode (**3**), where you can choose the method of outputting the image – bitmap (black and white), grayscale, RGB, CMYK, etc. – or split an image into "channels" for working on or modifying individual colors (**4**); Image (**5**), which offers a range of controls for adjusting an image, such as changing its resolution, flipping or rotating it, modifying its input and output levels, color curves, brightness, contrast, color balance, hue and saturation levels, etc.; Filter (**6**), where you can apply a wide range of special effects to an image by using customizable "filters," many of which are supplied by third-party software developers (**7**); Select (**8**), which gives a range of controls for modifying or saving selections; Window (**9**), where you can "zoom" in or out of an image or select one of a variety of "floating" windows.
Among the latter are: Info window (**10**), which gives a "read-out" of an image at the exact position of the cursor as it is dragged across the image, the position of the cursor, and the RGB and CMYK color values; Palette (**11**), where you can define and select colors for modifying an image or for painting; Brushes (**12**), for selecting a shape and size of brush, although further brush controls are available through the tool palette.
The Tool palette (**13**), contains a range of tools, among them a variety of selection tools, a "magic wand" tool for selecting areas of an image with a similar pixel value to that where the wand is positioned, a cropping tool, a pen tool for drawing object-oriented lines, a blend tool for creating graduated tints, an "eyedropper" tool for selecting specific pixel colors, an airbrush tool for simulating airbrush effects, drawing and painting tools, a "rubber stamp" tool for duplicating groups of pixels and applying them to another area of the image, a "droplet" tool for blurring or sharpening specific areas of an image, and a "smudge" tool which, as its name suggests, smudges parts of the image by blending pixels into one another as the tool is dragged across it.

Type design on a computer Several applications are available for creating entire typeface families. They can also be used to create logos, etc., so that they can be incorporated into a font. As well as designing new fonts, you can modify any existing font that you possess. Fonts can be generated in either PostScript Type 1 or TrueType formats. Rough sketches of a letterform can be scanned in and then used as a guide for drawing the character. The outline letterforms are created using Bézier curves in the same way as in drawing applications.

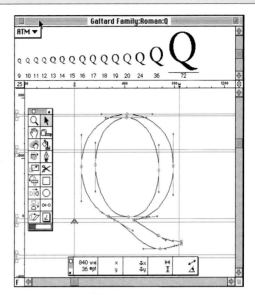

and limited rendering effects.

Rendering applications enable you to apply the surface appearance of a material such as wood, metal, or marble to an object, and to manipulate the intensity, color, and direction of the light source illuminating the object. However, rendering can be very slow.

Advertising If you work in advertising, you will find very little software tailored specifically to your design needs. Although the leading application, **Multi-Ad Creator** (Multi-Ad Services, Inc.), offers sophisticated page makeup, drawing and painting features, and quite powerful typographic control in a single package, it is quite common for advertising studios to use a page make-up application in preference.

Type design and manipulation Font technology on computers is a complex subject and is discussed in greater detail in Chapter 6 (p.96). But the computer is of huge benefit to the typographic designer when it comes to typeface design. Using a suitable application, it is a relatively straightforward matter to create an entire typeface from scratch and then use it as you would any other font. It is also easy to modify every character of any existing font installed on your computer and then use it as a new typeface. **FontStudio** (Letraset) and **Fontographer** (Altsys Corp.) are applications which are both capable of either generating new faces or modifying existing ones. Both applications are also very useful for drawing logo designs.

Font manipulation programs are available, that enable you to produce extensive typographic effects. These applications, in addition to offering powerful effects features, usually incorporate a library of ready-made effects which you can use to suit your needs.

Multimedia With the growing number of titles being published on CD-ROM-related media, multimedia is a becoming an increasingly important source of work for computer-based graphic designers. However, the medium presents a huge creative challenge with the need to integrate all the aspects that make up the whole – graphics, music, narration, photography, and video sequences, for example.

Software for multimedia comes in the form of "authoring" programs that allow you to write or modify program "scripts" (a simplified form of program language) depending on the complexity of the project. Many applications include extensions to the scripting language in the form of "external commands" (XCMDs) and "external functions" (XFCNs), that enable the application to perform specialized commands or functions, such as adding an extra menu or controlling a hardware device. Multimedia applications range from the basic **Hypercard** (Claris Corp), through the more sophisticated **SuperCard** (Aldus Corp.) application, to powerful animation packages such as **Authorware Professional** (Macromedia, Inc.) and **MacroMind Director** (MacroMind, Inc.), which also has built-in painting tools.

Word processing Although most page makeup applications provide adequate text-editing features, you may sometimes be required to provide text in a format that your client can work with. For this reason, it is best to equip yourself with one of the most widely used applications. Among these are **WordPerfect** (WordPerfect Corp.), **WriteNow** (T/Maker Co.), and the most widely used of all, **Microsoft Word** (Microsoft Corp.).

Other applications There are hundreds of other items of software, most having little design relevance. However, some can be of considerable use to designers: **Persuasion** (Aldus Corp.) and **PowerPoint** (Microsoft Corp.) both provide the means to create customized slide presentations, and some CAD and architecture applications go far beyond what mere modeling programs can achieve. There are many other peripheral applications, including those for essential tasks such as optical character recognition, which allow you to use a scanner to input typewritten text into your computer. **OmniPage Professional** (Caere, Inc.) is an example.

Utilities There are thousands of little applications, called utilities, designed to increase the efficiency with which the computer performs. Some of the more useful are listed here:

Adobe Type Manager (ATM) (Adobe Systems, Inc.) This renders PostScript Type 1 fonts smoothly on screen (by using the outline printer font file), replacing the awful "jaggies" of the bitmapped screen fonts that you would otherwise get (see p.98). This utility is absolutely essential unless you are going to use only TrueType fonts.

Adobe Type Reunion (Adobe Systems, Inc.) This utility shortens what would otherwise be very long font menus; it organizes them by family, with submenus for font variations such as italic or bold.

Suitcase II (Fifth Generation Systems, Inc.) This font-management utility enables you to open or close fonts on your computer easily.

QuicKeys (CE Software) This utility enables you to assign keyboard shortcuts to menu items or to repetitive actions.

Virus protection A virus is a mischievously written program that copies itself from computer to computer (usually via floppy disks, but also over networks) where it can wreak havoc by, for instance, causing repeated crashes or files to vanish. Fortunately, there are many utilities available for detecting and eliminating such viruses.

File compression These are useful for creating space on your hard disk, archiving files (storing old jobs that you need to keep), and transporting large files, say, to a service bureau.

Backup utilities The golden rule in computing is: back up your files. Regularly, and without question. To make the chore of backing up as painless as possible, there are several specially designed backup utilities, the choice depending upon what media you are backing up to (hard disk, removable disks, tape streamers, floppy disks, etc).

6
TYPESETTING
Hot metal/Phototypesetting/Digital typesetting/
Page make-up systems/Imagesetters

Of all the graphic crafts affected by the development of technology – most particularly by the introduction of desktop computers – none has been so radically changed as the typesetting industry. Typesetting – as a separate part of the reprographic process, carried out in isolation from design – is declining at a rapid rate, with users – such as designers – now possessing equipment which is both affordable and capable of producing high quality typesetting. Those designers without computers are now finding that their typesetting houses are switching over to the same equipment as that used by designers with computers. Indeed, in many cases, the emphasis in typesetting houses has switched from offering the services of skilled typographers to one of merely offering output services (albeit valuable ones) – designers no longer go to a typesetter for their typesetting, but to a service bureau.

From the graphic designer's point of view, these changes have come as something of a mixed blessing; while computers may have opened up a whole new world, potentially bringing typographic finesse totally within our control, so a whole new set of problems has also cropped up, requiring that we use much of our precious time in pursuit of matters which were once never the concern of graphic designers. For example, before we started using computers, all we had to do was to choose between typesetting houses. Now we may be required to choose between font vendors. And, having made our choice of typeface, we may find that we are also offered a choice of font "format." We then discover that a typeface in a set of about eight styles (light, roman, semi-bold, and bold, with their respective italic variations, for example) is very expensive – it may even cost more than the fee for the job. And, to top it all, we discover that to get the full mix of styles and weights, we must purchase not one, but two font sets (or more – an entire typeface, Helvetica 25 through to Helvetica 95, for example, may be split into three sets). The next dilemma is getting all those 20,000 words of typewritten manuscript into our machine (see p.86). Having input the text into our computer, formatted it to our desired specifications, and printed out a proof, we discover that there is something not quite right about the kerning, or about the character or word spacing on justified text. But now we can't go back to the typesetter to get it fixed – we've actually got to do it ourselves. By now you may be forgiven for wondering whether you are a designer or a typesetter.

However, typesetting on your own computer is far from a negative experience. If you discipline yourself to stay within certain parameters, you will encounter few problems and will come to rejoice at the typographic control you now have over your work.

The final, printed result of modern computer-generated typography differs little in its vernacular from that produced by movable pieces of type – even if typographic tastes and the *means* of generating letterforms have changed.

Hot metal The first significant change after the introduction of movable type came with the invention, patented in 1884, of the Linotype machine by the German-born American engineer Ottmar Mergenthaler. This was the first keyboard-operated composing machine to employ the principle of a "matrix" – a single master containing a complete character set, one for every size and style of a typeface – from which molten metal was used to cast type. Each line of type was cast as a single, solid piece (hence the name "Linotype"), called a "slug."

One year after the patenting of the Linotype machine came the Monotype process, invented in 1885 by Tolbert Lanston of Ohio. This process consisted of a keyboard-operated composing machine which cast type as individual letters, using large numbers of matrices (which was only feasible due to the invention of a mechanical punch cutter by L.B. Benton).

Hot-metal machines are rarely used today except for very specialized requirements.

Phototypesetting In the 1950s, photomechanical typesetting machines were introduced, and they employed matrices stored as negatives on glass disks or strips. Output was produced photographically onto bromide paper. Some phototypesetting machines are still used for generating large characters, such as headlines.

Digital typesetting The first digital typesetting machines appeared in the early 1970s. Letterforms made up of digitized data were generated on the screen of a cathode ray tube (CRT), from which an image was projected onto photographic film or paper. This method of generating digitized type has gradually been replaced by the laser imagesetter, which was first introduced in the mid-1970s.

The desktop computer, in the form of the Macintosh, arrived in 1984, but it wasn't until the late 1980s that it began to be taken seriously by the various graphic arts industries. Not only was it now possible to set type directly from the desktop, but it was also possible to arrange that typesetting in its final position on page – all on the same machine and without the operator requiring knowledge of complex computer codes.

On all computers now capable of quality output, the amount of control the user has over word and letter spacing is almost limitless. Most page make-up applications offer numerous alternative hyphenation and justification permutations, which means that, just as the medieval scribe determined his own criteria for spacing lines of text, so the modern graphic designer must also be well-versed in the parameters of esthetic acceptability of word and character spacing, instead of relying, as we have done for many years, on the skill of the typesetter and the sophistication of his machines.

The first fonts on computers were bitmapped fonts which were designed to be both displayed on screen and printed. Unfortunately, the printing quality of bitmapped fonts left a lot to be desired, but it was not long before the introduction of PostScript resolved this problem.

PostScript PostScript is the proprietary "page description language" (PDL) of Adobe Systems Inc. A page description language is the program that the printer uses to interpret data from the computer into a form that the printer can use to print from. The PostScript PDL is used to describe graphic images, such as tone images, tints, rules, etc., as well as fonts, to a printer, so a PostScript printer is still a necessary piece of equipment even when non-PostScript fonts (TrueType, for example) are used.

On the computer, PostScript fonts have two "parts" – screen fonts and printer fonts (one for each style – italic, bold, etc.).

Screen fonts These are bitmapped fonts that are designed to display the font on-screen in a variety of fixed sizes. Before the introduction of "ATM" (see below), bitmapped screen fonts gave an ugly, stepped appearance – called "jaggies" – when they were rendered on-screen.

Printer fonts These are "outline" fonts containing data that describes the outline shapes of type characters, from which any size can be drawn and filled in by the output device (printer fonts may also be called "scalable" fonts). The advantage of outline fonts is that, as well as providing a single set of data for any size, they can be output at any resolution, whether it be the 300dpi of a laser printer or the 2540dpi of an imagesetter.

Adobe Type Manager (ATM) This utility made a huge impact on the computer world generally, but more particularly on its use by designers as a typographic tool. As far as the user is concerned, all ATM does is to draw a font on the screen by using the data contained in the printer outline font file, resulting in a smooth screen-rendering of the type design. This did away with the need for bitmap screen fonts (although not entirely – one bitmapped font is still required so that the font name appears in font menus). ATM is now included as part of the operating system on some computer platforms.

TrueType For a variety of reasons, not least to avoid paying licensing fees to Adobe for the use of PostScript, Apple deemed it necessary to develop their own outline font technology, which they named "TrueType."

There are two main distinctions between TrueType and PostScript.

Below Computer fonts are constructed from an outline shape of the type design (**1**), and this outline is used by printing devices to generate typesetting. However, so that a font can also be displayed on a monitor, letterforms need to be constructed of pixels: to create the pixelated, or "bitmapped," shape, a program called Adobe Type Manager (ATM) uses the technique of "hinting" (opposite) to render the fonts as closely as possible to the printed version (**2**). Without ATM, fonts would appear distorted and jagged on screen (**3**). Fonts can be made even smoother on screen by using a technique called "antialiasing," in which gray pixels are added in appropriate places (**4**). The examples below are shown next to their 60pt equivalent.

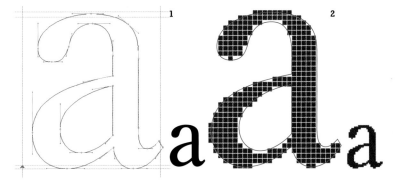

The first is that TrueType fonts are rendered both on screen and by the printer from a single set of outline data. Thus there is no need for a separate bitmapped screen version, not even for font menu purposes – unlike ATM, which requires a screen font in order to display the name of the font. The second is that TrueType fonts can be printed on any printer, whether it is PostScript or not – although TrueType is not a PDL, so PostScript is still needed by a printer to output graphics.

The use of a single file, either in TrueType or PostScript formats, for screen and printer rendering reduces the possibilities for error – for example, the number of characters in a line of text displayed on screen using a bitmapped version may not be the same as that output by a printer using the outline version.

Traditionally, each size of metal type was cast from its own matrix, and because of this, changes could be made to the design of a face at different sizes in order to adjust optical aberrations that may occur when a face is enlarged or reduced. The problem with outline fonts on a computer, whether they are TrueType or PostScript, is that each size of a font is scaled from a single set of data, ignoring the fact that, to achieve optimum results, it may be necessary to make changes to the design of a font at different sizes. However, this inadequacy of the current font formats may be redressed by the introduction of TrueType Optical Scaling and Adobe's Multiple Master (MM) formats, which offer a choice of design for different sizes of the same font – although the real purpose of MM is to make the transfer of files between different computers less problematical if, for instance, a font is missing from one computer.

Imagesetters High-quality output, whether it is bromide paper for camera-ready art or fully process-separated final film for imposition and platemaking, is produced on a machine called an imagesetter. Imagesetters work by means of a digitally controlled laser beam raking a photosensitive material such as bromide paper or film, thus exposing an image onto the material. Imagesetters are either flatbed – in which case the laser beam is projected via a series of mirrors and prisms onto the photosensitive material, which moves forward, one scan line at a time – or drum, whereby the film or paper, wrapped around a glass drum, is exposed by a rotating

Left Normally, a screen font will instruct a pixel to turn on if more than half the area of the pixel is covered by the font, resulting in anomalies (**5**). A "hinted" character, on the other hand, knows how the character should *look* – that both stems of an "n" should be the same width (**6**).

5 | 6

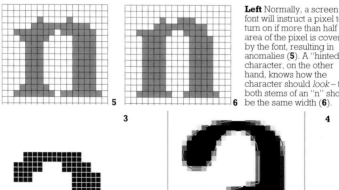

3 | 4

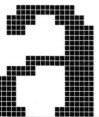

laser exposure assembly, while the photosensitive material remains stationary. Drum imagesetters are thought to create fewer registration problems than flatbed types, because the material remains stationary and because the laser light source remains at a constant distance from the paper.

The process of a light beam raking the surface of a material is known as "rasterizing." So that the imagesetter can understand the page description language (PDL) code, such as PostScript – which is used to "describe" the image to a printing device and thus translate it into machine code – it must contain, or have access to, a "raster" controller, or "raster image processor" (RIP). Desktop

Hyphenation and justification Computer applications allow almost limitless features for controlling the way space is apportioned between words and characters in justified and unjustified text. In justified text the program will attempt to insert spaces according to an optimum value, but failing that will space out a line according to a defined minimum and maximum value. In unjustified text, only the optimum value is used. Usually, the optimum word space represents the normal space width of a font. Using default values in justified text with a short column measure may result in inconsistent spacing from line to line, and it is often necessary to modify the values.

Word spacing
Minimum: 100%
Optimum: 100%
Maximum: 150%

Character spacing
Minimum: 0%
Optimum: 0%
Maximum: 20%

Lorem ipsum dolor sit amet, consectetuer adipiscing elit, sed diam nonummy nibh euismod tincidunt ut laoreet dolore magna aliquam erat volutpat. Ut wisi enim ad minim veniam, quis nostrud exerci tation

Word spacing
Minimum: 95%
Optimum: 100%
Maximum: 105%

Character spacing
Minimum: -3%
Optimum: 0%
Maximum: 3%

Lorem ipsum dolor sit amet, consectetuer adipiscing elit, sed diam nonummy nibh euismod tincidunt ut laoreet dolore magna aliquam erat volutpat. Ut wisi enim ad minim veniam, quis nostrud exerci tation ullam-

Horizontal scaling is a distinctive feature of computer-generated typography, whereby fonts are scaled along their horizontal axes only. While this facility can be useful, it should not normally be used as a substitute for fonts that have a specially designed condensed or expanded version – the exaggerated distortions of horizontally scaled letterforms rarely surpass the esthetic properties of the real thing.

Univers 67 Bold Condensed, no horizontal scaling

Univers 65 Bold, 83% horizontal scaling

laser printers have RIPs built into them.

Imagesetter resolution Although both are laser printers, an imagesetter differs greatly from a desktop laser printer; it is more precise, it produces a photographic, rather than toner-based, image, and it possesses greater RAM. Most important, it is able to reproduce an image at much higher resolutions than a laser printer, with the consequent advantage of extremely high-quality output. Normally, typographic matter will be output from an imagesetter at 1270dpi or 1800dpi (a typical laser printer outputs at 300dpi) – any higher resolution will be indiscernible and may slow down output to such an extent as to negate the quality versus cost ratio.

Tracking values When text is output, by laser printer or imagesetter, it is scaled from a single outline printer font (p.98), and the character spacing values are standard, regardless of output size. You may wish to adjust the spacing between characters ("tracking," as distinct from kerning, which involves pairs of characters) in some cases, depending on the characteristics of the typeface and the effect you want. Tracking values are normally expressed in fractions of em, the definition of which depends on the application being used. Values can be expressed as finely as 0.00005 em ($\frac{1}{20,000}$ em).

Lorem ipsum dolor sit amet, consectetuer adipiscing elit, sed diam nonummy nibh euismod tincidunt ut laoreet dolore magna aliquam erat volutpat. Ut wisi enim ad minim veniam,

7pt Gill Sans, +0.05 tracking

Lorem ipsum dolor sit amet, consectetuer adipiscing elit, sed diam nonummy nibh euismod tincidunt ut laoreet dolore magna aliquam erat volutpat. Ut wisi enim ad minim veniam, quis nostrud exerci tation

7pt Gill Sans, 0 tracking

Lorem ipsum dolor sit amet, consectetuer adipiscing elit, sed diam nonummy nibh euismod tincidunt ut laoreet

10pt Gill Sans, +0.025 tracking

Lorem ipsum dolor sit amet, consectetuer adipiscing elit, sed diam nonummy nibh euismod tincidunt ut laoreet dolore

10pt Gill Sans, 0 tracking

Lorem ipsum dolor sit amet, consectetuer adipiscing elit, sed diam

14pt Gill Sans, -0.025 tracking

Lorem ipsum dolor sit amet, consectetuer adipiscing elit, sed

14pt Gill Sans, 0 tracking

Lorem ipsum dolor sit amet, consectetuer adipiscing elit, sed diam nonummy nibh

12pt Gill Light, no horizontal scaling

Lorem ipsum dolor sit amet, consectetuer adipiscing elit, sed

12pt Walbaum, no horizontal scaling

Lorem ipsum dolor sit amet, consectetuer adipiscing elit, sed diam nonummy nibh euismod

12pt Gill Light, 80% horizontal scaling

Lorem ipsum dolor sit amet, consectetuer adipiscing elit, sed diam nonummy nibh

12pt Walbaum, 80% horizontal scaling

Lorem ipsum dolor sit amet, consectetuer adipiscing elit, sed diam nonummy nibh euismod tincidunt ut laoreet dolore magna

12pt Gill Light, 60% horizontal scaling

Lorem ipsum dolor sit amet, consectetuer adipiscing elit, sed diam nonummy nibh euismod tincidunt ut

12pt Walbaum, 60% horizontal scaling

7
REPRODUCTION
Halftone image formation/Color reproduction/
Computers and reproduction/Scanning resolution/
Output resolution/Tint charts

In its broadest sense, reproduction is the duplication of an image by any means. However, in the printing business, it is generally used to describe the photomechanical or digital conversion of an illustration or photograph so that it can be used in any of the various printing processes.

Halftone image formation When printing by letterpress, lithography, or screen, ink is transferred to the surface to be printed in a layer of uniform density. This is fine for areas of solid color, but if graduations of tone are required, such as in a photograph, the original must be broken up into a pattern of dots. Each dot varies in size to give the optical illusion of continuous tone when printed small enough not to be detected by the eye when viewed at a normal reading distance.

In conventional reproduction, the conversion into dots is made by placing a screen between the original subject and the film negative. The screen itself can be one of two types: a conventional glass cross-line screen or a vignetted contact screen. The cross-line screen consists of two pieces of glass, each one having had parallel grooves etched into its surface, which are filled with opaque pigment. The two pieces are sealed together with the lines intersecting at right angles to create square windows in a lattice pattern of opaque lines. This is placed a few millimeters in front of the photographic film, allowing incoming light to spread slightly behind the screen. The gap between film and screen is crucial since it is the spread of light – dictated by its intensity as reflected from the subject – which determines the final size of the dot. For instance, the highlights from a subject reflect the most light and the resulting image on the film – in negative – will be an opaque area with pinpricks of tiny windows which will eventually print – in positive – as small dots, with the area surrounding them predominantly white. The opposite happens in the dark areas of the original. The same principle applies to all the intermediate tones, but in varying proportions; the illusion of different shades of gray in a printed subject is the result of the arrangement of different size dots, their center points exactly the same distance from each other.

Vignetted contact screens employ the same principle of converting the intensity of light into different sized dots, but in a different way. Instead of a lattice pattern of lines, the screen consists of dots – each one vignetted (solid at its core, but fading away gradually toward its circumference until it disappears completely). This

A screen is used to reproduce a halftone original (**above**). If this is enlarged (**right**), the halftone dots become clearly visible. The lightest areas are black dots on white, and the shaded parts are white on a black background.

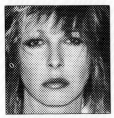

A screen angled at 90°

A screen angled at 45°

Left Halftone screens must be placed at an angle of 45°, so that the pattern of dots is harder to detect by the eye. If the screen is placed at 90°, the rows of dots form a noticeable pattern. Screens vary in coarseness (**below**), ranging from 55 lines per inch through to 300 lines per inch.

55 lines per inch
20 lines per centimeter

65 lines per inch
26 lines per centimeter

85 lines per inch
35 lines per centimeter

100 lines per inch
40 lines per centimeter

120 lines per inch
48 lines per centimeter

133 lines per inch
54 lines per centimeter

150 lines per inch
60 lines per centimeter

175 lines per inch
70 lines per centimeter

200 lines per inch
80 lines per centimeter

1 Halftone, printed black only

2 Halftone, printed magenta only

3 Black halftone over 30% magenta flat tint

4 20% magenta halftone over black halftone

5 40% magenta halftone over black halftone

6 60% magenta halftone over black halftone

7 80% magenta halftone over black halftone

8 100% magenta halftone over black halftone

9 Cyan, magenta, and yellow tritone, no black

Duotones There are a number of ways in which you can achieve a wide variety of effects if you are limited either by the number of printing colors available to you, or by only having a black-and-white original. This can be done

by the "duotone" method – reproducing images by combining two colors, usually black and one other. Strictly speaking, a duotone is a monochrome halftone image made from the same original, but to two different tonal ranges, so that when printed – in different shades of the *same* color – a greater tonal range is produced than is possible with a single color. However, the term is generally used,

wrongly, to describe a "duplex" halftone – which is two halftones made from the same original, but printed in two different colors.

The most basic type of halftone is black-and-white, where the subject will obviously only appear in shades of black (**1**). In a monochrome color halftone, the black is replaced by another color, and the result is an image in shades of the color and white (**2**). To create a flat tint halftone, a black-and-white halftone is combined with a flat color tint, producing a duller result than a duotone (**3**). The effect of the two colors in a duotone image can be controlled by varying the strength of either color (**4–8**). Further effects can be achieved by printing a monochrome original in each of the three process colors, but at varying strengths ("tritone," **9**). If a color original is available, it can be separated into local colors by the use of filters (**left**).

screen is placed in direct contact with the film emulsion; the size of dot is determined by the intensity of light passing through each dot. In monochrome reproduction, the screens are positioned with the rows of dots running at 45° angles to the page, which makes them less noticeable to the eye.

The distance at which dot centers occur between each other on a screen is measured in terms of their frequency per inch or centimeter. Thus a screen with 133 rows of dots (lines) to each inch (54 per centimeter) is referred to as a 133 screen (54 screen), but because of the wide use of both imperial and metric measurements, it is usually safer to be specific. Screens are available in a variety of sizes, ranging from 55 lines per inch (20 lines per centimeter) to 300 lines per inch (80 lines per centimeter). The finer the screen, the finer the detail in a printed subject.

The coarseness of a screen depends entirely upon the printing process and the porosity and smoothness of the paper to be used. Newsprint, for instance, with its high absorbency, is only suitable for coarser halftone screens of say, 65 lines per inch (26 lines per centimeter), whereas very smooth coated art paper can produce a high-quality reproduction with screens as fine as 200 lines per inch (80 lines per centimeter).

Color reproduction In its crudest sense, the term "color printing" can be applied to anything which is printed in more than one color – and in some cases, anything printed in any single color except black. More often it is used to denote the reproduction of full-color originals. Because each color in the printing process has to be applied by a separate printing surface, reproduction is achieved by the use of three "process" colors – cyan, magenta, and yellow, with black used as well to add finer detail and greater density in dark areas. Consequently, any original that has been presented in color first has to be separated into separate pieces of film, each one representing a different color.

Originals for color reproduction can be grouped into two main types – those consisting of solid areas of color without intermediate tones ("line originals") and those in which the subject appears as full-color continuous tone. The latter can exist as any form of hand-created art – such as a watercolor painting – on a flat surface (called "flat artwork" or "flat copy"), as full-color prints on photographic paper, or as color transparencies. A flat original is reproduced by light being reflected from it, whereas light is shone through a transparency.

In printing, nearly all colors can be obtained by mixing cyan, magenta, and yellow inks in their correct proportions, which are determined by the size of the halftone dots on each piece of film. Photographic color originals produce more faithful reproduction, since the same principle of simulating full color is employed, with color film emulsion consisting of cyan, magenta, and yellow dyes.

In some high-quality reproduction work such as fine art paintings, the standard "tri-chromatic" process colors cannot achieve faithful results and need to be supplemented by one or two – and, though rarely, even more – additional colors such as lemon yellow because this color cannot be achieved with process yellow alone.

The simplest use of color printing is by reproducing line originals as solid colors. Depending on the limitations of the job specification, there need be no restriction on the number of colors used, since any number of inks – each applied by a separate plate or block – can be used to match the original. If the design is to be printed in the process colors, overlapping solid colors can be used

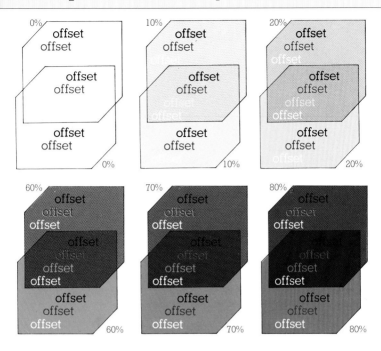

to create a much greater range of colors than just cyan, magenta, yellow, and black – cyan and yellow, for instance, can be used to produce green. Different shades of the solid colors can even be achieved by using screen tints.

The easiest way of presenting conventional line artwork for color reproduction is to produce a black representation of each respective color on a transparent overlay. If the original is presented in full-color, a separation process must be used. To separate a color original into its process color components, it is necessary to make a negative for each respective color by photographing the original through a color filter which has been matched to the standard inks and also to the respective parts of the color spectrum.

To explain this, some understanding of the color components of light is required. White light is formed by a combination of all of the colors of the spectrum, and these can be broken down into three main color sectors – red, green, and blue. Since these colors are added together or overlapped to create white light, they are known as "additive" primaries. If one of the primary colors is taken away, a different color is produced. Hence the combination of red and green, without blue, makes yellow, whereas red and blue without green produces magenta, and green and blue without red give cyan. The three colors made in this way – cyan, magenta, and yellow – are known as "subtractive" primaries.

In the color separation process, the negative for each of the process colors (subtractive primaries) requires the use of a filter of the appropriate additive primary color. Thus to make a negative record of the yellow component of an original, a blue filter is required, the effect of which will be to absorb all wavelengths of light reflected from the yellow components. The result is that yellow is not recorded on the photographic emulsion – whereas the blue reflects light and is recorded. Similarly, a green filter is used to record magenta (in negative), and a red filter for cyan. To separate black,

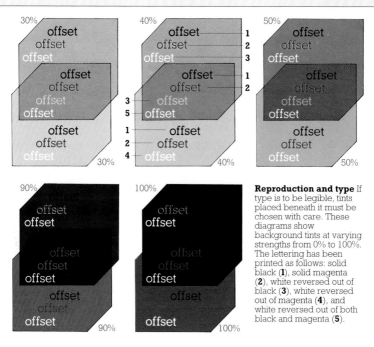

Reproduction and type If type is to be legible, tints placed beneath it must be chosen with care. These diagrams show background tints at varying strengths from 0% to 100%. The lettering has been printed as follows: solid black (**1**), solid magenta (**2**), white reversed out of black (**3**), white reversed out of magenta (**4**), and white reversed out of both black and magenta (**5**).

either a combination of all three filters is used, according to the color bias of the original, or no filter at all.

To produce separated negatives for printing, a halftone screen must be introduced. There are various ways of doing this, but they are all referred to as being either indirect or direct. The indirect method involves a two-step process. An accurate continuous tone record of the primary colors is produced as a "continuous tone separation negative" which is then used to make a positive image, the halftone screen having been introduced at this stage. In the direct method the halftone screen is introduced at the initial separation stage, without first making a continuous tone negative. Thus, the negative is already screened.

It is always extremely difficult, if not impossible, to produce perfect color reproductions when printing separated subjects. This is because pigmented printing inks are not pure; they do not reflect or absorb all incidental light accurately. Thus the color must be corrected by adjusting the negative or positive separation films. This is done either by photographic "masking," skilled hand-retouching, or if an electronic color scanner has been used, by using appropriate color correction software.

To make color halftone reproductions, each color negative or positive is photographed through the same screen. In order to avoid a screen clash, known as moiré, the screen lines are set at different angles to each other – usually about 30° between each. This produces the desired "rosette" pattern – imperceptible except under a magnifying glass – giving the appearance of smooth variation in tones when viewed at a normal reading distance.

Most types of original can be used for color halftone reproduction (though not color negatives), and an unwanted color bias – if slight – can usually be corrected at the filtration stage, especially if a scanner is being used. Contrast can also be improved, although never up to the standard that a perfect original would produce.

Generally, transparencies produce better results than reflective flat originals, because the light path is direct and does not suffer from the subsequent degradation suffered by reflected light. The best results are obtained from transparencies in which the density range is not too great, the details clear in both the shadows and highlights, definition good, and the color balance neutral with no bias in any particular direction.

Computers and reproduction Generally speaking, most designers who use computers deal with the problem of halftone reproduction, particularly color, traditionally – by leaving it up to the operators of high-end color scanners. A desktop scanner can be used to scan images – or even hand-drawn line tracings of images – at low resolution which are then used as guides for position only, with the final origination undertaken by conventional methods.

Color reproduction generated by desktop scanners is improving steadily, and in some situations – such as in multimedia applications, where the end result is a video display – it may be deemed acceptable, but it still comes nowhere near the quality demanded by most graphic designers. Even using desktop scanners, if you consistently work with large numbers of images, you will need powerful data storage facilities, a powerful computer – and eons of time.

However, although truly high-quality desktop color reprographics

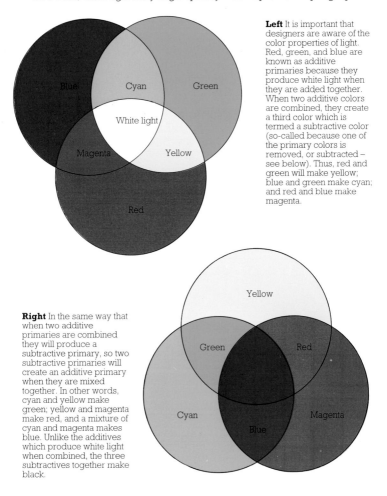

Left It is important that designers are aware of the color properties of light. Red, green, and blue are known as additive primaries because they produce white light when they are added together. When two additive colors are combined, they create a third color which is termed a subtractive color (so-called because one of the primary colors is removed, or subtracted – see below). Thus, red and green will make yellow; blue and green make cyan; and red and blue make magenta.

Right In the same way that when two additive primaries are combined they will produce a subtractive primary, so two subtractive primaries will create an additive primary when they are mixed together. In other words, cyan and yellow make green; yellow and magenta make red, and a mixture of cyan and magenta makes blue. Unlike the additives which produce white light when combined, the three subtractives together make black.

may still be some way away, facilities are already in place that enable you to take advantage of the fact that a computer can be linked to a repro scanner to produce final page film.

This is done via a "gateway link," whereby your completed document is passed to the repro house who, having previously scanned your color originals, electronically strip the images into your page. The gateway itself is usually a hardware/software combination which converts your computer-generated document into a form that enables the high-resolution repro scanned images to be placed into your page layout – just as the RIP does in an imagesetter. A typical gateway system is Crosfield's **Lightspeed StudioLink** which provides the link to the Crosfield Studio System. Another gateway is Scitex's **Visionary**, which is based on QuarkXPress and is designed to interface with the Scitex Response System. An increasingly important gateway link is provided by Aldus Corp's **Open Prepress Interface** (OPI) technology, which is now supported by the leading page make-up and prepress applications.

Scanning resolution When you use a gateway link, an original is scanned at a appropriately high resolution, and a low resolution (72dpi) file can be automatically generated, which is returned to you so that you can show the exact crop and final position on the layout. The low-resolution scan is replaced by the high-resolution

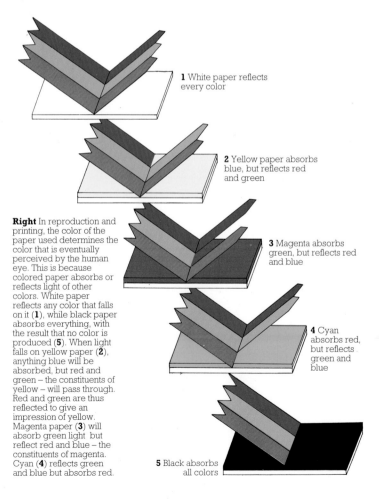

1 White paper reflects every color

2 Yellow paper absorbs blue, but reflects red and green

Right In reproduction and printing, the color of the paper used determines the color that is eventually perceived by the human eye. This is because colored paper absorbs or reflects light of other colors. White paper reflects any color that falls on it (**1**), while black paper absorbs everything, with the result that no color is produced (**5**). When light falls on yellow paper (**2**), anything blue will be absorbed, but red and green – the constituents of yellow – will pass through. Red and green are thus reflected to give an impression of yellow. Magenta paper (**3**) will absorb green light but reflect red and blue – the constituents of magenta. Cyan (**4**) reflects green and blue but absorbs red.

3 Magenta absorbs green, but reflects red and blue

4 Cyan absorbs red, but reflects green and blue

5 Black absorbs all colors

The scanner So that a full color image can be printed by the four-color printing process, it must first be scanned and separated into each of the four process colors. In principle, the way this works is simple. Images are scanned by a high-intensity light or laser beam, which, via color filters and a computer converts them into individual screened films for each color. These films can be either positive or negative, according to requirements.

Scanning transparencies The transparencies are first fixed with tape or adhesive lacquer to the glass cylinder, or drum, of the scanner (**1**). The accuracy of modern scanners means that the slightest flaw or scratch on a transparency will be picked up and magnified. This is a particular risk with 35mm transparencies and, for this reason, it is common for such transparencies to be floated in oil on the surface of the drum if a substantial enlargement is required (**2**). The drum is then fitted to the scanner and rotated at high speed, and the operator keys in the desired settings on the scanner's control panel (**3**). Light – usually a laser beam – passes through a system of lenses to illuminate the image which is then analyzed as the scanning head moves along the surface of the drum. The signals are passed to a computer which transmits the color data in digital form to an imagesetter, which converts it into light signals which are exposed onto film and then processed (**4**).

The film used produces a "hard" dot, meaning that the opportunity to hand-retouch the film is limited – if the dots are slightly etched away, their area remains the same, as opposed to soft dots which become smaller. Many operators can tell the accuracy of the color by visual examination of the film even before proofing. Normally, very little correction is needed, though proofs are correctable up to between 5% and 10% on hard film (20% on soft). Often, it is quicker and cheaper to re-run the images than correct. The reason why color correction is still necessary even

1

2

3

4

5

with this sophisticated system – is simple: with the pigments currently available, it is impossible to produce a perfectly pure printing ink since each ink absorbs some of the light it should reflect. Color correction compensates for undesirable absorption of color by the inks.

High-end scanning can be expensive, therefore it is cost-effective for transparencies to be "batched" so that the optimum number of transparencies of a median size can be fitted to the drum at the same time. Their densities, however, should also be similar, since the scanner will be set to average this out.

Scanning artwork The scanning of artwork is carried out in exactly the same way as the scanning of transparencies. However, you should remember that the scanner is even more sensitive because of the amount of light artwork will reflect, and this will affect the way certain colors react to light – some colors are difficult or impossible to reproduce. These include turquoise – a slightly warmer color than

cyan – and orange-reds. Lemon yellow and fluorescent colors are impossible to reproduce by the four-color process method, while excessive amounts of "process" white on artwork tends to make the color read-out, the basis for computation, inaccurate.

When preparing artwork for the scanner, it is advisable to use flexible board as its base, so that the artwork can be wrapped around the drum without being damaged. If artwork is presented on rigid board, the scanner operator may try to strip it off its backing – so that it is flexible enough to be mounted around the scanner drum – with the consequent risk of tearing. Also, if paint is applied too thickly, it may crack when wrapped around the drum. To avoid risk of damaging artwork, it is common for color separation houses to make a transparency of it, but doing so increases the likelihood of color inaccuracies.

Electronic page make-up and desktop computers Computers were used for page make-up for some years before the arrival of the desktop computer. Then, as now, the machines used were sophisticated and powerful, and allowed operators to work with multiple high-resolution image files – something that is still difficult on all but the most capacious and powerful desktop computers.

Desktop computers, on the other hand, were, until relatively recently, used mainly for typesetting work, images being restricted to line illustrations and simple monochrome halftones.

However, there is now less of a distinction between the capabilities of high-end electronic page composition (EPC) systems (**5, opposite**) and desktop computers, and you can combine the power of sophisticated color scanning equipment and the skills of their operators with the work you do on a computer.

A "gateway" link (**6**), a hardware/software setup, such as Open Prepress Interface (OPI) technology, is designed to take advantage of appropriate technology at every stage of production, from desktop computer to final film. You use the originals as low-resolution scans, probably done on a

desktop scanner, for design purposes (**7**). When you have established image sizes, you send the originals for high-resolution scanning (**8**). Output is stored on high-capacity disks or tape (**9**). A low-resolution version is sent to you for positioning on your layouts (**10**). When you send your layout for output as film, the gateway setup automatically replaces the low-resolution scans with the stored high-resolution versions and converts your layout files to the maker's format of the high-end system (**11**). Cleaning up, if required, is made on an electronic page composition system (**12**) before output to final film (**13**).

Blue filter

Green filter

Red filter

Yellow printer

Magenta printer

Cyan printer

Yellow proof

Cyan proof

Yellow proof

Yellow+magenta

Yellow+magenta+cyan

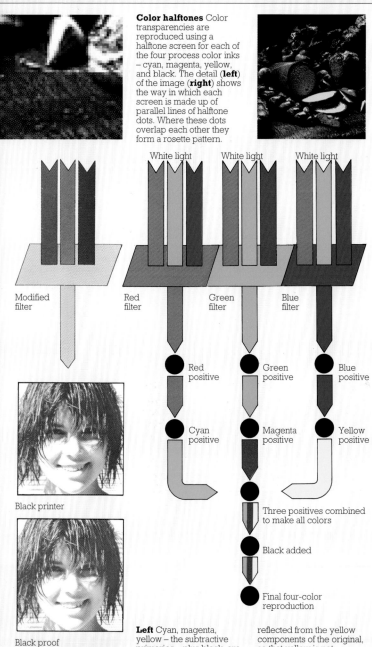

Color halftones Color transparencies are reproduced using a halftone screen for each of the four process color inks – cyan, magenta, yellow, and black. The detail (**left**) of the image (**right**) shows the way in which each screen is made up of parallel lines of halftone dots. Where these dots overlap each other they form a rosette pattern.

Modified filter

White light White light White light

Red filter Green filter Blue filter

Red positive Green positive Blue positive

Cyan positive Magenta positive Yellow positive

Three positives combined to make all colors

Black added

Final four-color reproduction

Black printer

Black proof

Yellow, magenta, cyan+black

Left Cyan, magenta, yellow – the subtractive primaries – plus black, are the four process colors used in color printing. They print as tiny dots of color which combine to give the color of the original. To make film that will produce the required color, a filter of the respective additive color is used (**above**). Thus, to make a negative film for the yellow, a blue filter is used. This absorbs all the wavelengths of light reflected from the yellow components of the original, so that yellow is not recorded on the film. When developed, the "black" part of the negative will represent everything in the original that is not yellow, and the clear part therefore includes all the yellow components of the original. Similarly, a green filter will produce a negative for the magenta, and a red filter a negative for cyan. Black is nearly always added at the end.

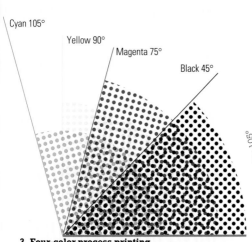

Cyan 105°
Yellow 90°
Magenta 75°
Black 45°

3. Four-color process printing

2nd color 75°
Black 45°

1. Two-color printing

3rd color 105°
2nd color 75°
Black 45°

2. Three-color printing

Screen angle One most important aspect of color halftone printing is making sure that the screens for each color are positioned correctly. For two-color printing (**1**), the black screen should be placed at an angle of 45° – the least visible angle – and the second-color screen at 75° These two screens remain at the same angles for three-color printing (**2**), but an additional screen (for the third color) is placed at 105°. In four-color printing (**3**), the black screen is angled at 45°, the magenta at 75°, the yellow at 90°, and the cyan screen at 105°. The most visible angle is 90°, and for this reason yellow – the lightest color – is always

positioned there. **Above** If the halftone screens are set at the wrong angles, an undesirable screen clash, called "moiré," occurs.

Below Most color proofs have a color bar included on them. It is totally independent of the actual image and is used by everyone involved to check the quality of the colors on the proofs. There are various makes of color bar, and, although they look different, they all share common elements. The bar shows the process colors in various forms so that accuracy of the color separation can be checked against the original with the minimum of interference from the proofing process. The amount of ink on the proof is indicated by the solid colors, and fine lines ("slur" gauge) are used to check that the paper was stable during proofing.

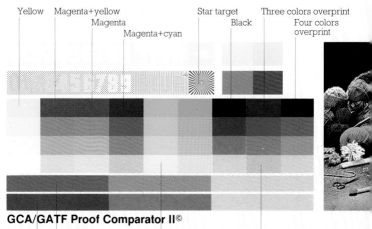

Yellow
Magenta+yellow
Magenta
Magenta+cyan
Star target
Black
Three colors overprint
Four colors overprint

GCA/GATF Proof Comparator II©

Gray balance
Neutral gray
Percentage screen patches
Gray balance patches

4-color, no color removal

Cyan+magenta+yellow

Black

Achromatic 4-color

Cyan+magenta+yellow

Black

4-color, undercolor removal

Cyan+magenta+yellow

Black

Undercolor removal
(UCR) This is a technique in which the gray and neutral tones in cyan, magenta, and yellow are removed and replaced with black. This is done to reduce the amount of ink overall, thus reducing costs (black is cheaper than colored inks) and allowing more control on the press. Conventional UCR subtracts equal amounts of cyan, magenta, and yellow from shadows and dark colors, which are then replaced by adding black. "Achromatic" reproduction reduces the complementary colors as well as shadows and middle tones, which are replaced by greatly increased black. This helps to reduce "tracking" problems on press, where two halves of the same image may be on different parts of a sheet.

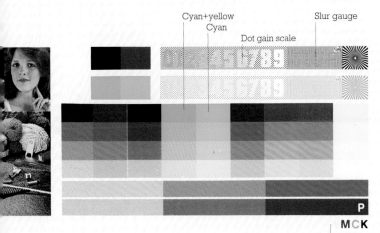

Cyan+yellow
Cyan
Dot gain scale
Slur gauge

P

M C K

Stripper's color identification

version prior to final output. Using this method still means that you need to know the final size that you want the image to be, since the scan resolution is set at the time of scanning, and any subsequent enlargement may reveal pixelation (10 percent enlargement may just about be acceptable). Repro scanner input resolution is typically 300dpi; while this may seem very low compared to imagesetter output, it must be remembered that the typical halftone screen ruling for color images is only 150lpi, and higher input resolution is really only required for very fine halftone screen rulings, such as those over 200lpi. Another confusion may arise when repro scanner operators refer to scanned images as "contones" (continuous tone images) – a relic of the days when mechanical color separations produced continuous tone negatives prior to halftone screening – whereas, in fact, the images will already have been digitized.

Output resolution Tints and halftone screens will normally be output on imagesetters at resolutions of 2540dpi for screens of 150 lines per inch, or more if the halftone screen is finer. This is

Right These symbols are widely used to mark corrections on color proofs. Always write instructions neatly and make any expansion to the marks clear (**below**). A subject marked for reproofing (**2**) normally requires re-separating unless the whole sheet is unacceptable, in which case the sheet would be reproofed. Detail and modeling (**5**) refers to highlights and details that need enhancing. Hardness (**6**, **7**) refers to subjects where edges of color, shape or tone are too hard or too soft. Register (**10**) refers to when the film for a color has been wrongly stripped. Its edges should align exactly with other colors. If an individual subject is out-of-register, but the others are not, it is "out-of-fit." Slur (**11**) is a proofing defect which occurs when ink "skids," causing the halftone dots to take on an elongated shape

Instruction	Marginal mark
1 Passed for press	
2 Reproof	
3 Reduce contrast	
4 Increase contrast	
5 Improve detail or modeling	
6 Too hard, make softer	
7 Too soft, make sharper	
8 Rectify uneven tint	
9 Repair broken type, rule or tint	
10 Improve register	
11 Correct slur	

Process color	Increase	Reduce
Cyan	C+	C–
Magenta	M+	M–
Yellow	Y+	Y–
Black	K+	K–

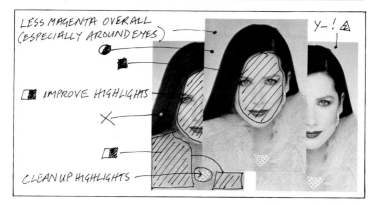

LESS MAGENTA OVERALL
(ESPECIALLY AROUND EYES)

Y – !

IMPROVE HIGHLIGHTS

CLEAN UP HIGHLIGHTS

because imagesetter resolution only determines the quality of solid black since imagesetters cannot print grays. Imagesetter resolution, then, controls the quality of line and halftone dot – the higher the resolution, the better the quality of halftone dot and thus the opportunity to reproduce the original image with greater fidelity. However, final image quality depends on the relationship between input resolution, imagesetter resolution, and halftone screen ruling.

Problems with high resolution concern the time it takes to output such files. The higher the resolution, the longer it takes to run out – a single, large image of around 30Mb may take as long as one hour to output four pieces of film. Documents of smaller sizes, but containing multiple images, may take even longer.

Tint charts Many jobs involving color reproduction require the use of flat areas of color. In four-color printing, these are made up from cyan (C), magenta (M), yellow (Y), and black (K) – the four process colors. Such tints are created by screening a solid color into a percentage of that color, typically in 5% increments, and then combin-

The correct version (**1**)

Too much contrast (**3**)

Not enough contrast (**4**)

Loss of detail (**5**)

Detail too hard or sharp (**6**)

Detail too soft (**7**)

Too much yellow

Too much cyan

Too much magenta

Too little yellow

Too little cyan

Too little magenta

ing them with a percentage tint of one, or more, of the other colors. Conventionally, tint laying was carried out by hand, involving a long and laborious process, which consequently made tint laying very expensive – a luxury, even. Nowadays, however, it is possible to specify and lay, using a desktop computer, complex tints in infinitesimal percentages – in a matter of seconds. Although it is relatively simple to specify a tint, it is still necessary to make a selection from a chart showing the complete range of combined colors. Even a computer cannot replicate the precise shade of a tint produced by the vagaries of the printing process. Such charts need to be printed with a high degree of precision, since normal good printing may deviate from optimum fidelity by as much as 10%. There are also other factors to be taken into consideration, such as the type of paper upon which the chart is printed and the inks used to print them.

Color tints The four process colors – cyan, magenta, yellow, and black – can be printed in an almost unlimited number of combinations to produce flat tints. Tints of each process color are always expressed in percentages, usually in 10% increments – a convention largely left over from the pre-computer era, when each tint was laboriously laid by hand, involving many hours of work for even simple tint-laying. However, the wide use of computers in page make-up and planning now means that tints can be laid in increments of 1% – or less, if the computer application permits – without involving extra work. The examples (**below**) show combinations of solid process colors, together with combinations of those colors broken down into percentages.

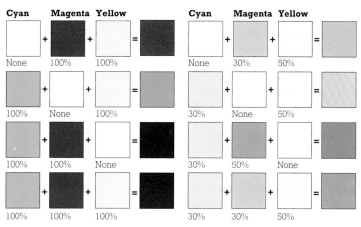

Cyan	Magenta	Yellow			Cyan	Magenta	Yellow	
None	100%	100%			None	30%	50%	
100%	None	100%			30%	None	50%	
100%	100%	None			30%	50%	None	
100%	100%	100%			30%	30%	50%	

Tint charts To select and assess a process color tint, it is essential that you refer to a printed sample of that color, preferably on paper similar to that which you will use for the job. The following pages contain charts which show 1,330 tints made up from cyan, magenta, and yellow. There are also three charts which show tints of each of the process colors combined with black (K). The charts are similar to commercially available ones, and are simple to use: the percentage of yellow in each chart is given in the top left corner of the chart (**1**) – this is the amount of yellow in every tint patch in that chart; magenta is shown along the top, and cyan down the lefthand edge. In the example (**below**), the selected tint consists of 50% yellow (**1**), 10% magenta (**2**), and 30% cyan (**3**). It is specified to the origination house as 30C + 10M + 50Y.

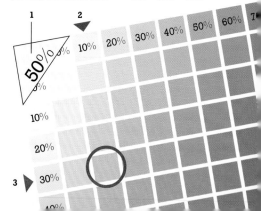

C+K	0%	10%	20%	30%	40%	50%	60%	70%	80%	90%	100%
0%											
10%											
20%											
30%											
40%											
50%											
60%											
70%											
80%											
90%											
100%											

M+K	0%	10%	20%	30%	40%	50%	60%	70%	80%	90%	100%
0%											
10%											
20%											
30%											
40%											
50%											
60%											
70%											
80%											
90%											
100%											

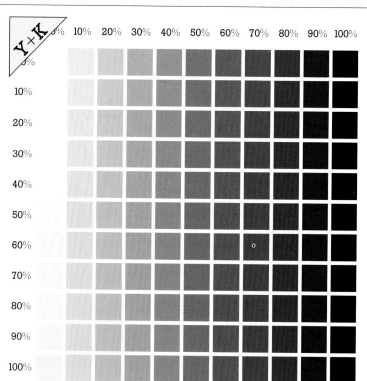

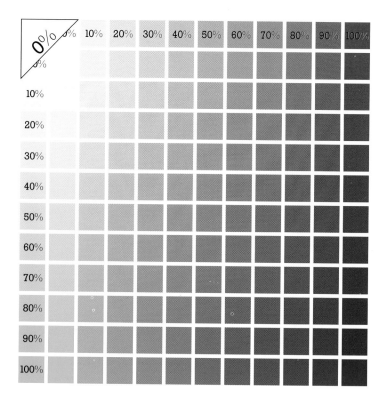

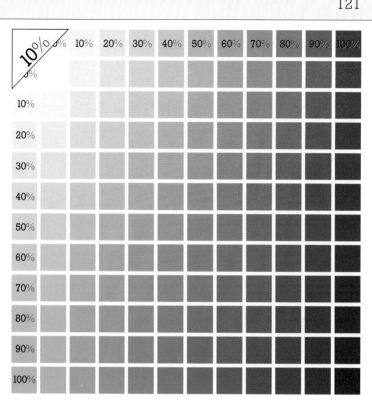

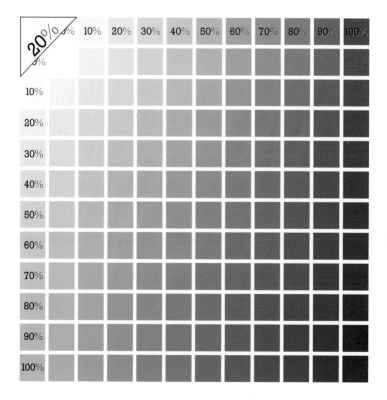

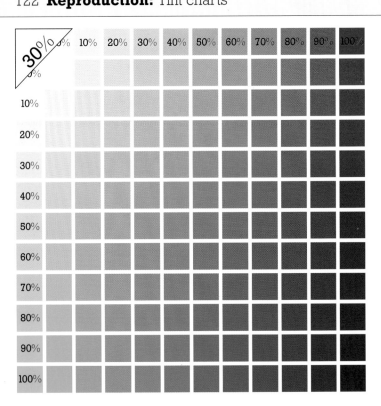

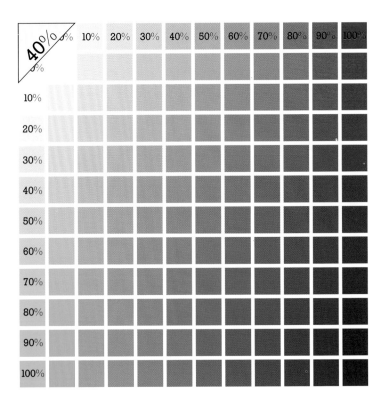

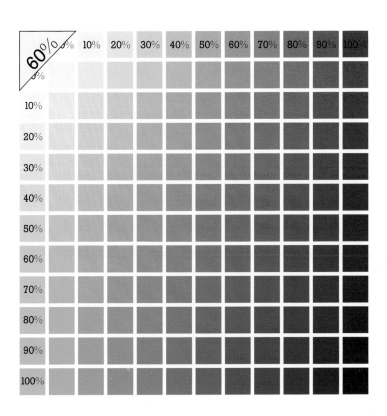

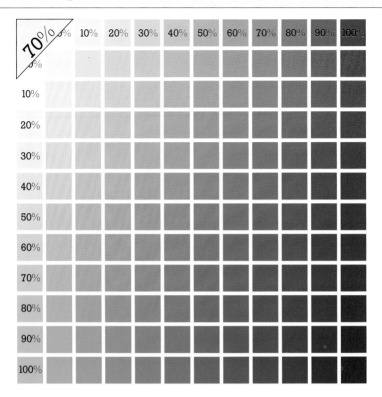

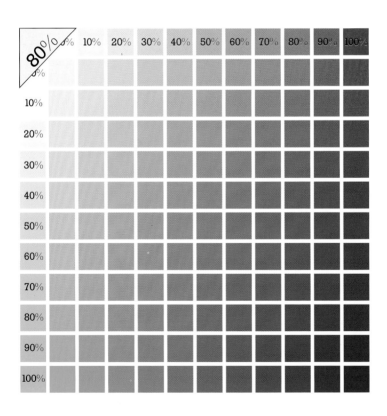

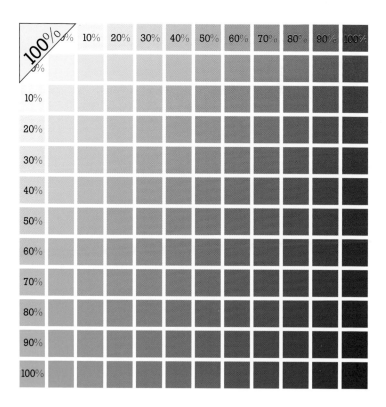

8
PRINT PRODUCTION
Letterpress/Lithography/Gravure/Screen printing/
Collotype/Flexography/Die-stamping/Thermography/
Imposition/Scoring and perforating/Folding/Embossing/
Die-cutting/Stitching/Binding/Varnishing/
Blocking/Paper

There are four principal methods in which ink can be transferred onto a surface in order to duplicate an image – by relief, plano-graphic, intaglio, or stencil printing.

In the relief method, paper is pressed onto raised areas of wood or metal, the surface of which has been inked. Commercially, this process is called letterpress printing. Planographic printing, or lithography, works on the principle that grease and water do not mix – image areas are made to attract ink and non-image areas to repel it. Intaglio printing employs a process of transferring ink onto the paper from very small cells of different depths which are recessed into the printing surface. Gravure is the commercial process using the intaglio principle. Printing from stencils is possibly the earliest known form of duplication – ink is simply passed through the remaining apertures of a cut-out shape. These shapes are held by a fine mesh, or screen, and consequently the process is called screen printing.

Letterpress One of the earliest commercial printing processes, widely used until very recently, this method is being supplanted by processes which can be linked more readily to modern photo-graphic and computer production methods – although the letter-press-derived processes are still used for special requirements, such as flexography (see below). A letterpress printing surface may consist of just pieces of type or, alternatively, the type can be used in conjunction with photoengraved plates. These plates – which may be zinc, magnesium, copper, or plastic – are used if a line or halftone illustration is to be included. They are usually produced by specialist platemakers, and, having been mounted on a base material – the whole assembly called a "block" – they are locked together with the type in a framework called a forme.

A line plate is coated with a layer of light-sensitive material which, when dry, is exposed to a powerful light source through a photo-graphic negative of the original subject. The areas of coating struck by the light become hard and will not dissolve in the acid which is subsequently used to etch away the non-image areas. The coated areas are left in relief so that the plate image is formed.

To make halftone plates, the photographic image is screened to break the subject up into a pattern of dots which vary in size, thus producing a range of different tones. Plates can be duplicated by making a mold, or to produce plates made of a thermoplastic material – polyvinyl, for instance – on a hydraulic press. The resulting plates are flexible and can be wrapped around a cylinder for rotary letterpress printing.

To print letterpress, the type of machine used is either platen, flatbed, or rotary. The platen press is the simplest machine, which operates by bringing two flat surfaces together. The forme is secured in the bed of the press and is inked by rollers when the platen opens. The paper is held on another flat surface; when the platen is closed, it brings the paper into contact with the forme under pressure.

With the flatbed press, the forme lies on a horizontal bed and travels under the inking rollers while the paper is pressed against the type by a rotating impression cylinder. Flatbed presses are now more commonly used, with modifications, by carton manufacturers for cutting and creasing.

A two-color flatbed press carries two formes, two inking systems, and two impression cylinders; the paper is passed automatically from one cylinder to the other. Flatbed perfecting presses are simi-

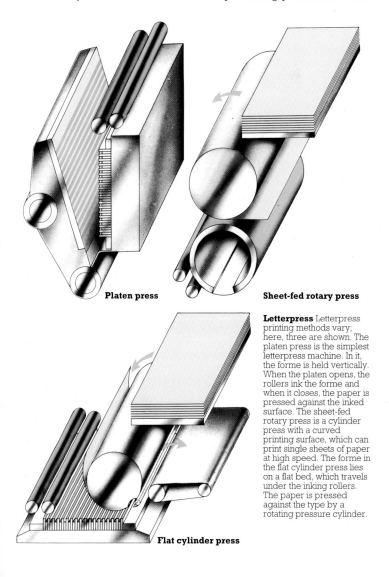

Platen press

Sheet-fed rotary press

Flat cylinder press

Letterpress Letterpress printing methods vary; here, three are shown. The platen press is the simplest letterpress machine. In it, the forme is held vertically. When the platen opens, the rollers ink the forme and when it closes, the paper is pressed against the inked surface. The sheet-fed rotary press is a cylinder press with a curved printing surface, which can print single sheets of paper at high speed. The forme in the flat cylinder press lies on a flat bed, which travels under the inking rollers. The paper is pressed against the type by a rotating pressure cylinder.

lar to two-color flatbed presses, but the paper is turned over for the second printing. These machines were generally used for printing books.

The rotary press, like the flatbed press, employs the use of an impression cylinder, but, as it was designed for high-speed work, it printed on every revolution of the cylinder from a curved forme on another cylinder, as opposed to every other revolution as with the flatbed press.

Rotary presses were sheet-fed or web-fed (printing on both sides of a continuous web of paper passing from one cylinder to the other) and could produce fine-register, high-quality work at fast speeds, making long runs economical. Sheet-fed presses could produce up to 6,000 impressions per hour, while web-fed presses operated at speeds of more than 500 meters per minute. A modern development of letterpress printing is the wrap-around rotary press, which prints from a one-piece shallow relief plate fastened around a press cylinder. This is used for general commercial printing, folding cartons, labels, and business forms.

Lithography The most important and widely used printing process today is lithography, with applications ranging from small office duplicating presses to massive machines used to print magazines, books, and newspapers. Unlike letterpress, the image areas on the printing surface do not stand up in relief. This is because lithography works on the principle that grease – on the image areas – attracts ink, while water – on the non-image areas – repels it. Thus, water plays as important a part as all the other elements in the lithographic process since the plate must first be dampened before it is inked.

Lithographic ("litho") presses use a rotary method of printing, with the printing plate – made of strong, thin sheet metal, plastic, or even paper – being wrapped around a revolving cylinder. Although plates can be made from a great variety of materials, the most common are those made of aluminum – combining strength, lightness,

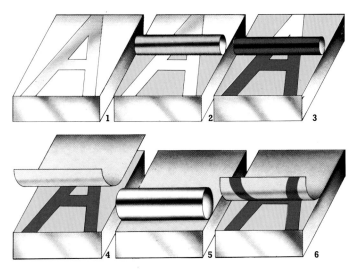

Lithography Lithography, or planographic printing, is based on the mutual repulsion of grease and water. The part of the plate to be printed is treated with a greasy medium (**1**) and rinsed. The plate is then dampened with rollers (**2**) and coated with ink (**3**), which sticks to the greasy image. Paper is positioned (**4**) and the plate run through the press (**5**) to produce the print (**6**).

and excellent lithographic qualities with economy.

The printing image on commercial litho plates is produced by photographic methods, using a (usually) presensitized plate coated with a light-sensitive material. The sensitized plate is placed in contact with a photographic film image and exposed to high-intensity light. The types of coating on a plate can be "negative-working" or "positive-working," depending on whether it is exposed to a negative or positive film image.

After exposure the plate is treated with an emulsion developer which consists of lacquer and gum-etch in a solution of acid. After developing, the plate is thoroughly rinsed with water to leave a hard stencil image on the plate, which is then coated with a protective solution of gum arabic. Plates can be baked to give longer life. The finished plate is mounted or wrapped around the plate cylinder of the press and clamped into place. In the press it comes into contact with two sets of rollers – one for dampening, the other for inking. The dampening rollers apply a solution of water, gum arabic, and acid to the plate; this prepares the image to accept the ink when it comes into contact with the ink roller, and to repel it on the non-image areas, which are damp.

The plate then comes into contact with the "blanket" cylinder which, being made of rubber, prevents the delicate litho plate from being damaged through contact with an abrasive paper surface. The rubber responds to irregular surfaces, making it possible to print on a wide variety of papers – from newsprint to heavily textured papers to fine art papers. Because the printing plate does not actually come into contact with the paper, the process is widely known as "offset" litho.

Offset litho printing relies as much on its chemical as on its physical properties. Therefore successful results depend not just on mechanics and on the skills of the printer, but on such things as conducive atmospheric conditions. As already mentioned, water is a vital part of the process, and if the air is too damp, print quality is

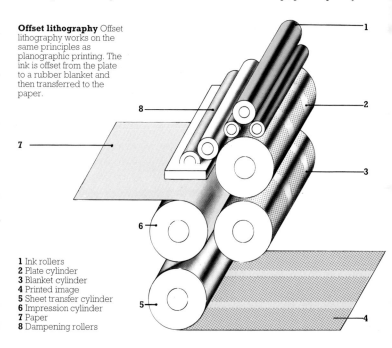

Offset lithography Offset lithography works on the same principles as planographic printing. The ink is offset from the plate to a rubber blanket and then transferred to the paper.

1 Ink rollers
2 Plate cylinder
3 Blanket cylinder
4 Printed image
5 Sheet transfer cylinder
6 Impression cylinder
7 Paper
8 Dampening rollers

affected. Excess dampening of the plates may give the printed sheet a "flat" quality, so that the colors lack density and "lift" (the degree to which ink appears to lie on the surface of the paper, as opposed to being absorbed into it).

The speed at which the printing presses run can also affect the final quality more in offset litho printing than in other processes. This book, for instance, will have been run at a relatively slow speed (approximately 5,500 sheets per hour, as opposed to the maximum of around 12,000), producing a good result despite having been printed in a country with very high humidity. Of course, ink and paper type are also important factors in determining print quality – as is air conditioning.

Offset presses are either "sheet-" or "web-" fed, the former being machines which print, as the name suggests, one sheet of paper at a time, as distinct from the latter, which prints on paper fed from a continuous roll, or "web." The largest sheet-fed presses are capable of printing runs of around 100,000 or more at speeds of about 12,000 sheets per hour on sheets of paper up to 49 x 74in., or larger. Web fed offset presses run at speeds of up to 50,000 impressions per hour and are consequently used for long runs, usually in excess of 100,000 copies.

At the other extreme from four-color, high-volume, and high-quality offset litho printing presses are the so-called "small offset" presses which are used for printing limited circulation material such as "in-house" material, price lists, forms, sales lists, and so on.

Gravure Gravure is an intaglio printing process in which ink is drawn out from small cells sunk into the printing surface. This process can be used with equal success on papers of different qualities, ranging from newsprint to coated art paper. Though used mostly for printing magazines and packaging, gravure is also used for such diverse applications as printing cellophane, decorative laminates, wallpaper, postage stamps, and reproductions of fine art pictures.

There are three main types of cell structure – conventional

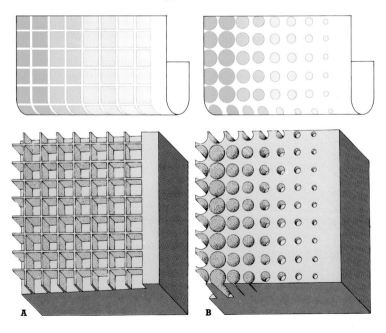

A   B

Intaglio printing In this process, the image to be reproduced is etched or incised beneath the surface of the printing plate (**1**). Ink is applied with a roller and a thin, flexible steel blade, known as a "doctor blade," is drawn across the plate to remove surplus ink from the non-printing areas (**2**). Paper is put on the plate (**3**) and pressure applied by a rubber-coated roller (**4**). This forces the paper into the recesses on the plate to pick up the image. The design is transferred and the finished print removed (**5**).

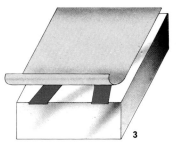

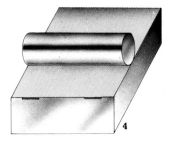

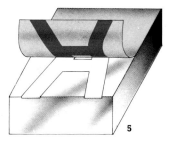

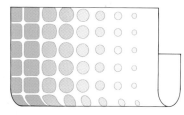

Gravure As well as its other uses, gravure printing (**left**) is particularly suited to the production of long runs because of the durability of the plates. On a conventional gravure plate (**A**), the cells vary in depth, but have the same surface areas. In variable surface, variable depth gravure (**B**), the size of the cells varies as well as the depth. This form of gravure is suitable for long-run periodical printing. Variable area direct transfer gravure (**C**) is widely used in the printing of packaging and textiles. As the image areas do not vary in depth only limited tones are available. The enlarged details above each example clearly show the individual effects of each method. They also demonstrate the basic gravure principle of printing in thousands of dots.

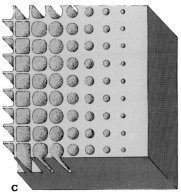

C

Sheet-fed gravure

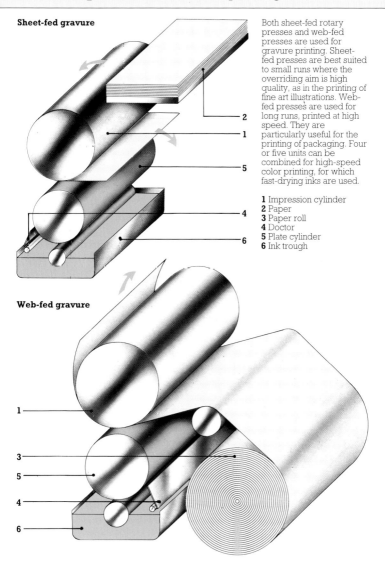

Web-fed gravure

Both sheet-fed rotary presses and web-fed presses are used for gravure printing. Sheet-fed presses are best suited to small runs where the overriding aim is high quality, as in the printing of fine art illustrations. Web-fed presses are used for long runs, printed at high speed. They are particularly useful for the printing of packaging. Four or five units can be combined for high-speed color printing, for which fast-drying inks are used.

1 Impression cylinder
2 Paper
3 Paper roll
4 Doctor
5 Plate cylinder
6 Ink trough

gravure, variable area direct transfer, and variable area, variable depth. With conventional gravure, the surface size of the cells is equal although the depth of each varies; it is used for high-quality jobs of short runs. Variable area direct transfer cells are all of the same depth, but with different surface sizes; this process is used widely for packaging and textile printing. With variable area, variable depth cells (or invert halftone gravure), the size as well as the depth of the cells varies, thus producing wider ranging, more durable tones, particularly suitable for printing color periodicals in large quantities.

There are various methods of engraving a surface. In electro-mechanical engraving, a scanning head "reads" the image to be reproduced, from which signals are used to control a diamond engraving head which cuts out the cells. Another method uses a laser beam to break up a selected area according to the strength of signal received from the scanning head. Pages created on a desktop computer can be read directly by an electronic engraving machine.

Gravure printing surfaces are usually made of a thin, highly polished copper skin which has been electroplated onto a solid steel cylinder. This skin may be chromium plated after engraving to protect it against hard wear during long print runs. If the surface is to be engraved by conventional methods rather than by scanning, the image is transferred from positives of both text and pictures by the use of a sensitized gelatin transfer medium called carbon tissue. This is exposed to bright light in contact with a gravure screen (consisting of transparent lines surrounding tiny opaque squares).

The positives are then exposed – in contact with the carbon tissue – to a diffused light which passes freely through the positive where the tones are light. Consequently, the gelatin on the carbon tissue becomes harder on these areas. The tissue is mounted onto the cylinder, and when the paper backing is removed, it is "developed" in warm water to wash away any unhardened gelatin, while the remaining gelatin forms an acid resist.

The cylinder is etched in solutions of ferric chloride, the rate of penetration depending on the thickness of the gelatin resist. A graded etching is produced by using a series of solutions of progressively decreasing concentration. The process etches the image below the surface of the plate so that it will retain the ink. At this stage, a first proof is usually taken, and corrections to tone and color can be made by rolling up the cylinder with a stiff ink. This permits local etching, needed to achieve the desired finish.

Electronic engraving is cheaper and more accurate than chemical methods, and is helping to reduce gravure preparation costs, enabling the process to compete at shorter runs than previously.

The finished cylinder is mounted onto the rotogravure press and "made ready" – positioned and locked in register below the impression cylinder. Register can be controlled automatically by using an electric eye, which guarantees accurate color reproduction. The printing surface is inked by rotating the cylinder through a trough of printing ink. Any excess ink is removed from its surface by a flexible "doctor" blade so that non-image areas remain clear.

In web-fed gravure, the paper is fed through the press continuously, passing between the etched cylinder and the impression cylinder, which has a hard rubber surface. This applies considerable pressure, forcing ink from the etched recesses of the cylinder onto the paper, thus transferring the image. Sheet-fed gravure presses employ the same method as web-fed machines; each revolution of the cylinder prints a single sheet. Gravure is an expensive process and alterations are difficult to make, so it is only really economical for long print runs.

Screen printing One of the simplest and cheapest forms of printing is by using stencils. A stencil is held in position by placing it on a fine mesh or screen which is stretched very tightly over a wooden or metal frame. Traditionally the screen was made from silk and the process was called "silkscreen printing," but synthetic materials are now used in preference to silk, and the process now tends to be known as "screen printing."

In commercial screen printing, the most common method of producing stencils is by photographic means, although knife-cut stencils – cut directly from layouts – are still used occasionally. There are two methods of photographically preparing stencils – direct and indirect. Direct stencils are made by exposing a screen mesh coated with light-sensitive emulsion to a film positive of the image

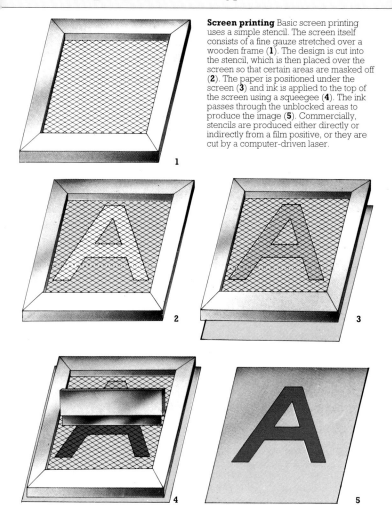

Screen printing Basic screen printing uses a simple stencil. The screen itself consists of a fine gauze stretched over a wooden frame (**1**). The design is cut into the stencil, which is then placed over the screen so that certain areas are masked off (**2**). The paper is positioned under the screen (**3**) and ink is applied to the top of the screen using a squeegee (**4**). The ink passes through the unblocked areas to produce the image (**5**). Commercially, stencils are produced either directly or indirectly from a film positive, or they are cut by a computer-driven laser.

by using ultraviolet light. The emulsion in the image areas is hardened by the light, leaving soluble emulsion in the image areas which is subsequently washed away with water. The same basic principle applies to indirect stencil-making, the difference being that the stencil is exposed and washed out or developed before it is applied to the screen.

Once the screen has been prepared, it is scraped to remove any excess emulsion that may have built up. The paper to be printed is positioned accurately under the screen by aligning corresponding register marks in the corners. When the screen and the paper have been assembled on the frame, the printing process itself, known as "pulling" the print, can take place. Printing ink is drawn across the screen with a rubber squeegee. The action of the squeegee presses the screen into contact with the paper – onto which the ink is forced through the unmasked areas of the mesh. Versatility is a major advantage of the process – it can be used to print on almost any surface, including wood, glass, metal, plastic, and fabrics.

One of the chief characteristics of screen printing is the thickness of the ink on the printed surface – sometimes up to 10 times as heavy as that of letterpress – but modern ink technology has reduced the ink film thickness considerably. Although screen printing equipment can be used to print at relatively high speeds and can be specially designed to suit almost any requirement, much of it is done on hand-operated presses.

Collotype Like lithography, collotype printing (sometimes called "photogelatin") is a planographic process. It is now rarely used, and only a handful of printers in the world offer collotype printing services. However, this process is the only one which can produce high-quality black-and-white or color continuous tone prints without the use of a screen.

The image is carried by a film of gelatin which has been made light-sensitive with potassium or ammonium bichromate (called, confusingly "dichromate"). The gelatin, carried by a thick sheet of plate glass, is placed in contact with a photographic negative and exposed to light. The gelatin hardens according to the amount of light reaching it – the harder the gelatin, the more capable it is of accepting ink.

As with lithography, the process depends on water repelling grease, so the unexposed parts of the gelatin are kept moist with water and glycerine so that they repel the ink. This gives a result rather like that of a photograph in that it achieves gradations from the deepest black to the lightest shades of gray.

The machines used for printing are special collotype presses similar to litho machines, but they run at particularly slow speeds; it may take two days to produce 2,000 copies – the maximum that can be taken from one plate. However, the process can produce extremely high-quality results and is used for printing small runs of fine art reproductions.

Flexography This process is a derivative of letterpress using flexible plates and thin, fluid inks that dry by evaporation (sometimes assisted by heat). The plates are made from rubber or photopolymer, and the image is raised as in conventional letterpress.

Most flexographic presses are web-fed, and many machines are four-color presses. Flexography's main use is for packaging – printing on cellophane, plastics, and metallic films; it can be used to print on virtually any material which will pass through the press. It is also used to produce newspapers and paperbacks; these publications are filmset and use photopolymer plates.

Photopolymer plates are made from negatives, much in the same way as letterpress blocks. The plate material is given a light-sensitive coating that is exposed through the negative. The light hardens the image area, while the background (non-image) area remains soft and can be dissolved away to leave the image area in relief.

Die-stamping This process, like gravure, is an intaglio process, where a steel or copper plate is engraved by hand or etched using photographic techniques to create a recessed image. Ink is deposited in the recesses of this "female" die, and a "male" die of cardboard, or plastic (previously made from the female die by pressure) presses the paper onto it to deposit the ink and simultaneously produce a bas-relief effect. The paper or cardboard is raised in the image area and indented on its back.

Copper is cheaper to prepare than steel and is therefore used for shorter runs. Most of this work is done on hand presses, but power-driven presses, known as "die-stampers," are used for runs of 1,000 or more. This technique can also be used for "blind embossing," where a raised image is produced, but no ink is applied.

The process is used for high-quality business cards, letterheads,

Imposition This refers to how the pages are arranged on each side of a printed sheet, so that they read correctly in the right order when cut, folded and trimmed. The illustrations (**below**) show the commonest forms of imposition scheme and the illustrations (**right**) show the corresponding folding methods. Sufficient margins are left for trimming – normally ⅛in. (3.175mm) to ¼in. (6.350mm).

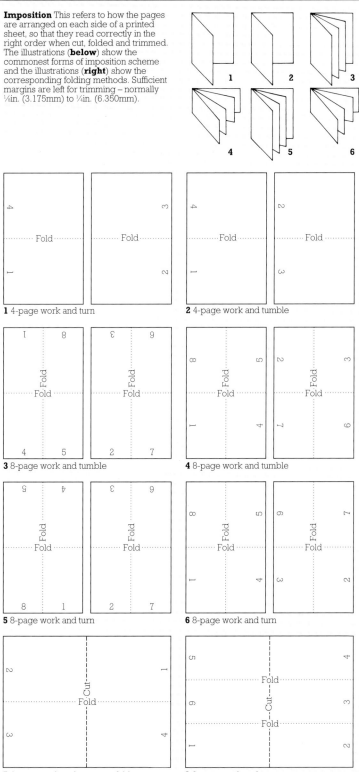

1 4-page work and turn

2 4-page work and tumble

3 8-page work and tumble

4 8-page work and tumble

5 8-page work and turn

6 8-page work and turn

7 4-page work and turn, one fold

8 6-page work and turn

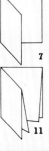
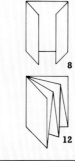
7
8
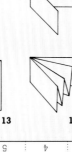

9

10

11
12
13
14
15

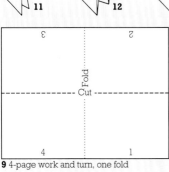

9 4-page work and turn, one fold

10 8-page work and turn

11 8-page work and turn

12 12-page booklet work and turn

13 12-page booklet, three parallel folds

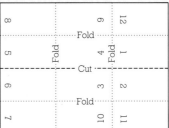

14 16-page oblong booklet

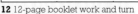

15 16-page booklet

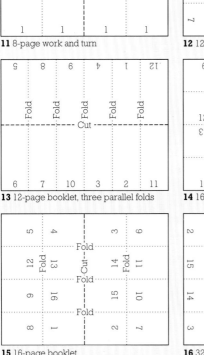

16 32-page section (16 pages to view)

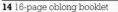

and invitations, where the glossy bas-relief effect adds distinction. Rotary versions of this process are used in banknote and security printing.

Thermography This process produces a glossy, raised image by using infrared light. The image is first printed either by letterpress or litho using an adhesive ink which is coated with a fusible resin containing pigment or a metallic powder. When passed under infrared light, the coating is fused to give a hard image. The result is glossy and simulates the results of copper engraving, but is coarser and much cheaper. It is commonly used for invitations, business cards, and letterheads.

Imposition Perhaps the most important aspect of print production to graphic designers is that of the position of the printed page on a sheet. The way in which pages can be "imposed" (placed in position on a printing plate) varies considerably, and knowledge of how the printed sheets are to be folded is essential to guarantee that the pages appear in the correct order.

This whole procedure can be particularly vexing to designers, and before planning any job which involves complex color fall – such as an uneven distribution of four-color pages among single-color pages – you should consult the printer first, since the size of the machine to be used will dictate how many pages can be printed on a sheet. If you use a computer, software is available which automatically configures your designed pages to the correct imposition.

If a job is to print evenly – such as four-color throughout – then imposition need not necessarily concern you, but if, say, a job is to print "four backed two" (4 x 2 – four-color pages backing onto two-color ones) the way the color actually falls is paramount to the design of the piece. Knowledge of imposition will reveal to you that a seemingly rigid distribution of 4 x 2 in fact allows considerable flexibility as to where those four-color pages actually occur. For instance, a publication of 192 pages printing 4 x 2 (as this book is) means that you have 96 pages of four-color and 96 pages of two-color to play with. If the book is to be printed on sheets of 32 pages (16 pages on each side, or "16 to view") six sheets will be required to print the job. This means that the color pages can be printed in a number of combinations with the two-color. Three sheets, say, may be printed 4 x 4, leaving the remaining three to print 2 x 2, or, alternatively, one sheet may print 4 x 4, another 2 x 2, and the remaining four 4 x 2.

Further flexibility is possible if the sheets are slit after printing, or if the job is printed as "work and turn." This is when all the pages are printed on one side of the sheet, which is then turned over to print the other side. The number of pages on a sheet depends on the page size related to the sheet or machine size. While most printers print and bind in multiples of 16 pages, it is also common for them to work in multiples of 20 or 24.

Imposition not only affects the position of color pages throughout a publication, but also – because of the position of each page on the sheet – the degree to which color can be corrected on machine. Balancing the color of two halves of a double-spread picture, for instance, can be extremely difficult if each half appears on opposite sides of the sheet and out of line from the direction the sheet comes off the machine. Color correction is obviously easier to control if the two halves appear on a portion of the sheet passing through the same part of the inking process of the press.

Scoring and perforating Scoring is done on board or thicker grades of paper to facilitate folding. In letterpress printing, a scoring rule can be part of the printing forme on the press. In offset printing, perforating rules can be stuck around or across the cylinder, or scoring wheels can be brought into the operation between the printing unit and delivery of the sheets or done on a scoring machine.

Perforating can be carried out similarly, using a perforating rule in the forme on a letterpress machine or a perforating rule or wheel on an offset machine. The same separate machine used for scoring will also perforate. Scoring and perforating can be done while die cutting is carried out.

Folding Thick paper should not be used for folders of more than eight pages, and they should be planned with great care. If a book is to include a fold-out page, allowance must be made for the page to fold-in, which must be slightly smaller – at least ¹⁄₁₆in. – than the trim size; the fold must not project beyond the trim size; otherwise, it will be trimmed off.

Embossing This is normally carried out on letterpress printing machines or die-stamping machines. "Blind-embossing," the creation of a raised image without ink, is often used for letterheads. Paper or board can also be embossed overall on special roller-embossing machines either before or after printing.

Die-cutting This is known also as "cutting and creasing." A forme is made consisting of knives – blunt for creasing and sharp for cutting – and placed in the bed of a converted letterpress machine or a special cutting-and-creasing machine. The process is used mainly for cartons, where irregular shapes have to be cut out and the box corners scored.

Stitching There are two principal methods of stitching – saddle-stitch and side-sewing (which is also called stab-stitch). Saddle-stitching is used for publications of up to ³⁄₁₆in. in bulk. Folded sections are positioned on a "saddle" underneath a mechanical head and a wire staple or thread stitch is forced through the spine of the book. Although it is a cheap method of binding, saddle-stitched publications lie flat when opened.

For books of greater bulk, side-sewing is used. The folded sheets are gathered (placed one on top of the other), and the stitches are forced through from first page to last. The stitching is about 3mm from the spine and will not permit the book to be opened flat.

Binding Of the many different types of binding available, probably the most common is "perfect" – also called "unsewn" and "thread-less" – binding. In this, the folded and gathered sections have the back fold trimmed off and the pages are glued by their back edges to the cover. An allowance of ¹⁄₄in. (6mm) must be made for the trim at the backs and for the gutter margins. The minimum thickness for a perfect bound book is about ¹⁄₄in. (6mm) – any less and the pages may fall apart.

Covers for perfect bound work should only be laminated or varnished on the outside – glue will not adhere to a gloss-coated surface, unless a strip of uncoated paper has been specially left for the glue. Publications which have covers consisting of the same paper as its insides are described as having "self" covers. These may be the same size as the text pages ("cut flush") or may overlap them, and in either case they may require some reinforcement. This can be achieved by a "French fold" – double thickness paper, folded at the top – or as a "wraparound" cover in which the paper is folded at the foredge and turned inward. The latter may be given additional support by wrapping the cover around a sheet of stiff cardboard.

Case-bound work, in which the text pages are glued into covers

Bookbinding Methods of bookbinding vary according to the nature of the job and the materials used. The various elements involved in the binding of a conventional jacketed hardback (**right**) are: endpapers (**1**), headbands (**2**), dust jacket (**3**), spine (**4**), case (**5**), metallic foil stamping (**6**), and tailbands (**7**). This form of binding is known as edition binding; paperbacks are perfect bound, a preprinted cover being glued to the spine.

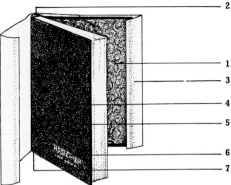

Edition binding and perfect binding are the conventional forms of binding for hardbacks and paperbacks respectively (**left**). In edition binding, the sheets are folded into 16- or 32-page signatures to be collated and sewn by machine. The edges are trimmed and the sewn-back edge coated with glue (**1**). This is then rounded and a strip of gauze glued to the backbone to overlap on both sides (**2**). Finally, book and cloth cover (**3**) are placed on a casing-in machine, which pastes the endpapers and fits the cover. In perfect binding, the folded and collated pages have the spine edge roughened so that the binding glue adheres strongly (**4**). A lining is placed over the backbone and the cover glued firmly in place (**5**). Quarter binding and half binding (**below**) are more luxurious versions of edition binding. In both, leather – or a similar substitute – is used to strengthen the spine; in half binding, patches are also used to reinforce the corners.

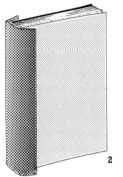

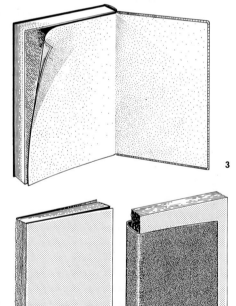

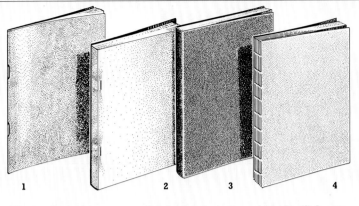

There are four main stitching methods (**above**). Saddle-stitch binding is the most common (**1**). In this, the book is opened over a "saddle" and stapled along the back fold. In side-wire stitching (**2**), wire staples are inserted from the front, about ¼in. (6mm) from the back edge, and then clinched at the back. In thermoplastic binding, the gathered signatures are trimmed along the back edge and bound with a hot plastic glue (**3**). In sewn-thread binding (**4**), the gathered signatures are sewn individually, then sewn together again.

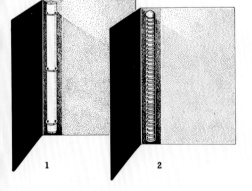

Ring binding (**left**) allows a book to lie absolutely flat when it is opened. The loose-leaf post or ring binder (**1**) is based on two or four rings, riveted to a stiff cover. These springs open so that ready-drilled paper can be inserted. The multiple ring binder (**2**) works on exactly the same principle, but uses many more rings.

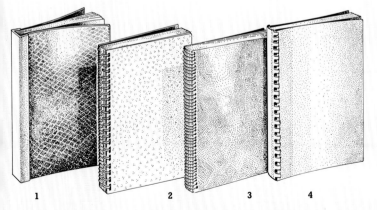

In one version of mechanical binding (**above**), a plastic gripper is fitted tightly over the spine to hold the pages together (**1**). In open-flat mechanical binding, holes are drilled through covers and pages, which are then bound together with a wire or plastic coil. Examples include the Wire-0 (**2**), spiral (**3**), and plastic comb (**4**). Because the pages lie flat when the book is opened with these three forms of binding, they are ideal for reference manuals or notebooks.

made of boards wrapped in cloth, is used extensively for more expensive trade books. This method of binding can range from wholly mechanized mass-produced publications to specialized hand-tooled work. A wide variety of finishes is available, from real leather to imitation cloth. Alternatively, a case-bound book may have a printed cover which is glued onto the boards instead of cloth, and this may sometimes eliminate the need for a dust jacket.

Varnishing A gloss finish can be achieved by applying lacquer or varnish after printing. This can be done by printing varnish on the normal printing machine or by "spirit varnishing" on a special machine. Very high gloss can be achieved by using an ultraviolet (UV) cured lacquer. In this process, the lacquer is applied by a roller and then dried with UV lamps. Most paperback books and many cartons have this finish.

Blocking (Foil stamping) The case of most books is impressed either with its title or a design, or both. This may be done by blocking (stamping) the case with a metal die forced into the cloth through gold or metallic foil. Metallic foils are available in a variety of finishes which are produced by vaporizing aluminum with colored dyes. Black, white, and other colors are also available – either in a matt or in a bright, polished finish.

The finesse of a blocked design depends heavily on the material onto which it is being stamped. A coarse canvas cloth, for instance, will respond better to a simple, clearly defined image, whereas a smooth, paper-covered board will accept designs with a high degree of intricacy.

Paper The choice of paper for a printed work is as much an integral part of the design as every other aspect. Generally, paper types are grouped according to the purpose for which they are to be used and also according to the printing process that is to be employed. Of each group, or classification, there are hundreds of different qualities – each manufacturer may produce several different qualities of papers for the same specific use.

Understanding the characteristics of paper requires some knowledge of how it is made. One of the main constituents of paper is cellulose fiber, which is normally obtained either from wood, rags, or old paper, or any combination of these. In the past, many other

Paper Every designer should have a basic knowledge of the common types of paper and their suitability for various jobs. Good quality halftones, for instance, should be printed on a coated art paper to reproduce to best effect. Conversely, rough surface antique papers, though they reproduce text well, are not suitable for halftones. This chart gives a selection of common paper types and a guide to their best uses.

Paper	Comments	Uses
Antique	Subdivided into two types – antique laid, if mold marks show, otherwise antique wove	Text books. Not suitable for halftone reproduction or large line plates
Newsprint	Made from mechanical woodpulp. Cheap, discolors rapidly	Newspapers, cheap leaflets, proofing
Mechanical	Made from mechanical woodpulp. If polished, subdivided into super-calendered (SC), machine-finished (MF), and machine-glazed (MG), depending on how polishing is done	Cheap leaflets, booklets, magazines. SCs print tones up to 100 screen; MFs to 85 screen
Woodfree	Does not contain woodpulp. Strong, with good color. Bulks well	General and magazine printing Lithography if hard sized
Artboards	Boards covered with lining paper on both sides	Packaging

sources of fiber were used, such as grasses, bamboo, and cane – the nature of the raw fiber determined the type of paper produced.

Softwoods such as pine, spruce, and fir have relatively long fibers, which give added strength to the paper. Timber is reduced to pulp either by mechanical or by chemical means. The former, being simpler and more economical, produces weaker, less permanent papers such as those used for newspaper printing. Chemically produced pulp gives a much stronger, brighter, and more permanent quality than mechanically produced ("ground-wood") pulp, but the yield is smaller and more expensive.

The pulp is washed, screened for impurities, bleached, and finally beaten and is then delivered to the mill or factory in the form of bales of fiber. At the mill, fillers, size (glue), and dyes are added. The most common additive is china clay, which adds bulk to the more costly cellulose; it also improves the color and opacity of paper and is used to size the surface of high gloss papers.

The pulp is further broken down in a pulper, where it is mixed with water to form a slurry called furnish. After further mechanical and chemical treatment, the furnish is pumped into the first stage ("wet end") of the papermaking system. Here it is diluted again, then moved to a mechanism ("flow head" or "head-box"), which feeds it onto an endless, moving wire. This conveys it through a series of presses, where most of the water is squeezed out.

It next moves to the drying section of the machine, which consists of a series of heated rollers. At the end of the drying section, the surface of the paper is smoothed and finished by being passed under chilled heavy iron rollers. These exert enough pressure to compress the surface fibers – a process known as calendering. The degree of the smoothness of the paper is determined by the number of calenders, or "nips," the paper runs through – the more calenders, the higher the final gloss.

Certain types of paper – particularly the more expensive, high-quality grades – are treated with fluorescing agents to increase their whiteness. The end product is a continuous sheet of paper, known as a "web," which can be used at once, in reel form, or it can be transferred to another machine which cuts it into sheets for sheet-fed presses.

Paper	Comments	Uses
Art	Coated with china clay to give it smoothness. In imitation art, the clay is mixed with the wood pulp. Often polished, though some are matt	Halftones, especially four-color printing. Frequently used for offset lithography. Reproduces up to 150 line line screen; imitation art to 120 line screen
Chromo	Very smooth, usually matt and coated on one side	Proofing four-color halftones. Reproduction proofs
Cast-coated	Very smooth, highly polished	Packaging, labels, booklet covers
Cover papers	Strong, fold and wear well. Available in plain and embossed finishes. Usually colored	Book and pamphlet covers
Cloth-lined board	One side lined with linen or cloth for strength. Depending on quality of paper, cloth can be sandwiched between lining papers	Covers
Cartridge	Tough wove, similar to Antique, although smoother. Offset cartridge specially designed for offset lithography	Booklets, brochures, drawings. Print litho well. Reproduce letterpress halftones to 85 screen

9
GLOSSARY

With the advance of technology, the designer's vocabulary now needs to include many new printing and computer terms. This glossary has been compiled with a view to explaining as many of these as possible. Terms relating to systems that are no longer in use have largely been omitted.

Key: *com:* computer; *fin:* finishing/binding; *pap:* paper; *pho:* photography; *pri:* printing; *rep:* prepress; *typ:* typography/typesetting; Terms that have their own entry in the glossary are written in SMALL CAPS.

A

AA *abb* AUTHOR'S ALTERATION.

Absorbency (*pap*) The ability of a material to suck in liquid or moisture.

AC *abb* AUTHOR'S CORRECTION.

Accent (*typ*) A mark added to a letter to denote pronunciation in a given language. The most common are boll â, grave è, acute é, cedilla ç, circumflex â, tilde ñ, barØ, umlaut ä.

Access time (*com*) Of disk drives, the average combined seek time (the time taken for the drive head to reach data being accessed) and latency time (the time taken for the data sector to rotate beneath the READ/WRITE HEAD).

Accordion fold (*fin*) Method of paper folding in which each fold runs in the opposite direction to the one before it to form a pleated effect.

Acetate see CELLULOSE ACETATE.

Additive colors The primary colors of light red, green, and blue that may be mixed to form all other colors in photographic reproduction.

Aerate (*pri*) To use an air stream or manual riffling to separate paper SHEETS to be fed mechanically through a printing machine.

Against the grain (*fin*) Folding or marking paper at right angles to the GRAIN (1).

Agate (*typ*) Type size of 5.5 POINTS.

Agate line (*typ*) Measurement of space in newspaper advertising, denoting 0.25in. depth by one COLUMN width.

Airbrush, airbrushing A mechanical painting tool producing a fine spray of paint or ink, used in illustration, design, and photographic retouching.

Albumen plate (*pri*) Lithographic plate with PHOTOSENSITIVE surface coating, originally made from albumen.

Algorithm (*com*) A set of predetermined procedural steps for solving a specific problem.

Aligning numerals (*typ*) see LINING FIGURES.

Alignment The arrangement of type or other graphic material to make things level at one horizontal or vertical line.

Alphabet/alphabet length (*typ*) A measure derived from the length in POINTS of the 26 alphabet letters set in LOWER CASE. Thus 39 CHARACTERS (1) have a measure of 1.5 alphabets.

Alphanumeric set (*typ*) A full set of letters and figures, possibly also including punctuation marks and certain commonly used symbols.

Ampersand The sign (&) used in place of the word "and."

Analog computer (*com*) A computer using a physical variable, like voltage, to represent numbers in arithmetical calculations.

Angle bar (*pri*) The metal bar of a WEB-FED printing press that turns paper between two units of the press.

Aniline (*pri*) Oily liquid from a nitrobenzene base used in preparing dyes and aniline ink, a volatile, quick drying printing ink.

Animal-sized (*pap*) Describes paper which has been hardened or sized with animal glue or gelatin by passing the finished SHEET through a bath of glue.

Animation A method of film-making that produces movement by rapid projection of a series of sequential still images, often drawings or cartoons.

Annex A supplement to a technical publication bound with the main BODY of the text

Annotation (**1**) A type label added to an illustration. (**2**) Explanatory notes printed in the MARGIN of a text.

Anodized plate (*pri*) A plate used in OFFSET printing, specially treated to harden the surface so it will resist wearing down in the press.

Antialiasing (*com*) A technique which reduces the jagged effect of bitmapped screen images by averaging the density of pixels at the edges of images with their background, thus softening the stepped appearance of the image.

Antihalation backing (*rep*) A protective coat on the non-EMULSION side of a film or plate that prevents light from reflecting back into the emulsion.

Antiquarian (*pap*) The largest known size of handmade paper, 53 x 31in. (1350 x 790mm).

Antique paper (*pap*) Paper with a rough, lightly sized finish used mainly for books, booklets, and folders.

Aperture (*pho*) Opening behind a camera lens that allows light to reach the film. The size of the aperture is governed by the DIAPHRAGM and measured by the F-NUMBER.

Application (com) A PROGRAM written to create or manipulate DATA for a specific purpose, such as word processing or page layout, but which is distinct from non-application programs such as UTILITY programs or SYSTEM software.

Application heap (com) The portion of RAM set aside for use by any or all APPLICATIONS.

Apron (pri) Extra white space allowed at the MARGINS of text and illustrations forming a FOLDOUT.

Aquatint (pri) An INTAGLIO process that allows reproduction of even or graded tones.

Arabic numerals (typ) The numerical symbols 1 2 3 4 5 6 7 8 9 0. See also ROMAN NUMERALS.

Art see ARTWORK.

Artificial intelligence (AI) (com) A term describing PROGRAMS that deduce, to a specific set of rules, a solution from original and subsequent criteria provided by you – in other words, the program learns by its own experience. Such programs are sometimes called "expert systems." Used in, among other things, programs for writing other programs, and industrial processes.

Art-lined envelope (pap) Envelope with a plain colored or patterned lining of extra-fine paper.

Art paper (pap) Paper with a hard smooth surface caused by an even coating of china clay compound on one or both sides.

Artwork MATTER other than text prepared for reproduction such as illustrations, diagrams, and photographs.

As to press Term used in production of GRAVURE printed magazines for proofs showing final position of color images.

ASA abb American Standards Association. An ASA number appears on film stock to provide a basic quantity from which the length and F-NUMBER of an EXPOSURE can be calculated.

Ascender (typ) The section of a LOWER-CASE letter rising above the X-HEIGHT, i.e., the upper part of an h or d.

ASCII (com) Acronym (pronounced askee) for the American Standard Code for Information Interchange, a standard by which most computers

assign CODE numbers to letters, numbers, and common symbols.

Aspect ratio (com) A term used in COMPUTER GRAPHICS to denote the ratio of width to height in a figure or letter.

Assembled negative (rep) Negative of line and HALFTONE COPY used in preparing a printing plate for PHOTOLITHOGRAPHY.

Asynchronous (com) A communications method in which operations start at varying or irregular intervals, as when the end of one initiates the beginning of another.

Author's alteration/ correction Changes in COPY made by the author after TYPESETTING, but not those made necessary by printer's errors.

Author's proof GALLEY PROOFS checked and marked by the typesetter's READER to be read by the author, who may then make any necessary correction.

Autoflow (com) The facility, in some APPLICATIONS, to flow text automatically from one page to another or from one box to another.

Autopositive (pho) Photographic materials designed to provide a POSITIVE (1) image without a NEGATIVE being required.

Auxiliary roll stand (pri) A second stand holding a paper roll in a WEB-FED press, allowing continuous printing while the first roll is replaced.

AVA abb Audio Visual Aids. The term refers to teaching and display equipment such as projectors, tape recorders, VIDEO players, etc.

A/W abb ARTWORK.

B

Back (fin) The part of a book nearest the fold or the edge at which the pages are bound.

Back jacket flap Section of a BOOK JACKET folded inside the back COVER of a HARDCOVER book.

Back lining (fin) A paper or fabric strip fixed to the back of a book before CASING IN.

Back margin (fin) The MARGIN of a page nearest to the SPINE of the book.

Back matter see END MATTER.

Back step collation (fin) To COLLATE a book by referring to marks printed on the back fold of each SECTION (1).

Back to back (pri) Printing on both sides of a

SHEET. See BACK UP.

Back up (**1** pri) To print the second side of a sheet of paper. Backed refers to the sheet when it has been backed up. Also called "perfecting." (**2** com) To make a duplicate of a disk, application, or document as a precaution against losing the original.

Backbone see SPINE.

Background (**1** com) Description of a program which runs at the same time as another is running in the foreground, as when two or more programs are open. (**2** pho) In an illustration or photograph, the part of the image that appears farthest from the viewer or on which the main subject is superimposed.

Background processing (com) The facility of a PROGRAM running in the BACKGROUND (1), to process DATA without interfering with the program operating in the foreground.

Bank paper (pap) A light, uncoated paper used for making carbon copies.

Banker envelope The most common type of envelope, having a top flap along the longer edge of the rectangle.

Banner A main HEADLINE across the full width of a page.

Bar code A pattern of vertical lines identifying details of a product, such as country of origin, manufacturer, and type of product, conforming to the UNIVERSAL PRODUCT CODE (UPC) – there are several different formats for product coding.

Barn doors (pho) Flaps attached to a spotlight or floodlight to direct the fall of light.

Bas relief Three-dimensional design in which the image stands in shallow relief from a flat background.

Base alignment (typ) In computer typesetting, the automatic alignment of type of different sizes on a common BASE LINE (1).

Base artwork ARTWORK requiring the addition of other elements, such as HALFTONE positives, before reproduction.

Base film (rep) The basic material for contact film in platemaking for PHOTOMECHANICAL reproduction, to which film positives are stripped.

Base line (**1**) An imaginary line on which the bases of CAPITALS rest. (**2**) The last line of space on a page containing type MATTER.

Base material Material forming the support for a coating or plating.

Base stock (*pap*) Accumulated material from which different types of papers can be made.

Basic size (*pap*) A standard size for a particular type of paper, though the SHEET may be cut larger or smaller.

Basic weight (*pap*) The designated weight of a REAM of paper cut to a given standard size.

Bastard (**1** *pri*) A substandard or abnormal element. (**2** *pri*) A letter foreign to the FONT in which it is found. (**3**) A general term meaning a non-standard size of, for example, type or paper.

Bastard title see HALF-TITLE.

Baud (*com*) The unit of measure equating to one unit per second describing the speed of DATA transfer, by – say – a MODEM, sometimes inaccurately referred to as BIT RATE (two or more bits can be contained in a single event). The greater the baud rate, the faster the transmission of data.

Bearoff (*typ*) Adjusting spacing in type MATTER to correct JUSTIFICATION and COMPOSITION of the copy.

Begin even (*typ*) Instruction to printer to set first line of COPY FULL OUT.

Below the line Advertising term describing costs of promotional items other than the advertisement itself.

Ben Day prints (*rep*) A series of mechanical tints in the form of celluloid sheets that are used in blockmaking and LITHOGRAPHY to add texture, shading, and detail to line drawings.

Bézier curve (*com*) In OBJECT-ORIENTED drawing APPLICATIONS, a mathematically defined curve between two points (Bézier points). The curve is manipulated by dragging, from an anchored point, control handles (sometimes called ''guidepoints'') which act on the curve like magnets.

bf (*typ*) abb BOLD FACE. Instruction to printer to set COPY in bold type.

Bible paper (*pap*) A very thin paper that is also tough and opaque, used mainly in printing Bibles and prayer books.

Bibliography List of publications providing

reference material on a particular subject, usually included in the END MATTER of a book.

Bimetal plate (*pri*) LITHOGRAPHIC plate used in long runs; the printing area is of copper while the non-printing sections are of aluminum or steel.

Binary code (*com*) The code by which sets of data are represented by BINARY DIGITS.

Binary digit (BIT) (*com*) 1 or 0, the only figures used in BINARY SYSTEM.

Binary system (*com*) Numbering system using only two digits, 0 and 1 (binary = of, or involving, pairs), rather than the decimal system of 0-9 or hexadecimal system (16). It is a particularly useful system for computers since the values of 0 and 1 can be represented variously by the presence or absence of electrical current, positive or negative voltage, a large or small mark, or a black or white dot on a MONITOR.

Binder's board (*pap*) Heavy paperboard covered with cloth, used in binding HARDCOVER BOOKS.

Binder's die (*fin*) see BRASS.

Binding edge (*fin*) see SPINE.

Binding methods (*fin*) Methods of securing the leaves of a book, MANUSCRIPT, or brochure. Mechanical binding methods include PLASTIC COMB BINDING, ring binding, and metal clasp attachments. Bookbinding methods include smyth-sewn, side-sewn, SECTION-SEWN, and PERFECT BINDING.

Bit (*com*) abb BINARY DIGIT. The smallest unit of information your computer uses. It is expressed as 1 or 0, meaning on or off, yes or no, positive or negative, something or nothing. Eight bits are required to store one alphabet character.

Bit density (*com*) The number of BITS in a given area or length of magnetic tape.

Bit-depth (*com*) The number of BITS used to define a DEVICE's capability to reproduce grays or colors – the greater the bit-depth (say, 32-bit), the more colors you will have available.

Bit map (*com*) At its simplest, a text CHARACTER or graphic image made up of dots. In fact, a bit map is the set of BITS that represents the position and BINARY state (on or off) of a

corresponding set of items to form a bit image such as on a MONITOR.

Bitmapped font (*com*) A font made up of bitmapped letters, characterized by their jagged edges, as distinct from the smooth edges of an OUTLINE FONT used by printers.

Bitmapped graphic (*com*) An image made up of DOTS, or PIXELS, as distinct from an OBJECT-ORIENTED graphic.

Bit rate (*com*) The number of BITS per second (DATA and non-data) carried by a communications channel. Sometimes, inaccurately, referred to as BAUD rate.

Black art see BASE ARTWORK.

Black letter (*typ*) Old style of typeface based on broad-nib script, also called Gothic (UK) and Old English (US).

Black out see BLACK PATCH.

Black patch (*rep*) A piece of black (or red) material used to mask the image area on reproduction line copy, leaving a WINDOW in the NEGATIVE (1) for STRIPPING (1) in a HALFTONE.

Black printer (*pri*) Term for the film printing black in the COLOR SEPARATION process.

Blad Sample pages of a book produced in booklet form for promotional purposes.

Blanc fixe (*pap*) Barium sulfate, a white filler used with china clay for coating paper.

Blank (*pap*) Thick paper used for posters and advertising display.

Blanket (*pri*) A sheet made of rexine or rubber that covers the impression cylinder of a printing machine. Also, a similar sheet used to cover the FLONG when casting a STEREOTYPE PLATE (1).

Blanket cylinder (*pri*) The cylinder of an OFFSET press that transfers the ink image to the paper.

Blanket to blanket press (*pri*) An OFFSET printing press in which paper is fed between two blanket cylinders to print both sides at once.

Bleed (*pri*) That part of an image that extends beyond the TRIM MARKS on a page. Illustrations that spread to the edge of the paper allowing no MARGINS are described as bled off.

Blind emboss (*fin*) To make an impression without foil or ink, such as on the CASE (1) of a book.

Blind folio (*pri*) Page number counted for

reference or identification but not printed on the page itself.

Blind P The CHARACTER ¶, used to indicate new paragraphs. Also called a "paragraph mark" or "reverse P."

Blind stamping see BLIND EMBOSS.

Blinding (pri) Poor surface condition on an apparently sound printing plate that causes a substandard image.

Blister card (fin) Form of display packaging in which goods are mounted on card and protected by a transparent plastic bubble.

Block (**1** pri) HALFTONE or line illustration engraved or etched on a zinc or copper plate, for use in LETTERPRESS printing. (**2** fin) A metal stamp used to impress a design on a book COVER. The verb to block means to emboss a book cover. (**3** typ) A group regarded as a unit, usually referring to DATA or MEMORY in which data is stored.

Block book (fin) A book made by RELIEF PRINTING from page-sized wood blocks, before the advent of movable type.

Block letter (typ) A SANS-SERIF CHARACTER (1) traditionally cut in a wooden block, that can be used for embossing or printing.

Block printing see RELIEF PRINTING.

Blues, blueprints (pri) Low-quality PROOFS for initial checking, printed as white lines on a blue ground. See also OZALID.

Blurb The description of a book or author printed on the jacket or on promotional material.

Board, circuit board (com) The name given to the support upon which CHIPS and other components are mounted. A printed circuit board (PC board) is one that has been stamped with metallic ink to connect the components. A motherboard, or logic board, the main board in a computer, bears the CPU, ROM, RAM, and expansion slots. A board that plugs into an expansion slot is often called a card.

Body (**1** typ) The shank of a piece of type. (**2**) The main portion of a book, excluding PRELIMS or appendices.

Body copy/matter/type (**1**) Printed MATTER forming the main part of a work, but not including HEADINGS, etc. (**2** typ) Body type refers to

the actual type used in setting a text.

Body size (typ) POINT measurement of a body of type.

Bold, bold face (typ) Type with a conspicuously heavy, black appearance. It is based on the same design as medium weight type in the same FONT.

Bolts (fin) The folded edges of a SHEET or SECTION (1) that will be trimmed off.

Bond paper (pap) Standard grade of evenly finished paper used for writing and typing. It can also be printed upon.

Book block (fin) A book that has been FOLDED AND GATHERED and stitched, but not CASED IN.

Book face (typ) Old term for a particular TYPEFACE, but now used to mean any type suitable for the text of a book.

Book jacket The printed paper COVER folded around the CASE in which a book is sold.

Book paper (pap) A general classification of papers suitable for book printing.

Book proof (pri) IMPOSED PROOFS or PAGE PROOFS put together in book form.

Bookbinding (fin) see PERFECT BINDING, smyth-sewn, side-sewn, SECTION-SEWN.

Booklet A publication larger than a PAMPHLET, but of not more than 24 pages.

Boot(**ing**) (**up**) (com) The process of starting up a computer.

Border A continuous decorative design or RULE arranged around MATTER on a page.

Bottom out To arrange text so there are no unsuitable breaks at the bottom of a page, or so that the page does not end with a WIDOW.

Bounce lighting (pho) A method of lighting a subject in studio photography by reflecting light from the walls, ceiling, or a suitable reflector.

Bowl (typ) The curved part of a type CHARACTER (1) that encloses the COUNTER.

Box, box rule (typ) An item of type or other graphic MATTER ruled off on all four sides with a heavy RULE or BORDER.

Box feature/story Information in a book presented separately from the running text and illustrations and marked off with a BOX RULE.

Boxhead In a table arranged in COLUMNS (2), the HEADING to each column appearing under the main

heading.

bpi (com) abb BITS per inch. See BIT DENSITY.

Brace (typ) A sign used to group lines or phrases, appearing as }.

Bracketed type (typ) Type in which the SERIF is joined to the main stem in an unbroken curve.

Brackets see PARENTHESES.

Brass (fin) A bookbinder's engraved plate used to block a book COVER.

Breve A mark indicating pronunciation of a short vowel (˘).

Bristol board (pap) Fine board made in various thicknesses and qualities, usually with a smooth finish and used for drawing and printing.

Broad fold (fin) Method of paper folding in which the GRAIN (1) runs along the shorter dimension after folding.

Broadside/broadsheet (pri) Old term for a sheet of paper printed on one side only.

Brochure A PAMPHLET or other unbound, short publication with stitched pages.

Broken images (pri) Prints produced when a PHOTOMECHANICAL (1) plate is damaged or worn.

Bromide (**1** pho) A photographic print on paper coated with light-sensitive silver bromide emulsion. (**2** typ) General term for high-quality output from an imagesetter, made on photographic paper rather than film.

Bronzing (fin) Producing a gold or metallic effect by applying powder to a SHEET treated with special printing ink.

Brownprint see VANDYKE PRINT.

Buckram (fin) A sized, coarse cloth used in BOOKBINDING.

Buffing (pri) The final polishing of a reproduction plate before ETCHING.

Bulk (**1**) The thickness of the assembled pages of a book, excluding the COVERS. (**2** pap) The thickness of a SHEET of paper related to its weight.

Bulldog Printer's term for the first daily edition of a newspaper.

Bullet (typ) A large dot used to precede listed items or to add emphasis to particular parts of a text.

Bundle (pap) Two REAMS of paper (1,000 SHEETS).

Bundling (pri) In BOOKBINDING, the tying together of SIGNATURES (2).

Burn through (rep) Exposure of film caused by light penetrating a MASKING

(1) material.

Burnout (*rep*) The MASKING (1) of COPY being exposed in a reproduction process, to make space for new insertions.

Bus (*com*) A series of wires or paths along which information is shared within a computer or between one DEVICE and another.

By-line The name of the author that appears above an article.

Byte (*com*) A unit of information made up of eight BITS (0s and 1s), which can represent any value between 0 and 255 (256 is the total number of possible configurations of eight 0s and 1s). One byte is required to make up a single text CHARACTER.

C

© The mark agreed by the Universal Copyright Convention (UCC) to signify, when accompanied by the date of publication and COPYRIGHT owner's name, that an item is protected by international copyright laws.

C-type (*pho*) A term for a photographic color print produced directly from a NEGATIVE. It refers to a method of processing developed by Kodak.

CAD (*com*) *abb* Computer aided design. A term describing any design that is carried out with the aid of a computer. However, the term is more usually applied to design in technical and architectural contexts, particularly where the three-dimensional capabilities of specific CAD applications are utilized, enabling the user to develop complex structures.

Calender (*pap*) A column of metal rollers at the dry end of a papermaking machine through which the paper passes under pressure. This action closes the pores and smoothes the surface.

Caliper (**1** *pap*) A measurement of thickness in paper or board expressed as thousandths of an inch (mils) or millionths of a meter (microns) (**2** *pap*) The instrument that can measure such a thickness.

Calligraphy The art of fine writing, the term deriving from the Greek words meaning "beautiful handwriting."

Cameo (**1** *typ*) A term for TYPEFACES in which the CHARACTERS are reversed to show white on a dark ground. (**2** *pap*) A brand of dull, coated paper suitable for the printing of HALFTONES or ENGRAVINGS.

Camera ready A term applied to ARTWORK, COPY, or PASTE-UP that is ready for reproduction.

Camera shake (*pho*) Movement at the point of exposure in use of a hand-held camera that may cause distortion or lack of focus in the image.

Cancel (*pri*) To cut out and replace a wrongly printed LEAF (2) or leaves.

Cancelled numeral (*typ*) A figure crossed through with a diagonal stroke used in mathematics.

Cap line (*typ*) An imaginary horizontal line running across the tops of CAPITALS.

Capital, cap (*typ*) The term for UPPER-CASE letters, deriving from the style of inscription at the head, or capital, of a Roman column.

Caps and smalls (*typ*) Type consisting of CAPITALS for initials and SMALL CAPS in place of LOWER-CASE letters.

Caption Strictly speaking, the descriptive MATTER printed as a HEADLINE above an illustration, but also generally used to refer to information printed underneath or beside a picture.

Carbon arc lamp (*rep*) A strong light source used in some forms of PHOTOMECHANICAL platemaking.

Cardboard (*pap*) As distinct from the common type of paperboard, a thick paper made in various colors for display graphics.

Cardinal numbers Numbers as in sequential counting, 1 2 3, etc, as opposed to ordinal numbers which indicate placement, first, second, etc.

Caret, caret mark (*typ*) Symbol (∧) used in preparing COPY and PROOF correcting to indicate an insertion.

Caricature A drawing of a person or thing showing deliberate distortion with comic or satirical intent.

Carry forward/over (*typ*) see TAKE OVER.

Carton (*fin*) A box container designed to be flattened out when not in use.

Cartouche A decorative device used to enclose a title or name.

Cartridge paper (*pap*) A general purpose, rough surfaced paper used for drawing, wrapping, OFFSET printing, etc.

Case (**1** *fin*) The stiff COVER of a book, consisting of two boards, a HOLLOW, and a binding material. (**2** *typ*) A box with separate compartments in which pieces of type are kept. This is the origin of the terms LOWER and UPPER CASE.

Cased/case bound (*fin*) A HARDCOVER BOOK, that is, one with stiff outer COVERS.

Casein (*pap*) A substance obtained from curdled milk, used as an adhesive in the manufacture of COATED PAPER and sometimes as a binder for paint.

Casing in (*fin*) To insert a book into its CASE (1) and paste it down.

Cast coated paper (*pap*) Art paper with an exceptionally glossy, enamel finish.

Casting-off (*typ*) Making a calculation as to how much space MANUSCRIPT COPY will take up when printed in a given TYPEFACE.

Catchline (*typ*) The temporary HEADING for identification at the top of a GALLEY PROOF.

Cathode ray tube (CRT) (*com*) The standard video display device consisting of a vacuum tube producing information display electrostatically, as in televisions and computer MONITORS.

CCD (*com*) *abb* Charge-couple device. A means of translating light into data in a scanner or non-tube video system.

CD (*com*) see OPTICAL DISC.

CD-I (*com*) *abb* Compact disc interactive. A MULTIMEDIA standard allowing sound and video to be stored on the same CD, which can then be played back in a special CD player that uses an ordinary television set as a MONITOR.

CD-ROM (*com*) *abb* Compact disc read only memory. Non-erasable storage systems of huge capacity – around 650Mb, which is enough space for a type foundry's entire font library.

CD-ROM-XA (Extended architecture) (*com*) A CD-ROM which runs the CD at high speed, thus enabling the use of REAL-TIME video sequences. A CD-ROM-XA drive will read CD-ROM, CD-I, and Kodak's Photo-CD discs.

Cel (**1**) *abb* CELLULOSE ACETATE. (**2**) In ANIMATION, a transparent SHEET the proportion of the film frame on which one stage of the sequence is drawn.

Cell (**1** *pri*) A recessed

DOT in a PHOTOGRAVURE plate forming part of the image for inking. (**2**) see CEL. (**3** *rep*) A MASK (1) used in photographic methods of reproduction.

Cellophane Transparent CELLULOSE ACETATE film that is thin and very flexible.

Cellulose acetate Plastic sheet material, usually transparent or translucent, available clear or colored and with a shiny or matt finish. It is used as the basis of ARTWORK and overlays, and is the base material of some photographic films.

Center fold/spread The center opening of a SECTION (two pages) where one plate may be used to print facing pages with following page numbers. Center spreads are also called "naturals."

Centered (*typ*) TYPE which is placed in the center of a sheet or type measure.

Centered dot (*typ*) A raised dot used as a decimal point between figures.

Central processing unit (CPU) (*com*) Generally used to mean the central computer, built around a CPU CHIP (itself often referred to, probably more correctly, as the CPU), that performs the computer's calculating functions and to which other DEVICES are connected.

cf (*abb*) Confer, a Latin word meaning compare. cf is used to refer to a FOOTNOTE in text.

Chain lines/marks (*pap*) Lines running through LAID PAPER, caused by the wires of the papermaking machine.

Chalking (*pri*) A printing fault caused by ink soaking into the paper and leaving pigment deposited on the surface.

Change bar A vertical rule in the MARGIN of a revised technical publication indicating a part that varies from the original text.

Chapter drop The level at which text begins underneath a chapter heading.

Character (**1** *typ*) An individual item cast in type, such as a letter, figure, punctuation mark, sign, or space. (**2** *com*) A set of BITS in data processing which represents a figure, letter, etc.

Character assembly (*typ*) An alternative term for TYPESETTING, especially in reproduction methods not using metal type.

Character count (*typ*) The number of CHARACTERS (1) in a piece of COPY, or in a line or paragraph.

Character generator (*com/typ*) A system of HARDWARE or SOFTWARE that provides a FONT for computer composition.

Chart A graphic demonstration or display of information on values and qualities.

Chemical pulp (*pap*) Processed wood PULP used in high-quality printing papers.

Chip, microchip (*com*) A small piece of silicon impregnated with miniaturized computer circuits. Chips comprise the basis of computer functions in the form of CPUs or MEMORY chips.

Choke (*rep*) A method of altering the thickness of a letter or solid shape by overexposure in processing or by means of a built-in option in some computer applications.

Chroma The intensity or purity of a color.

Chromo (*pap*) A printing paper heavily coated on one side.

Chromolin (*rep*) A fast proofing system in which powder is used instead of ink.

Chromolithography (*pri*) Lithographic printing in several colors by traditional techniques.

Chuck (*pri*) The core supporting a paper roll in a WEB-FED printing press.

Chute delivery (*pri*) A particular method of delivering printed material from a press.

Cibachrome (*pho*) Agfa process, a direct method of obtaining photographic color prints.

Cicero (*typ*) A European unit for measuring the width, or MEASURE of a line of type and the depth of the page. One Cicero = 4.511mm or 12 DIDOT POINTS. See also PICA.

c.i.f. (*abb*) Cost, insurance, freight. A commercial term denoting that a price quote includes delivery.

Circular Advertising MATTER in the form of a single LEAF or folded SHEET.

Circular screen (*rep*) A photographic screen that can be adjusted to prevent MOIRÉ patterns in color reproduction.

Circumflex see ACCENT.

Classified ad Newspaper or magazine advertisement without illustration, sold by the line.

Clean proof (*pri*) A PROOF which is free from errors.

Cliché (*pri*) The French term, also used elsewhere in Europe, for a block, stereotype, or ELECTROTYPE.

Clock speed/rate (*com*) The number of instructions per second, regulated by the pulses of a quartz crystal, that can be processed by a computer's central processing unit. The pulse frequency is measured in MEGAHERTZ (millions of cycles per second) – the more megahertz, the faster the clock speed. Clock speed determines such things as the speed of screen redraw and RAM or disk access.

Close up (*typ*) An instruction to delete a space, i.e., bring CHARACTERS (1) together.

Closed h (*typ*) An ITALIC "h" in which the shorter stroke curves inward, as in *b*.

Closed section/signature (*fin*) In either case, one where BOLTS are uncut.

Club line A short line ending a paragraph, which should not appear at the top of a page in a book.

CMY *abb* Cyan, magenta, and yellow. Color model based on the subtractive color theory that is used, in some computer applications, to produce spot colors which have been mixed from these colors.

CMYK (*rep*) Abbreviation for the process colors of CYAN (C), MAGENTA (M), yellow (Y), and black, or "KEY" (K) inks used in FOUR-COLOR printing.

Coated paper (*pap*) A general term for ART, CHROMO, and enamel papers or similar groups in which the surface has a mineral coating applied after the body paper is made. It is also known as surface paper.

Cock-up figure/letter (*typ*) see SUPERIOR FIGURE/LETTER.

Cocked-up initial (*typ*) A BOLD-FACE CAPITAL that projects above the line of type.

Code (*com*) The instructions in a PROGRAM, written by a programmer, that make the program work. The efficacy of a program depends upon how well its code is written.

Codet (*rep*) see COLOR BAR.

Cold pressed (*pap*) A categorization of a type of paper surface. See NOT.

Collate (*fin*) To put the SECTIONS (1) or pages of a book in correct order.

Collotype (pri) A PHOTOMECHANICAL printing process suitable for fine detail reproductions. Printing is done from a raised gelatin film on a glass support and gives CONTINUOUS TONE.

Colophon (**1** pri) An emblem identifying a printer or PUBLISHER, appearing usually on the SPINE and TITLE PAGE of a book. (**2** pri) An inscription placed at the end of a book giving the title, printer's name and location, and date of printing.

Color (typ) The light or heavy appearance of a particular TYPEFACE.

Color bar/codet (rep) A standard set of bars on PROOFS in FOUR-COLOR PROCESSING showing the strength and evenness of ink, and the registration of colors.

Color blind emulsion (rep) Photographic EMULSION sensitized to blue violet or ultraviolet light only.

Color break (rep) The edge between two areas of color in an image.

Color burnout (pri) A deterioration in the color of printing ink caused by chemical reactions in mixing or drying.

Color chart (pri) Chart used in color printing to standardize and select or match colored inks or tints used.

Color coder (pri) An instrument capable of comparing the intensity of printed colors, guaranteeing correct reproduction.

Color correction (rep) The adjustment of color values in reproduction to obtain a correct image.

Color filters (pho/rep) Thin SHEETS of colored glass, plastic, or gelatin placed over a camera lens to absorb or allow through particular colors in the light entering the camera.

Color model (com) In graphics APPLICATIONS, the manner in which colors can be defined or modified. The most common color models are RGB (red, green, and blue); HSB (hue, saturation, and brightness); or HLS (hue, lightness, and saturation); CMY; CMYK (process colors); and PANTONE® (spot colors).

Color negative film (pho) Film which provides a color image in NEGATIVE form after processing.

Color positives (rep) A set of screened positive COLOR SEPARATIONS.

Color reversal film (pho) A film which provides color images in positive form after processing.

Color separation (rep) Division of colors of a CONTINUOUS TONE multicolored ORIGINAL or LINE ORIGINAL into basic portions by a process of photographic filtration. The portions are reproduced by a separate printing plate carrying a color.

Color separations (rep) The images or pieces (SUBJECTS) to be separated in the COLOR SEPARATION process.

Color sequence (pri) The accepted order of printing the four process colors.

Color temperature A term describing the color composition of a light source. In photography measured in "degrees Kelvin," a system based on a supposed absolute darkness rising to incandescence.

Color transparency (pho) A positive photographic image produced in color on transparent film.

Color value The tonal value of a color as compared to a light-to-dark scale of pure grays.

Colored edges (fin) The edges or top of a book which have been colored with a brush-on fluid.

Column (**1**) A section of a page divided vertically containing text or other MATTER. It is measured by the horizontal width. (**2**) A vertical section in tabulated work.

Column inch/centimeter A measure of space used to calculate the cost of display advertising in a newspaper or periodical. The measure is one COLUMN width by one inch (or one centimeter) depth.

Column rule The light-faced RULE used to separate COLUMNS in newspapers.

Combination line and halftone (rep) A combined block or plate used to reproduce photographs with superimposed figures, letters, diagrams, etc.

Command (com) An instruction given to a computer by its operator.

Command line interface (com) A USER INTERFACE in which instructions are given by means of a line of (usually) keyboard COMMANDS. The opposite of GUI.

Commercial a (typ) The type symbol (@) used to mean "at."

Commercial art A term used to describe ARTWORK intended for use in advertising or promotion, as distinct from fine art.

Commercial color (com) The term describing color separations produced by DESKTOP scanners as distinct from high-resolution repro scanners.

Comp (**1**) abb COMPREHENSIVE. (**2** typ) abb COMPOSITOR.

Compose (typ) To set COPY in type.

Composing room (typ) The area of a printing works specifically designated for TYPESETTING and MAKE UP (2).

Composite artwork ARTWORK combining a number of different elements.

Composition (typ) Type which has been set in a form ready for reproduction by printing.

Composition size (typ) A description of any type up to a size of 14 points, used mainly in setting text.

Compositor (typ) The person responsible for setting type, whether by hand or machine process.

Comprehensive A LAYOUT of type and illustrative material produced to a good, but not finished standard. See PRESENTATION VISUAL.

Computer (com) A device or machine capable of processing information, expressed in logical terms, according to a predetermined set of instructions.

Computer graphics (com) The use of computers to generate an OUTPUT of information in graphic form, such as a picture, diagram, or printed CHARACTERS (1).

Computer input devices (com) Methods of transmitting COMMANDS to a computer in a prescribed form, i.e., keyboard, mouse, etc.

Computer languages (com) Coding systems developed to deal with specific types of communication with computers.

Computer output device (com) see OUTPUT DEVICE.

Computer terminal (com) The part of a computer system that provides communication by its operator – i.e., a keyboard for INPUT and a device for information display.

Concertina fold (fin) see ACCORDION FOLD.

Condensed (typ) A TYPEFACE with an elongated, narrow appearance.

Contact print, contacts (*pho*) Photographic print or prints made by direct contact with an original POSITIVE (1) or NEGATIVE at same size.

Contact printing frame (*rep*) see VACUUM FRAME.

Contact screen (*rep*) A conventional HALFTONE SCREEN made on a film base which has a graded DOT pattern. It is used in direct contact with a film or plate to obtain a halftone NEGATIVE from a CONTINUOUS TONE ORIGINAL. It provides better definition than the conventional glass screen.

Continuous fold (*fin*) A paper folding system to convert rolls of paper into ACCORDION FOLDS.

Continuous tone/ contone (*rep*) Photographs or colored ORIGINALS in which the subject contains continuous shades between the lightest and the darkest tones, without being broken up by dots.

Contrast (*pho*) The degree of separation of tones in a photograph in the range from black to white.

Contre jour (*pho*) A photographic term meaning to take a picture with the camera lens facing toward the light source.

Controlling dimension (*rep*) The width or height of an image taken as the basis for enlargement or reduction.

Converting (*pri*) To produce articles of stationery or packaging that require minimal printing.

Cool colors A relative term often used to describe blue, green, and other colors with a blue or green cast.

Copperplate printing (*pri*) An INTAGLIO process used in short-run printing, producing a sharp, but very black image.

Coprocessor (*com*) A microprocessor CHIP that assists the CENTRAL PROCESSING UNIT with data-intensive or specific activities, such as large databases or graphics tasks. Also called a floating-point unit (FPU)

Copy Any manuscript, typescript, transparency, artwork, or computer disk from which a printed image is to be prepared.

Copyboard (*rep*) see VACUUM FRAME.

Copyfitting (*typ*) see CASTING-OFF.

Copyholder A person who reads aloud from ORIGINAL COPY while another

checks and marks the PROOF.

Copyright The right of the creator of an original work to control the use of that work. While broadly controlled by international agreement (UNIVERSAL COPYRIGHT CONVENTION – UCC), there are substantial differences between countries, particularly regarding the period for which a work is protected by copyright. In the U.S. copyright of an intellectual property is generally established by registration; in the U.K. it exists automatically by virtue of the creation of an original work. Ownership of copyright does not necessarily mean ownership of the actual work (or *vice versa*), nor does it necessarily cover rights to that work throughout the world (the rights to a work can be held territory by territory).

Copywriting A term applied to writing of COPY specifically for use in advertising.

Corner marks (*rep*) The marks on a printed SHEET acting as TRIM, or CROP, MARKS, and also sometimes as REGISTER MARKS.

Corporate identity/ housestyle The elements of design by which a company or other institution establishes a consistent and recognizable identity through communication, promotion, and distribution material. See also LETTERHEAD, LOGOTYPE.

Corrigendum, corrigenda A note inserted in a publication after printing to correct an item or items in the text.

Cosmetics (*com*) A term occasionally used to describe the general appearance of a computer-generated image, such as sharpness, tonal contrast, etc.

Counter (*typ*) The inside area of the TYPEFACE i.e., the center of an "o" or space between the "vertical strokes of an "n."

Counter-mark (*pap*) A WATERMARK of the papermaker's initials placed opposite the normal watermark

Cover (*fin*) The paper, board, cloth, or leather to which the BODY (2) of a book is secured by glue and thread.

Cover papers (*pap*) Papers for the COVERS of books, pamphlets, etc.

cpi (*typ*) *abb* CHARACTERS (1) per inch. In copyfitting,

the number of type characters per inch.

cpl (*typ*) *abb* CHARACTERS (1) per line. In copyfitting, the number of type characters per line.

CPU (*com*) *abb* CENTRAL PROCESSING UNIT.

Crash (**1** *com*) A more-or-less serious breakdown of an electronic system caused by the failure of a component or by a reading head damaging the surface of a DISK. (**2** *pri*) To number a multi-part set of forms on carbonless paper by letterpress-printing the top sheet of a made-up set so that the number appears on the other sheets of the set. (**3** *fin*) Muslin cloth used for lining the spine of a book during binding.

Crash finish (*pap*) Paper which has a coarse linen-like finish.

Crease (*fin*) see SCORE.

Creasing (**1** *fin*) A linear indentation made by machine in thick paper providing a hinge. (**2** *pri*) A printing fault producing deep creases.

Credit/courtesy line A line of text accompanying an illustration giving the name of an organization or individual supplying the picture or ARTWORK.

Crimping (*fin*) see CREASING (1).

Crop The part of a photograph or illustration that is discarded after it has been trimmed.

Cropped (*fin*) A term applied to a book with overtrimmed MARGINS.

Cross front (*pho*) The description of a camera in which the lens can be moved laterally in relation to the film.

Cross-head Subsection, paragraph HEADING, or numeral printed in the BODY (2) of text, usually marking the first subdivision of a chapter.

Cross line screen (*rep*) see HALFTONE SCREEN.

Cross section Illustrator's view of an object showing it as if cut through to expose the internal workings or characteristics.

Cross-stemmed W (*typ*) One in which the central strokes cross rather than meet.

Crow quill A term referring to a very fine pen, derived from the original use of a cut crow's quill.

CRT (*com*) *abb* CATHODE RAY TUBE.

C/T (*pho*) *abb* COLOR TRANSPARENCY.

Curl (*pri*) Measurement of

the height to which the edges of the paper will curl, especially applied to those that must be used in wet or damp processes.

Cursive (*typ*) A running script where the letters are formed without raising the pen.

Cursor (*com*) see POINTER.

Curved plate (*pri*) A plate used in a ROTARY PRESS that curves around the PLATE CYLINDER.

Cut (**1** *pri*) A shortened version of woodcut, used to describe a relief or block print. (**2** *pri*) A metal relief plate from which an image is printed. (**3**) An instruction to an editor meaning "cut text to fit."

Cut and paste (*com*) The action of removing an item from a DOCUMENT and then pasting it elsewhere in the same, or another, document.

Cut dummy (*rep*) Cut PROOFS of illustrations used in sequence as a guide to MAKE-UP (2) of pages.

Cut edge (*fin*) The three edges of a book which are cut with a GUILLOTINE.

Cut flush (*fin*) A term describing a book with even COVER and pages, as the cutting is done after the cover has been attached.

Cutline (**1**) A CAPTION to an illustration. (**2** *rep*) An instruction to the printer to insert an illustration during MAKE-UP (2).

Cutout (**1** *rep*) An illustration from which the background has been removed to provide a silhouetted image. (**2** *fin*) A display card or book COVER from which a pattern has been cut by means of a steel DIE.

Cyan (C) (*rep/pri*) One of the four process colors used in four-color printing. This special shade of blue is sometimes called process blue.

Cylinder press (*pri*) A printing press in which the FORME is carried on a FLAT BED under a paper-bearing cylinder for an impression to be made at the point of contact.

Cyrillic alphabet CHARACTERS (1) used in writing or printing Russian.

D

Dagger (*typ*) A type CHARACTER (†) used to refer to FOOTNOTES in a text.

Daisy-chain (**network**) (*com*) The linking, in sequence, of several PERIPHERAL DEVICES to a computer.

Dampening (*pri*) Necessary process in LITHOGRAPHY of dampening

the printing plate to prevent ink from spreading.

Dandy roll (*pap*) A cylinder of wire gauze on a paper-making machine that comes into contact with the paper while it is still wet. The dandy impresses the WATERMARK and laid lines when required.

Dark field illumination (*rep*) A method of checking the quality of HALFTONE DOTS on film by viewing them in angled light against a dark background.

Dash (*typ*) A punctuation mark usually known as an EM DASH/RULE (—) or en dash/rule (–), as distinct from a hyphen (-).

Data (*com*) Any information, but in computing usually used to mean information processed by a program.

Data bank (*com*) Any place or computer where large amounts of data are stored for ready access.

Data bits (*com*) Communications bits that contain DATA, as distinct from the bits that contain instructions. Sometimes called character width.

Data bus (*com*) The path along which DATA is transmitted. The wider the bus, measured in BITS, the more data that can be transmitted simultaneously.

Data processing (*com*) The processing of information via a computer or other mechanical or electronic device.

Database (*com*) Virtually any information stored on a computer in a systematic fashion and thus retrievable. Generally used to mean programs where you can store large amounts of data (names, addresses, and telephone numbers), but retrieve small parts of it very quickly.

Dateline Type placed above a newspaper item giving date and place of its origin.

Datum (*com*) The singular of DATA, though data is now commonly accepted as a singular noun in computer usage.

Daughter board (*com*) Sometimes used to describe a circuit board that connects to a motherboard.

Dead matter (*typ/rep/pri*) Leftover MATTER that is not used.

Deadline The final date set for completion of a particular job.

Decal (*pri*) A printed

transfer image.

Deckle edge (*pap*) The rough uneven edge of handmade paper.

Dedicated (*com*) A system or equipment with a unique function that can be used only for that purpose and is not otherwise adaptable, such as a dedicated word processing computer.

Deep-etch halftone (*rep*) A HALFTONE image from which unwanted screen DOTS have been removed, so that areas of plain paper will be left on the printed SHEET.

Deep-etching (*pri*) The ETCHING of long-run LITHOGRAPHIC printing plates to reduce the printing areas of the plate to slightly below the surface.

Default (*com*) The settings of a PROGRAM in the absence of user-specified settings; in other words, the settings it came with until you change them.

Delineate To accentuate outlines in line ARTWORK by making them heavier.

Dentsitometer (*rep*) An electronic precision instrument used to measure the quantitive colors or density in a color TRANSPARENCY.

Density (**1** *typ*) Of type, the amount and compactness of type set within a given area or page. (**2** *pho/rep/pri*) Of a TRANSPARENCY or printed image, the measure of tonal values.

Depth of field (*pho*) The area in front of or behind the point of focus in a photographic image at which other details remain in acceptable focus.

Descender (*typ*) The part of a LOWER-CASE letter that falls below the x-HEIGHT as in g, q, and p.

Desktop (*com*) The name given to the environment in which you work on a computer screen.

Desktop publishing (DTP) (*com*) A term coined at the advent of the Apple Macintosh computer, before the potential of the machine in the professional design and reproduction industries was fully realized. Used to describe the activity of generating text, page layout, and graphics on a computer and then printing, the result.

Detail paper/layout paper (*pap*) A thin translucent paper with a hard surface used for LAYOUTS and sketches.

Developer (*pho/rep/pri*) The chemical used to

bring up an image on photographic film, paper, or plate.

Device (com) Short form referring to any PERIPHERAL DEVICE.

Diacritical mark (typ) A mark indicating the particular value or pronunciation of a CHARACTER (1). See ACCENT.

Diaphragm (pho) A sectioned adjustable disc behind a camera lens that can be opened or closed to fix the APERTURE.

Dialog box (com) A box that appears on a computer screen, usually in response to a command from the user, requesting information or approval in order to execute an action.

Diapositive (pho) A photographic TRANSPARENCY in which the image is positive.

Diazo(type) (rep) abb Diazonium. A method of printing from a transparent or translucent original onto paper, cloth, or film. The image is exposed onto a light-sensitive coating of diazo salts and dyestuff, and the print may be blue (called blues/blueprints), brown (browns/ Vandykes), or black. Also known as OZALIDS and dyelines, diazos are widely used in preprint stages for checking imposed film as well as by architectural and engineering draftsmen.

Didot point (typ) The European unit for type. It measures an 0.0148in. whereas an English point is 0.013837in.

Die (pri) An INTAGLIO engraved stamp used for impressing a design.

Die cutting (fin) To cut paper, card or board to a particular design with a metal DIE for packaging and display work.

Die stamping (pri) A form of printing where all the CHARACTERS (1) are in relief.

Differential spacing (typ) The spacing of each CHARACTER (1) of type according to its individual width.

Digitize (com) To convert anything, such as an image or a sound, into a form that can be electronically processed, stored, and reconstructed.

Digitizer (com) An INPUT device such as a tablet or camera that digitizes signals so that a computer can understand them.

Dimensions In describing representations of three-dimensional objects, the dimensions

used are length, width, and height.

DIN abb Deutsche Industrie-Norm. The code of standards established in Germany and widely used throughout the world to standardize such things as the size, weight, or speed-rating of certain materials and manufactured items that depend on universal compatibility.

Dingbat (typ) A decorative font, the modern form of decorations traditionally called printer's flowers, ornaments, and arabesques, that were added to pages by hand in hot-metal typesetting.

Dinky (pap/pri) A term referring to a half roll (WEB) of paper, halved by width not diameter.

Dinky dash (typ) see JIM-DASH.

Diphthong (typ) A term meaning two vowels pronounced as one syllable, also commonly applied to two vowels printed as a LIGATURE.

Diploma paper (pap) A fine paper made specially for printing of certificates, official documents, etc.

Direct color separation (rep) COLOR SEPARATION in which a HALFTONE SCREEN is used in the original separation to produce screened NEGATIVES directly.

Direct cost The costs of a project incurred directly from the job in hand, not including the normal overhead costs of a business.

Directional Term such as "left," "above," "top," appearing in a CAPTION to direct the reader to the relevant picture.

Directory (com) An invisible catalog of information about all the FILES on a DISK. The "volume directory" contains general information, whereas the "file directory" logs specific information such as where the files are stored on the disk.

Dirty proof (typ/rep/pri) A heavily corrected PROOF.

Dis, diss (typ) abb Distribute.

Disk/disc (com) A circular platter coated with a magnetic medium (unless it is an optical disc) on which computer data is stored. Disks may be rigid (hard) or flexible (floppy) and may be permanently installed in a computer, in a peripheral device, or in removable cases. Floppy disks are typically high

density (1.4MB) and are also called diskettes. The capacity of hard disks ranges from around 10MB to 2GB or more. Hard disks also come in a variety of removable cartridges with around 40-80MB capacity. For the purposes of this glossary, the spelling used is "disk" for magnetic media and "disc" for optical media, which is the spelling convention in general usage (although either spelling can be used to describe either media).

Disk drive (com) The HARDWARE that reads DATA to and from DISKS.

Disk drive head (com) see READ/WRITE HEAD.

Display advertisement Advertising MATTER designed to a size or quality to attract immediate attention.

Display board (pap) Heavy, dull finish, coated board in various colors.

Display matter/type (typ) Larger TYPEFACES designed for HEADINGS, etc., usually above 14pt in book work.

Display size (typ) The size of type used for HEADINGS, advertising MATTER, etc. It is always greater than 12 point so clearly distinguishable from BODY TYPE (2).

Distribution rollers (pri) The rollers on a printing press that control an even distribution of ink to the roller that contacts the FORME.

Dithering (com) A technique used by some INPUT and OUTPUT DEVICES to simulate grays by varying the pattern and proximity of black PIXELS to each other.

Ditto/prime marks (typ) Symbols indicating repetition of the MATTER directly above.

Doctor blade (pri) A device used in INTAGLIO printing processes to wipe excess ink from the surface of a plate. The blade is made of flexible metal.

Document (com) Any file created or modified with an application on a computer, such as a page layout or simply a letter. The document file is created on a DISK when text is entered or a line is drawn and then saved (when you save a document for the first time, a DIALOG BOX will appear, asking you to name the document and indicate where you want to put it).

Documentary A term used in movie or still photographic work to describe images that are concerned with true events.

Dodging (*pho*) A method of obtaining greater contrast when printing a photograph by the selective use of MASKING(2).

Dogleg Colloquial term for a LEADER LINE that is angled toward its point of reference.

Dot (**1** *rep*) The smallest basic element of a HALFTONE. (**2** *com*) See PIXEL.

Dot and tickle A colloquial expression for stipple technique in drawing.

Dot area (*rep*) The pattern of a HALFTONE, that is, both the DOTS and the spaces in between.

Dot etching (*rep*) The process of reducing the size of HALFTONE DOTS on negative or positive film, using chemicals, in order to modify the tonal values of a halftone image.

Dot for dot (**1** *pri*) Printing color work in perfect register. (**2** *rep*) A method of producing printing film by photographing a previously screened halftone image. Generally, on fine-screened images, a maximum limit of 10 percent enlargement or reduction is desirable.

Dot formation (*rep*) The pattern of DOTS in a HALFTONE SCREEN.

Dot gain (*rep/pri*) An aberration occurring during the reproduction chain from original to printed image, caused by the tendency of HALFTONE DOTS to grow in size. This often leads to inaccurate results, but if the dot-gain characteristics of a particular printing press are known, compensation can be made during reproduction. A dot gain scale – part of a COLOR BAR – is usually included on proofs to check this occurrence and is specified as a percentage of the size of the dot.

Dot loss (*rep/pri*) The devaluation or disappearance of a HALFTONE DOT on a printing plate, the opposite of DOT GAIN.

Dot matrix printer (*com*) A crude, but usually cheap, printer that uses a grid of pins to create characters, with hammers hitting the correct combination of pins for each letter.

Double burn/print down (*pri*) To use two or more negatives to expose an image onto a sensitized plate – often one for line

work and a second for halftones.

Double coated paper (*pap*) Paper with a heavy coating on one or both sides.

Double dagger (*typ*) A symbol (‡) used as a reference mark for FOOTNOTES to text.

Double digest fold (*pri*) One of the four basic folds forming a SHEET into a SIGNATURE in WEB OFFSET printing.

Double image (*pho/pri*) The appearance of two impressions of an image on one surface in printing or photography.

Double spread/page spread Two facing pages of a publication.

Download (*com*) To transfer DATA from a remote computer to your own. Opposite of UPLOAD.

Down stroke (*typ*) A heavy stroke in a type CHARACTER (1), originally the downward stroke of a pen in CALLIGRAPHY.

Down time (*pri*) Loss of time in a given job due to machine breakdown, etc., or when time is a chargeable factor.

Draft To compose COPY or an illustration in a basic form to be refined, or an item so prepared. A final draft is copy that is ready for typesetting or printing.

Drawdown (**1** *pri*) The evacuation of air from a VACUUM FRAME. (**2** *pri*) A smear of ink produced by a smooth blade on paper, used to check quality and tone.

Drawing application/ program (*com*) Drawing applications can be defined as those which are OBJECT-ORIENTED (they mathematically define lines and shapes), as distinct from painting applications which use BITMAPS – although some applications combine both.

Drawn on (*fin*) Describes a paper book COVER glued to the back of the book.

Driers (*pri*) Substances, usually metallic salts, that can speed up ink drying.

Drilling (*fin*) To make holes in paper or binding with a rotating DIE.

Drive (*com*) See DISK DRIVE.

Drive head (*com*) See READ/WRITE HEAD.

Driving out (*typ*) Arranging the spaces in a line of type to fill the line.

Drop (**1** *typ*) A gap, or margin, usually at the top of a page or column, before the printed image starts. (**2** *typ*) Of text, the number of lines in a column permitted by the

page grid.

Drop cap (*typ*) A large, sometimes decorative, initial at the beginning of a text or paragraph that drops into the lines of type beneath.

Drop down see CHAPTER DROP.

Drop folios (*typ*) Numbers printed at the bottom of each page, generally referred to simply as folios.

Drop letter (*typ*) see DROP CAP.

Dropout (*rep*) During reproduction, to use filters or other means to prevent an item from appearing on final NEGATIVE or POSITIVE film.

Dropout blue/color (*rep*) Pencil or other marker, used to write instructions on artwork, which makes a mark that does not reproduce.

Dropout/dropped out halftone (*rep*) Areas removed from a HALFTONE NEGATIVE, POSITIVE, or PLATE, by MASKING.

Dropped initial (*typ*) see DROP CAP.

Dropped-out type (*typ*) Type that is REVERSED OUT of its background.

Dropping-out (*com/rep*) The repro house term for the replacement of a low-resolution scan by a high-resolution scan, prior to final film output.

Drop shadow An area of tone forming a shadow behind an image or character, designed to bring the image or character forward.

Drop tone (*rep*) see LINE CONVERSION.

Drum (*rep*) An image carrier or recording device used in high-end electronic scanners.

Dry mounting The use of heat-sensitive adhesives.

Dry offset (*pri*) see LETTERSET.

Dry stripping (*rep*) STRIPPING (1) of a film after it has been processed and dried.

Dry transfer lettering (*typ*) CHARACTERS (1) transferred to the page by rubbing them off the back of a SHEET.

DTP (*com*) *abb* DESKTOP PUBLISHING.

Dual roll stand (*pri*) A stand supporting two WEBS fed simultaneously through a press to increase production.

Duck foot quotes (*typ*) see GUILLEMETS.

Duct (*pri*) The ink reservoir in a printing machine.

Ductor roller (*pri*) A roller carrying ink or water

between the FOUNTAIN roller and the DISTRIBUTION ROLLER.

Dull finish (*pap*) A matt paper finish. See also COATED PAPER.

Dull seal (*pri*) A term for paper stock which has an adhesive backing.

Dummy (**1** *pri*) The prototype of a proposed book or publication in the correct format, binding, paper, and bulk, but with blank pages. (**2**) A mock-up of a design showing the position of headings, text, captions, illustrations, and other details.

Duotone (*rep*) Strictly speaking, a monochromatic image consisting of two HALFTONES made from the same original to two different tonal ranges, so that when printed – in different shades of the same color – a greater tonal range is produced than is possible with a single color. However, the term is generally used, wrongly, to describe a DUPLEX HALFTONE.

Dupe *abb* DUPLICATE.

Duplex board/paper (*pap*) Paper or board of two layers pasted together to give a different color or surface quality on each side.

Duplex halftone (*rep*) Two HALFTONES made from the same original, but printed in two different colors. Generally called a DUOTONE, although this is technically incorrect.

Duplicate A copy of an ORIGINAL that is exact in every way and at exactly the same size.

Dust wrapper/jacket see BOOK JACKET.

Dutch paper (*pap*) Describes any DECKLE-EDGED paper produced in the Netherlands.

Dye-based ink (*pri*) Ink obtaining its color from ANILINE dye.

Dyeline (*rep*) see DIAZO.

E

E13B A type FONT of numerals and signs used in MAGNETIC INK CHARACTER recognition.

Ear The advertising space or spaces beside the front-page title-line.

Easel-binder A three-dimensional display stand with ring binding.

Edges (*fin*) The three CUT EDGES of a book.

Edition (*pri*) The whole number of copies of a work printed and published at one time, either as the first edition, or after some

change has been made (revised edition, second edition, etc.)

Edition bound (*fin*) see CASED BOOK.

e.g. *abb* Exempli gratia, a Latin term meaning "for example."

Eggshell finish (*pap*) The rough finish found on drawing paper and notepaper as a result of omitting CALENDERING.

Eight-bit (*com*) The allocation of eight BITS of MEMORY to each PIXEL, giving a screen display of 256 grays or colors (a row of eight bits can be written in 256 different combinations: 0000000, 00000001, 10000001, 00111100, etc.)

Eight sheet A poster size measuring 60 x 80in. (153 x 203cm).

Electrotype (*pri*) A duplicate printing FORME made in a galvanic bath by precipitating copper on a MATRIX.

Element (*com*) In some drawing applications, any object such as a shape, text, or image.

Elevation A drawing showing the vertical projection of an item of equipment or machinery or of an architectural structure.

Ellipse A regular oval shape corresponding to an oblique view of a circular plane.

Ellipsis (*typ*) A sequence of three dots (…) indicating that part of a phrase or sentence has been left out.

Elliptical dot screen (*rep*) A HALFTONE SCREEN with an elliptical DOT, producing more even changes in the middle tones of a halftone illustration.

Em (*typ*) Traditionally, the area (usually a square) taken up by a CAPITAL M, but giving rise to a linear measurement equal to the POINT size of the type being set, so a 6 point em is 6 points wide. A 12 point em is generally called a PICA, or pica em, and measures 4.22mm (0.166ins.) Half an em is called an EN.

Em quad (*typ*) A space in type that is the square of the type size.

Em rule/dash (*typ*) A punctuation mark usually known as an em dash/rule (—) or EN DASH/RULE (–), as distinct from a hyphen (-). An em dash is one em wide, while an en dash is half an em wide, the actual width depending on the size of type being set.

Embossing (*pri*) RELIEF PRINTING or stamping in

which DIES are used to raise letters above the surface of paper, cloth, or leather.

Emulation (*com*) The simulation of otherwise incompatible SOFTWARE or HARDWARE in order to make them compatible.

Emulsion (*pho/rep*) The light-sensitive coating of a photographic material.

Emulsion side (*pho/rep*) The matt side of photographic film which holds the EMULSION and which is placed in direct contact with the emulsion of another film or a PLATE when printing down to guarantee a sharp image. Normally, the emulsion on POSITIVE film is on the back of the film ("emulsion down"), while on NEGATIVE film, it is on the front ("emulsion up").

Emulsion speed (*pho*) see FILM SPEED.

En (*typ*) A measurement half the width of an EM, used in CASTING OFF.

En quad (*typ*) A space in type half the width of an EM QUAD.

En rule/dash (*typ*) A dash (–), half the width of an EM DASH/RULE.

Enamel paper (*pap*) see COATED PAPER.

End even (*typ*) Instruction to a typesetter to end a section of COPY with a full line.

End matter Parts of a book that follow the main BODY (1) of the text. See appendix, BIBLIOGRAPHY, GLOSSARY, INDEX.

End-of-line decisions (*com/typ*) The term used to describe a program's ability to hyphenate words and justify lines of text.

End papers (*fin*) The leaves of paper at the front and end of a book which cover the inner sides of the boards, securing the book to its CASE (1).

Engine sizing (*pap*) A method of sizing paper by the addition of emulsified resin to cleaned paper PULP.

Engraving (*pri*) The design or lettering etched on a plate or block and also the print taken from such a plate.

EO disc (*com*) *abb* Erasable optical. An optical disc that can be written to as well as read from.

EPS(F) (*com*) *abb* encapsulated PostScript (file). A standard graphics FILE FORMAT based on vectors (information giving both magnitude and direction).

Erratum An author's or printer's error discovered

after the book has been printed.

Esparto (*pap*) A long rough grass with soft fibers used for paper.

Et seq *abb* Et sequens, a Latin term meaning ''and the following.''

Etching (*pri*) A metal plate treated with acid and with certain parts protected by the application of a ground. It is also a print taken from the etched plate.

Even pages Left-hand pages, i.e., those with even numbers.

Even smalls (*typ*) SMALL CAPITALS used without a larger sized CAPITAL at the beginning of a word.

Even working (*pri*) A printed work divided into a number of SECTIONS of equal size, e.g., 16, 32, 48 pages.

Exception dictionary (*com*) A list of user-defined word breaks that are exceptions to the standard breaks contained within an application's hyphenation dictionary.

Exotic (*typ*) A traditional term for a TYPEFACE with CHARACTERS (1) of a language not based on LATIN (1) letterforms.

Expanded/extended type (*typ*) Type with a flattened rectangular appearance.

Expansion card/board (*com*) A circuit board that allows you to expand the capabilities of your computer, such as an accelerator.

Exploded view Drawing of an object showing its component parts separately, but arranged in such a way as to indicate their relationships within the object when assembled.

Export (*com*) The facility provided by some APPLICATIONS to save a FILE in an appropriate format for use by another application: a text file may be saved as an ASCII file or an illustration as an EPS file.

Exposure (*pho*) The amount of light allowed to contact a PHOTOSENSITIVE material. The exposure is the combination of length of contact and intensity of light acting upon the material.

Extract Material in a publication quoted from another published work. It is often made distinct from the main text by use of a smaller TYPEFACE or by indenting the extract.

F

F and G (*fin*) see FOLDED

AND GATHERED.

f-number/stop (*pho*) The notation for relative APERTURE, which is the ratio of the focal length to the diameter of the aperture. The numbers are marked on the device which sets the aperture size.

Face (*typ*) Traditionally, the printing surface of any type CHARACTER (1) it now means a group or FAMILY to which any particular type design belongs, as in TYPEFACE.

Facsimile see FAX.

Fadeout blue (*rep*) A light blue used in marking reproduction COPY. The blue is not registered by the camera.

Fadeback see GHOSTING (1).

Family (*typ*) The set of all the characters of a TYPEFACE design in all sizes and styles.

Fan fold (*fin*) see ACCORDION FOLD.

Fashion boards (*pap*) Simple body boards lined with good RAG PAPER on one side, and thin paper on the other to prevent warping.

Fast emulsion/film (*pho*) A PHOTOSENSITIVE material that records an image in a relatively short EXPOSURE.

Fat face (*typ*) A TYPEFACE with extreme contrast in the widths of thin and thick strokes.

Fat matter (*typ*) Term for COPY with a large proportion of spacing allowing rapid setting. Dense copy is known as lean MATTER.

Fatty (*rep/pri*) In conventional reproduction, the name given to the piece of film placed between the NEGATIVE (or POSITIVE) film and a plate in order to create TRAPS – the slight spread of two adjacent colors to achieve perfect registration.

Fax *abb* Facsimile. The electronic transmission of copy and artwork from one location to another, using telephone lines.

Feathering (*pri*) The method of biting areas of a plate using drops of acid, controlling their movement with a feather.

Featherweight paper (*pap*) A light bulky paper preferably with a high ESPARTO content made with little or no CALENDERING.

Feeder (*pap/pri*) Apparatus for feeding and positioning paper SHEETS in printing presses and paper processing machines.

Feint ruling (*pri*) Thin lines ruled on a SHEET as a writing guide.

Felt finish (*pap*) Paper finish applied in the manufacturing machine by felt that marks the paper roll.

Felt side (*pap*) The top side or printing side of paper. See also WIRE SIDE.

Felting (*pap*) The binding together of FIBERS in the wet PULP.

Ferrotype (*pho*) A photographic print made on a thin metal plate.

Fiber (*pap*) Plant matter composed of cellulose used as the basic element of paper-making material.

Field (*com*) In some APPLICATIONS (mainly DATABASES), a self-contained area into which DATA is entered and which is generally interactive with another field in the same (or another) RECORD, or the same field in another record.

File (*com*) A collection of DATA to which a name has been given and which is stored on a DISK. A file can be a DOCUMENT, a folder, an APPLICATION, or a resource.

File compression (*com*) The condensing of DATA within a FILE so that it is smaller, thus occupying less space on a DISK and being quicker to transmit over telecommunication lines.

File format (*com*) The way in which a PROGRAM saves DATA. In order to help you work on one job that requires the use of several APPLICATIONS, or to work with other people who may be using different applications to yours, file formats tend to be standardized. Typical file formats are TIFF (for BITMAPPED images), EPS (for OBJECT-ORIENTED images), and ASCII (for text).

Filler An extra figure or piece of COPY in a magazine or newspaper, put in to fill space in a page or COLUMN (1).

Fillet (*fin*) An embossed line used as a decorative device on a book COVER.

Filling in/up (*pri*) A fault in printing when ink fills spaces between HALFTONE DOTS or the COUNTERS of type to produce small areas of solid tone.

Film assembly/ stripping (*rep/pri*) The process of assembling film NEGATIVES (1) or POSITIVES (2) in correct positions for the preparation of printing PLATES.

Film negative (*pho/rep*) A photographic image on film in which the HIGHLIGHTS and SHADOWS are reversed.

Film positive (**1** *pho/rep*)

A black image on a background of clear or translucent film. (**2** rep) A POSITIVE (2) image on a film base made as a contact print from stripped NEGATIVES (1).

Film speed (pho) The rating given to photographic film so that an EXPOSURE can be calculated. The slower the speed, the finer the EMULSION, thus the better the quality of the photographic image. Film speed is indicated by an ASA or DIN number.

Filmsetting (typ) see PHOTOCOMPOSITION.

Filter (**1** com) A feature in many paint and image-editing APPLICATIONS that enables you to apply predefined (but sometimes editable) visual effects to an image.(**2** pho/rep) A tinted gelatin, glass, or CELLULOSE ACETATE sheet which may be placed in front of a camera lens to alter the color or quality of light passing through to the film.

Filter factor (pho) An increase in EXPOSURE necessary if a FILTER is used.

Final draft (typ) COPY fully prepared for TYPESETTING.

Fine rule (typ) A line of hair-line thickness.

Finial letter (typ) A CHARACTER (1) in certain TYPEFACES devised as the end letter in a word or line, not used elsewhere.

Finish (pap) The surface given to paper during manufacture.

Finished artwork see ARTWORK.

Finished rough see PRESENTATION VISUAL.

Firmware (com) A computer PROGRAM that can only be altered by replacing HARDWARE.

First generation copy A copy of a photograph or other item made directly from the original, as distinct from a copy made from another copy of the original.

Fish-eye lens (pho) A WIDE-ANGLE LENS that produces a distorted image with a pronounced apparent curve.

Fist (typ) The name given to an INDEX mark used in printing, shown as a pointing hand.

Fit (**1** typ) See letterspace/letterfit. (**2** rep/pri) The ALIGNMENT and REGISTER of individual areas of color or images within a printed page, as distinct from the register of the colors on an entire printed SHEET. Errors of fit occur in FILM STRIPPING, whereas errors of register occur in printing. Colors which do not fit are described as being "out of fit."

Fix, fixer (pho/rep) Colloquial term for a chemical used in photographic processing to make an image permanent. See HYPO.

Fixative A clear varnish solution that, sprayed over ARTWORK or a drawing, dries to a protective coating without altering surface qualities.

Fixed word spacing (typ) A standard space between characters and words, used for unjustified typesetting, as distinct from the variable spacing required for justified setting.

Flag see NAMEPLATE.

Flare (**1** pho) Non-image-forming light caused by reflection and scattering so that the quality of a photographic image is degraded. (**2** rep) Reflected light in PHOTOMECHANICAL reproduction that distorts or obscures the true image.

Flash exposure (rep) A second exposure in conventional HALFTONE processing that reinforces the DOTS in dark areas. These would otherwise run together and print solid.

Flat (**1** pri) An assembly of composite imposed film, used in preparing PLATES for printing. (**2** rep) A HALFTONE with too little contrast.

Flat bed cylinder press (pri) This press has the printing FORME on a plane surface as opposed to a curved printing surface. The forme is placed and moved to and fro under the cylinder.

Flat copy (rep) A PHOTOMECHANICAL image without a wide range of tonal values, such as a LINE ORIGINAL.

Flat plan (**1**) A diagrammatic plan of the pages of a book used to establish the distribution of color, chapter lengths, etc. Also called a flowchart. (**2**) A diagram or chart showing the sequence of events involved in a process or activity.

Flat tint halftone (rep) A HALFTONE printed over a background of flat color.

Flexography (pri) A method of printing from rubber or flexible plates.

Flimsy (pap) Semi-transparent paper used for layouts.

Flocking (pri) A decorative, slightly three-dimensional effect obtained in printing by blowing fibers over an adhesive ink base.

Flong (rep) The sheet of papier-mâché used to make a MOLD from a FORME for casting a STEREOTYPE PLATE.

Flop To reverse an image from left to right (horizontal flop) or top to bottom (vertical flop).

Floppy disk (com) see DISK.

Flowchart (**1**) A schematic diagram showing the sequence of a process or related series of events. (**2**) See FLAT PLAN.

Flowers (typ) Type ORNAMENTS used to embellish printed MATTER, for example, chapter HEADINGS, TITLE PAGES, etc.

Flush cover (fin) The COVER of a book cut to the same dimensions as the pages inside it.

Flush left/right (typ) See RANGED LEFT/RIGHT.

Flush paragraphs (typ) Paragraphs in which the first word is not indented but set flush with the vertical line of the text. See also FULL OUT.

Fly fold (fin) A folding method producing four pages from a SHEET.

Fly leaf (fin) Another term for END PAPERS, the part which is not stuck down.

Flyer A cheaply produced BROADSHEET or CIRCULAR for promotion purposes.

Flying paster (pri) An automatic mechanism on a WEB-FED press for running in a new web without interruption to the printing process.

f.o.b. abb Free on board. A commercial term denoting that a price quoted does not include delivery charge.

Focal length (pho) A property of a camera lens indicating its focusing ability. It is a measurement between lens and film when the image of a distant object is in sharp FOCUS in the camera.

Focus (pho) A point at which light rays converge. In photography, light rays are bent by the camera lens to converge on the film in such a way as to produce a sharp, clearly defined, but much reduced image of the subject.

Fog (pho) A gray blur obliterating part or all of a photographic image on film or paper, caused by uncontrolled EXPOSURE of the material to light.

Foil (**1** fin) Plastic film with a gold, silver, or metalized coloring, used to block designs, particularly onto packaging and book covers. (**2** rep) Clear, stable film used as a backing during film assembly.

Fold to paper (fin) A method of folding a SECTION (1) after printing by aligning the edges of the SHEET.

Fold to print (fin) A method of folding a SECTION (1) after printing by reference to page numbers or other matter printed on the SHEET.

Folded and gathered sheets/F and Gs (fin) Printed SECTIONS which are collated but not bound, and sent to the PUBLISHER for approval of printing before binding begins.

Folding (fin) see ACCORDION FOLD, FRENCH FOLD, GATEFOLD, PARALLEL FOLD, and RIGHT-ANGLE FOLD.

Foldout (fin) An extension to the LEAF of a book, making it wider than the standard page width so it must be folded back onto the page.

Foliation In book publishing, the practice of numbering leaves, that is alternate pages, rather than each page.

Folio (1) Technically, the number of a leaf of a book when it is not numbered as two separate pages. However, a folio number is generally said to mean a page number. (**2** pri) The size of a book that is formed when the sheet containing its pages is folded only once, thus making the pages half the size of the sheet. A folio-size book is generally said to mean a large-format book.

Follow copy (typ) Instruction to the TYPESETTER to follow the spelling and punctuation of a MANUSCRIPT, even If unorthodox, in preference to the HOUSE STYLE (1).

Follow on (typ) see RUN ON (2).

Font (typ) see FOUNT.

Foolscap (pap) A European standard size of printing paper $13^{1}/_{2}$ x 17in. (343x 432mm)

Foot The MARGIN at the bottom of a page or the bottom edge of a book.

Foot margin The MARGIN at the bottom of the page in a publication.

Footnotes Short explanatory notes, printed at the foot of the page or at the end of a book.

Fore edge, foredge (pri) The outer edge of a book parallel to the back.

Foredge margin (pri) The outer side MARGIN of a page in a publication.

Foreword Introductory remarks to a work or about the author.

Format (1) The size of a book or page or, in photography, the size of film. (**2** typ) To attribute type characteristics such as font, size, weight, tracking, leading, etc., to a text. (**3** com) The arrangement of sectors and empty directories on a disk in preparation for its initialization. (**4** com) In some applications, to specify paragraph, and other attributes such as indents, hyphenation, justification, tabs, etc.

Formatting
(**1** typ/com) See FORMAT (4). (**2** com) The process of preparing a new disk for use on a computer. When a disk is formatted, sectors, tracks, and empty directories are created, and the disk may be verified (a test of the integrity of the DATA blocks).

Forme, form (pri) Type matter and copy assembled into pages and locked up in a chase ready for LETTERPRESS printing

For position only (FPO) An instruction, to a repro house or printer, on layouts and artwork that an item is of inappropriate quality and is displayed only as a guide for positioning the properly prepared version.

Forty eight sheet (pap) A standard poster size, measuring 120 x 480in. (305 x 1220cm).

Forwarding (fin) The binding of a book after sewing and before CASING IN.

Foundry proof (pri) A PROOF from a FORME prepared for stereotyping or electrotyping.

Fount/font (typ) Traditionally, of metal type, a set of type of the same design, style, and size. On most computers however, a font is a set of characters, including letters, numbers, and other typographic symbols, of the same design and style – although some definitions of the term include, wrongly, all styles: light, roman, bold, etc.

Fountain (pri) A reservoir for ink supply in a printing press. The term is also used for a similar mechanism that supplies a solution for dampening the rollers of an OFFSET press.

Four-color process

(rep/pri) The printing process that reproduces full-color images by using three basic colors – CYAN, MAGENTA, and yellow plus black for added density.

Foxed The term is applied to book pages discolored by damp that has affected impurities in the paper.

Frame see BOX RULE.

Frame-based (com) A term sometimes used to describe APPLICATIONS which require you to create text or picture boxes in a DOCUMENT before text or pictures can be added.

Free line fall (typ) see RAGGED RIGHT and UNJUSTIFIED.

Freeware (com) Any SOFTWARE that is declared to be in the public domain and free of COPYRIGHT restrictions, as distinct from SHAREWARE.

French fold (fin) A term used to describe a SHEET of paper that has been printed on one side only and then folded twice to form an uncut four-page section.

French folio (pap) Thin, smooth-sized paper.

Fresnel lens (pho) A lens used to concentrate the beam of a photographic spotlight.

Friction feed (pri) A paper-feeding mechanism in a printing or copying machine using rubber rollers.

Fringe (rep) A halo seen to surround HALFTONE DOTS in the early stages of conventional film processing.

Front jacket flap The part of a BOOK JACKET that folds inside the front COVER of a book.

Front lay edge (pri) see LAY EDGES.

Front matter see PRELIMS.

Front projection A method of superimposing images in a photograph by projecting one image onto a two-way mirror placed between camera and subject.

Frontispiece An illustration facing the TITLE PAGE of a book.

Fugitive colors Colors or inks which are not permanent and which change or fade when exposed to light.

Full binding (fin) A BOOK-BINDING that is covered completely with the same material, such as full leather, full cloth.

Full-faced type (typ) see TITLING.

Full out (typ) Description of type set to the full measure, without indents.

Full-page display (FPD) (com) Name given to a 12in. (300mm) monitor (measured diagonally).

Full shadow (typ) A heavy outline to a letter or line of type.

Full space (typ) The horizontal space between two lines of type.

Full word wrap (typ) The transfer of a whole word to the following line to avoid a WORD BREAK.

Furnish (pap) The ingredients used in paper manufacture.

G

g/m2/gsm, grams per square meter A unit of measurement for paper used in printing.

Galley (typ) In conventional metal typesetting, the long shallow metal tray used by COMPOSITORS to hold type after it has been set.

Galley proof (typ) A proof of typeset text before it is laid out into a page design. The term derives from the days when metal type was proofed from a long, shallow, metal tray called a galley. Also called a "slip proof," the slip being the broad strip of paper on which a galley proof is printed.

Gang up (1 pri) To print a SHEET of paper with several different jobs, to be divided appropriately. (2 rep) To place a group of ORIGINALS of the same proportions together for reproduction.

Gang shooting (rep) In PHOTOLITHOGRAPHY, to make one NEGATIVE containing several pages of COPY for transfer to a printing plate. The pages are arranged to form a sequence that can be folded into page order.

Gatefold (fin) Two parallel folds dividing a sheet into three segments, in which both the outer segments are folded across the middle of the sheet in overlapping layers.

Gateway (link), router (com) A HARDWARE/SOFTWARE connection between dissimilar computer NETWORKS, enabling a user on one network to gain access to the DEVICES on another.

Gelatin process (pri) A duplication method using gelatin as the medium for transferring a carbon image as in GRAVURE printing.

Generation (rep) One stage of a process of reproduction.

Generic disk drive (com) A DISK DRIVE with a

mechanism that is common to many brands.

Ghosting (1 rep) To decrease the tonal values of the surrounding parts of an image in order to make the main object stand out more clearly. Also called "fadeback." (2) In illustration, particularly technical illustration, to depict parts of an image that would not normally be visible, such as parts of an engine covered by its casing.

Gigabyte (gig, Gb) (com) A unit of measure used to describe 1,024 MEGABYTES.

gigo, GIGO (com) abb Garbage In – Garbage Out. A principle in computer programming that poor quality INPUT produces equally poor OUTPUT.

Gilt edges/top (fin) The three edges, or top of a book, which are covered with gold leaf and rubbed down to prevent the absorption of dust.

Gloss ink (pri) A printing ink consisting of a synthetic resin base and drying oils. These inks dry quickly, without penetrating, and are suitable for use on COATED PAPERS.

Glossary (1) An alphabetical list giving the definition of terms, usually related to a particular subject. (2 com) In some word processing applications, the facility to insert frequently used text by means of a keyboard shortcut.

Glued back only (fin) Reference to a paper COVER which is glued to the back of a book only, leaving the sides loose.

Glued or pasted down to ends (fin) A paper COVER glued at back, with each side also glued or pasted to the first and last leaves of the book.

Glyphic (typ) A TYPEFACE originating from carved rather than scripted letters.

Gold blocking (fin) The stamping of a design on a book COVER using gold leaf and a heated DIE or block.

Golden section A formula for division of a line or area supposed to give harmonious proportions. If a line is divided unequally, the relationship of the two sections should be the same as that of the larger section to the whole. It is in practice a ratio of about 8:13.

Goldenrod (rep) An opaque, orange paper ruled with a GRID (1) used in preparing FLATS (1) for PHOTOLITHOGRAPHY.

Gothic (typ) see BLACK LETTER.

Grain (1 pap) In paper, the pattern of fibers and their prevailing direction in a manufactured sheet. (**2** pho) The density of tiny silver crystals in a photographic emulsion, sometimes used for graphic effect. (**3** pri) The roughness in the surface of some lithography plates that enables it to hold moisture.

Grain direction (pap) The direction the FIBERS lie in a SHEET of paper.

Graining (pri) The process by which a LITHOGRAPHIC plate is given a moisture-retaining surface. Abrasive powder and either glass or steel marbles are used. Mechanical agitation produces the required surface.

Grammage (pap) see G/M².

Graphic (1 typ) A TYPEFACE originating from drawn rather than scripted letter forms. (**2**) A general term used to signify any illustration or design.

Graphic design The arrangement, composition (design), and combination of shapes and forms based upon or involving two-dimensional processes such as typography, photography, illustration, video, motion picture, and various print methods. This does not exclude three-dimensional design, since the use of graphic design in three-dimensional forms is employed in many contexts, particularly packaging, product design, film, exhibitions, and architecture. Not to be confused with DESKTOP PUBLISHING.

Graphic user interface (com) see GUI.

Graphics tablet/ digitizing tablet (com) A computer input device that allows you to draw or write using a pen-like instrument as if you were working on paper.

Graticule A linear GRID (1) placed over an image to give reference to points on the image, such as lines of latitude and longitude on a map.

Gravure (pri) An INTAGLIO printing process in which the printing areas are below the non-printing surface of the printing plate. These recesses (CELLS (1)) are filled with a liquid ink, and the surplus is removed from the non-printing areas by the "doctor blade" before the paper "sucks" the ink from the cells.

Grayscale (1 *pho*) A tonal scale printed in steps of no-color through to black and used for quality control in both color and black-and-white photographic processing. (**2** *com*) Of MONITORS, the ability to display a PIXEL in a range of grays from white to black. (MONOCHROME monitors can only display black pixels, in which case grays can only be achieved by the varying density of black pixels to white pixels. See DITHERING)

Greek(ing) To indicate type by substituting rules or a gray tint for the letters themselves. This is common practice when preparing ROUGH VISUALS, or SCAMPS. On a computer, this is a feature of some APPLICATIONS (some also allow pictures to be greeked by substituting a flat gray tint) to speed up screen redraw.

Grid (1) A measuring guide used in book and magazine design to guarantee consistency. The grid usually shows such things as column widths, picture areas, trim sizes, etc. (**2** *com*) In some applications, a background pattern, usually invisible, of equidistant vertical and horizontal lines to which elements such as guides, rules, type, boxes, etc., can be locked, or "snapped," thus providing greater positional accuracy.

Gripper edge (*pri*) The edge which is caught by the GRIPPERS as a SHEET of paper is fed into a CYLINDER PRESS.

Gripper margin (*pri*) An extra MARGIN on a SHEET where it is gripped on the press, later trimmed away.

Grippers (*pri*) On printing presses, the short curved metal fingers attached to an operating rod which grip the sheet and carry it around the impression.

Groundwood (*pap*) A cheap wood PULP, such as that used to make NEWSPRINT.

Guards (*fin*) Narrow strips of linen or paper to which the inner MARGINS of single plates are pasted before sewing them with the SECTIONS of a book.

GUI (*com*) *abb* graphical user interface The feature of a computer system that allows you to interact with it by means of pointing at graphic symbols (ICONS) rather than by typing coded COMMANDS. Also called WIMPs or pointing

interface.

Guides (*pri*) see GRIPPERS.

Guillemets (*typ*) Quotation marks (« ») used in French and some German publications.

Guillotine (*fin*) A machine for cutting a large number of SHEETS of paper accurately.

Gum arabic (*pri*) A liquid used in platemaking processes. It dries to form a protective finish.

Gutter Strictly speaking, the space on a sheet, imposed for printing, including the foredges of the pages plus trim. Commonly, however, the term is given to the margin ("back margin") down the center of a double-page spread, or to the vertical space between adjacent columns on a page.

Gutter bleed An image allowed to extend unbroken across the central MARGINS of a DOUBLE SPREAD.

H

H & J, H/J (*typ*) *abb* HYPHENATION AND JUSTIFICATION.

Hairline rule (*typ*) Traditionally, the thinnest line that it is possible to print. In computer applications that list it as a size option for rules, it is usually 0.25 point thick.

Hairlines (*typ*) The very fine strokes of a TYPEFACE.

Hairspace (*typ*) Traditionally used of letterspacing, the term generally refers to a very narrow space between type characters.

Halation (*pho/rep*) In the highlights of an image, the undesirable spreading of light beyond its natural boundary, caused by overexposure or (in platemaking) poor plate contact during exposure.

Half-bound (*fin*) Used of case binding in which the back and corners are covered in one material and the rest of the sides in another, e.g. leather back and corners with paper sides.

Half sheet work (*pri*) The arrangement of plates so that each SHEET will be printed with two whole SECTIONS, half a sheet folding to one section.

Half-title (1) The title of a book as printed on the recto of the leaf preceding the title page. (**2**) The page on which the half-title appears. Sometimes called "bastard title."

Half up ARTWORK completed at one and a half times the size at which

it will be reproduced.

Halftone (1 *rep*) The process by which a continuous tone image is simulated by a pattern of dots of varying sizes. (**2** *rep*) An image reproduced by the halftone process.

Halftone blow up (*rep*) The enlargement of a HALFTONE NEGATIVE to coarsen the screened DOT pattern.

Halftone screen (*rep*) Conventionally, a sheet of glass or film cross-hatched with opaque lines. Also called a crossline screen or contact screen, it is used to translate a continuous tone image into halftone dots so that it can be printed. Computers – or rather, APPLICATIONS which offer a halftone screen feature – apply a halftone screen to an image by digital means, without the need for a physical halftone screen.

Hanging indent (*typ*) An arrangement in typeset text where the first line of each paragraph is set full out to the column measure and the remaining lines are indented to the right of the first line.

Hanging punctuation (*typ*) Punctuation marks allowed to fall outside the MEASURE of a piece of text.

Hard copy (1) A copy on paper of MATTER prepared for printing, used for revision or checking. (**2** *com*) A printout of a computer document, as distinct from a soft copy – a copy of a document to the same, or another, disk.

Hardcover book/ hardback book (*fin*) A CASED book with a stiff board COVER.

Hard disk (*com*) see DISK.

Hard dot (*rep*) A HALFTONE DOT in the second or third stage of conventional processing, with sharp edges.

Hard size (*pap*) Paper which contains the maximum amount of SIZE.

Hardware A term for equipment. It generally applies to the physical apparatus of a computer environment, as distinct from FIRMWARE (built-in PROGRAMS) and SOFTWARE (programs).

Head (1) The MARGIN at the top of a page. (**2** *com*) see READ/WRITE HEAD.

Head bolt (*pri*) The thickening of a fully folded SHEET before it is trimmed.

Head to foot arrangement (*pri*) The placement of COPY on either side of a SHEET to align the top of the first page with the bottom of the page overleaf.

Headband (*fin*) A cotton or silk cord glued or sewn to the top of the back of a book.

Heading The title introducing a chapter or subdivision of text. A crossheading, or crosshead, appears in the body of the text.

Headless paragraph A paragraph set apart from other text, but without a separate HEADING.

Headline (**1**) The line of type at the top of a page. A running headline, or running head, is often the title of the book, or a chapter contained within it, repeated on every page, the convention being for the book title to be printed on left-hand pages (VERSO) with chapter titles on the right-hand pages (RECTO). If running heads are at the bottom of the page, they are "footers." (**2**) The main title of a newspaper or magazine article.

Headpiece A decorative device added to a HEADING.

Heat set inks (*pri*) Ink designed to dry particularly quickly when the printed MATTER is passed through a drier.

Heavy (*typ*) An alternative term for BOLD.

Hertz (Hz) (*com*) The measurement of a unit of frequency. One hertz is one cycle, or occurrence, per second.

Hickie, hickey (*pri*) A common printing defect, visible as a spot surrounded by a blank halo, caused by a speck of dirt pushing the paper away from the printing plate.

High gloss ink (*pri*) A viscous ink that does not soak into paper and dries to a glossy surface.

High key (*pho*) A photographic image exposed or processed to produce light tones overall.

Highlight The lightest tones of a photograph or illustration.

Highlight halftone (*rep*) A HALFTONE plate in which DOTS appearing in HIGHLIGHT areas are etched out. See DROPOUT HALFTONE.

Hinting, hints (*com*) The set of instructions contained within Adobe PostScript Type 1 OUTLINE FONTS which modifies CHARACTER shapes so that they appear better when displayed or printed at low resolutions. Hinting is unimportant when fonts are printed at high resolution,

such as on IMAGESETTERS.

Holding line see KEYLINE.

Hollow (*fin*) The strip of brown paper placed in the center of a CASE to stiffen the SPINE.

Hologram An image with three dimensional illusionism created by the action of lasers.

Holograph In publishing, a MANUSCRIPT hand-written by the author.

Honing (*pri*) A technique of removing image areas from a printing plate by mechanical means.

Hooking (*fin*) A method of attaching a single LEAF to a SECTION (1) by means of a GUARD.

Horizontal scaling (*com*) In some APPLICATIONS, the facility to condense or expand type. By retaining the exact attributes of the source FONT, horizontal scaling distorts its appearance, and while the facility can be a bonus, it can also produce ugly typography.

Hot metal (*typ*) General term describing a now virtually obsolete method of typesetting which involved casting type from molten metal.

Hot-press lettering (*fin*) A method of laying down CHARACTERS (1) in metal foil on board, using type under heat and pressure.

Hot-pressed (*pap*) Paper glazed by heated metal plates.

House corrections PROOFS or script altered by the PUBLISHER or printer, as distinct from the author.

House organ A publication produced by a company for information to its own employees or customers.

House style (**1**) The style of spelling, punctuation, and spacing used by a publishing house to maintain a consistent standard and treatment of text throughout its publications. (**2**) See CORPORATE IDENTITY.

H/T (*rep*) abb HALFTONE.

Hue The distinguishing property of a pure color, not including any white or black.

Hygroscope (*pri*) A device for measuring how much humidity is picked up from the air by paper.

Hyphenate (*typ*) The use of a hyphen (-) to divide one word into syllables or to create a compound form from two or more words.

Hyphenation and justification (H&J; H/J) (*typ*) In typesetting, the routines of a computer application that distributes

spaces correctly in a line of type to achieve the desired measure in justified text. When this cannot reasonably be done without breaking words at the end of a line, hyphens will be introduced at a position determined by the application's built-in dictionary or H&J rules.

Hypertext (*com*) A programming concept that links any single word of text to an unlimited number of others.

Hypo (*pho*) abb Hyposulfate. A term applied to the FIXER used in photographic processing, though the solution used is in fact sodium thiosulfate

I

ibid abb Ibidem, a Latin term meaning "in the same place," used in notes to a publication to repeat a reference.

Icon (*com*) A graphic representation of an object, such as a DISK, FILE, folder or tool, or of a concept or message.

Ideal format (*pho*) A size of photographic NEGATIVE measuring 2⅜ x 2¾in. (60 x 70mm).

idem A Latin term meaning "the same," used as a reference in FOOTNOTES.

i.e. abb Id est, a Latin term meaning "that is."

Illustration (**1**) A drawing, painting, diagram, or photograph reproduced in a publication to explain or supplement the text. (**2**) A term used to distinguish a drawn image from one that is photographed.

Image (*rep*) The SUBJECT to be reproduced as an illustration on a printing press.

Image area (**1**) In design, the space within which a particular image is to fit. (**2** *pri*) The printing or ink-carrying area of a litho plate.

Imagesetter (*typ*/*com*) A high-resolution output DEVICE that is used to produce reproduction-quality COPY for printing, either as CAMERA-READY ARTWORK on photographic BROMIDE paper or as film NEGATIVES or POSITIVES.

Imitation cloth/leather (*fin*) A BOOKBINDING material usually of paper, made to simulate the look of leather or cloth.

Imperfection (*fin*) A book which has been incorrectly bound.

Import (*com*) To bring text, pictures, or other DATA into a DOCUMENT. Some

APPLICATIONS allow you to import material in a variety of FILE FORMATS such as ASCII (text) or EPS (graphics).

Impose/imposition (rep) To arrange pages – in the correct sequence and with the appropriate margins for folding and trimming – before platemaking and printing.

Imposed proof (rep) A proof of imposed pages prior to the final print run.

Impression (pri) All copies of a book printed at one time from the same type of plates.

Impression cylinder (pri) The cylinder of a ROTARY PRESS carrying paper into contact with the inked plate or BLANKET CYLINDER.

Imprimature A Latin term meaning "let it be printed." It used to be a statement to show that permission to print a work had been given by the appropriate authority.

Imprint The printer's imprint is the name of the printer and the place of printing (a legal requirement in many countries if the work is to be published). The publisher's imprint is the name of the publisher, usually printed on the title page of a book.

Imprint page The page of a book, often following the title page (title verso), carrying details of the edition, such as the printer's imprint, copyright owner, ISBN, catalog number, etc.

In pro (rep) abb In proportion. A term used to direct the enlargement or reduction of an original image.

Increment (typ) see LEADING.

Indentation (typ) Of type set to a narrower measure than the column measure, the term given to the distance that the beginning or end of the line is from the left or right edges of the column.

Index The section of a publication giving alphabetical listing of subjects, proper names, etc., mentioned in the book, with page references.

Index board (pap) Colored board made by machine, used for INDEX GUIDES.

Index guide (fin) The markers of a filing system designed to give ready access to items divided alphabetically or by subject. See STEP INDEX and THUMB INDEX.

Index letter/number A character or number used to key a reference between an illustration and the CAPTION or text.

India paper (pap) A very thin but strong opaque paper, made from rags and used for printing Bibles and dictionaries.

Indirect letterpress (pri) see LETTERSET.

Inferior character (typ) Letters or numbers set smaller than the text and set on or below the baseline, as H_2O. In many computer applications, inferior characters are called "subscript."

Initial (typ) A large CAPITAL often found at the beginning of a chapter. It is usually dropped to a depth of two or three lines below the first line.

Ink drier (pri) A chemical agent added to ink to speed drying and prevent smudging.

Ink duct (pri) The FOUNTAIN supplying ink to a printing press.

Ink squash (pri) A spread of ink outside the required details of an image, occurring during printing.

Inked art ARTWORK drawn up first in pencil for checking and then completed in ink.

Inkers (pri) The rollers on a printing press which apply ink to the plate.

Inline lettering (typ) Any TYPEFACE with a white line inside the shape that follows the outline of the character.

Input (com) Any data entered into a computer, by whatever means.

Input device (com) Any HARDWARE DEVICE capable of entering DATA into a computer; i.e., keyboard, SCANNER, DIGITIZER, etc.

Inset/insert A SHEET or part of a sheet placed inside another which is not part of the book's normal PAGINATION.

Intaglio (pri) A printing process, such as gravure, in which the image is below the surface of the plate.

Intensification (pho) Chemical methods of improving the DENSITY of a NEGATIVE.

Interactive (com) Term describing the immediate and reciprocal action between person and machine.

Interface (com) The physical relationship, or point of interaction, between systems and/or machines, or between person and machine

(which is called "user" or "human" interface).

Interleaving (**1** pri) Sheets of paper placed between newly printed sheets in order to prevent ink transfer. Also called slip-sheeting. (**2**) Blank pages between the printed pages of a book, provided for handwritten notes.

Interlinear spacing (typ) See LEADING.

Intermediate (rep) A transparent or translucent COPY of an ORIGINAL from which other copies can be made.

International paper sizes (pap) The standard range of metric paper sizes laid down by the International Standards Organization. The papers are designated A, B, and C series and are available in proportional sizes, divided in ratio to the largest sheet, A0 (trimmed – untrimmed sizes are prefixed with R, or SR for bled work), which is one square meter in area (841 x 1189mm): the shortest dimension of a sheet is equivalent to the longest dimension of the next size down.

Internegative (rep) A photographic NEGATIVE forming the intermediate stage in making a print from a FLAT ORIGINAL.

Interpolation (com) The term describing the technique of recreating the color values of PIXELS in BITMAPPED images which have been modified (i.e. by rotating or SKEWING). The interpolation is achieved by the ability of the PROGRAM to make estimates from known values of other pixels lying in the same or similar ranges. Interpolation is also used by some scanning and image manipulation SOFTWARE to enhance the resolution of images that have been scanned at low resolution – although advertised as capable of high resolution scanning, some scanners only scan at physically low resolutions (typically 300dpi), and use methods of interpolation to produce images of higher resolution (600dpi or more).

Interpreter (com) SOFTWARE used in programming that converts PROGRAM CODE into machine language. An interpreter converts a program one piece at a time, as distinct from a compiler, which converts a program in its entirety.

Introduction The opening

SECTION (2) of a book written either by the author as part of the text or by another person commenting on the purpose and content of the author's work.

Inverted commas (*typ*) A pair of commas printed above the BASE LINE of type ('') used to open or close a quotation. See QUOTES.

I/O (*com*) *abb* INPUT/OUTPUT.

iph (*pri*) *abb* IMPRESSIONS per hour.

Iris (*pho*) see DIAPHRAGM.

ISBN *abb* International Standard Book Number. A unique ten-figure serial number that appears on every book published and which identifies the language in which it is published, its publisher, its title, and a check control number. An ISBN is often included in the bar code on a book.

ISO *abb* International Standards Organization. A Swiss-based organization which has been responsible for standardizing many elements common to design, photography, and publishing.

Italic (*typ*) The specially designed sloping version of a roman typeface derived from handwriting and calligraphic scripts, intended to be distinctive from, but complementary to, that face. A version of italic, often called oblique or sloped roman, can be generated electronically on a computer, which slants the roman style to the right – which is what may happen when italic is specified for a font but no special italic is available for it.

Ivory board (*pap*) A smoothly finished white board used for ARTWORK and display printing.

J

Jacket The paper wrapper in which a book is sold.

Jaggie, staircasing (*com*) The term, technically called aliasing, given to the stepped appearance on MONITORS of BITMAPPED images and FONTS, particularly when they are enlarged, caused by PIXELS consisting only of straight, square sides

Jaw folder (*pri*) A paper folder, attached to a WEB-FED printing press, that cuts and folds a SIGNATURE.

Jim-dash (*typ*) A short RULE dividing items in a newspaper.

Jobbing (*pri*) Description of general printing, not specializing in any field (such as book work) and usually consisting of short runs.

Jogging (*fin*) To vibrate paper stock to bring the edges into line before trimming. A jogger may be attached to a printing press or form a separate unit.

Joint (*fin*) The flexible part of a CASE between the boarded side and the SPINE.

Jump (*typ*) In a publication, printed MATTER carried over to continue on a succeeding page.

Justification (*typ*) Spacing of words and letters so that each line of text finishes at the same point.

K

K, k (**1** *rep/pri*) The shorthand used to describe the process color black, deriving from the KEY, or black, printing plate in FOUR-COLOR PROCESS printing. Using the letter K rather than the initial B avoids confusion with blue, even though the abbreviation for process blue is C (CYAN).

(**2** *com*) See KILOBYTE.

Keep down (*typ*) Instruction to a compositor to keep text in LOWER CASE type.

Keep in (*typ*) An instruction to a COMPOSITOR to keep spaces narrow between words.

Keep out (*typ*) The opposite of KEEP IN, to use wide spaces between words.

Keep standing (*pri*) To keep plates ready for possible REPRINTS.

Keep up (*typ*) Instruction to keep text in UPPER CASE type.

Kern (*typ*) The part of a letter which overhangs the next.

Kerning (*typ*) Adjusting the space (usually reducing it) between a pair of type characters to optimize their appearance. Traditionally, in metal type, kerned letters were those that physically overhung the metal body of the next character and were particularly important in italic typefaces – the roman versions of most metal fonts being designed so that they did not require kerning. As distinct from TRACKING, which is the adjustment of space over several characters.

Key (**1** *rep/pri*) Any printing plate (traditionally the black, called the key plate) or piece of artwork

that provides a guide for the position and register of other colors. (**2** *com*) To input matter via a keyboard.

Key letters/numbers Letters or numbers forming a reference link between elements of an illustration and their description in a caption.

Key plate (*pri*) The plate that prints black ink in four-color process printing.

Keyline (**1**) An outline drawing on artwork, that may or may not form part of the artwork, indicating an area that is to be filled by a mechanical tint. (**2**) A line drawing on a page layout indicating the size and position of an illustration or halftone. (**3**) The outline on artwork that, when transferred to a printing plate, will provide a guide for the register of other colors.

Keystroke (*com*) The action of pressing a key, or group of keys, at a single time, whether or not it generates a character.

Kicker (*typ*) Newspaper or magazine term for a line of type appearing above or below the title of a feature.

Kill (*typ*) An instruction to delete COPY.

Kilobit (*com*) 1,024 BITS.

Kilobyte (K, Kb, Kbyte) (*com*) A unit of measurement representing 1,024 BYTES (8,192 BITS), which is used to describe the amount of MEMORY or STORAGE a computer or DISK may have. Since one byte represents a single CHARACTER, one kilobyte is roughly equivalent to 170 words. Strictly speaking, "kilo" means one thousand, but because computers use a BINARY SYSTEM (pairs of numbers) each number is doubled: 2; 4; 8; 16; 32; 64; 128; 256; 512; 1,024.

Kiss impression (*pri*) An IMPRESSION in which ink is put on paper by the lightest possible surface contact. This technique is necessary when printing on COATED PAPERS.

Klischograph (*pri*) A German electronic PHOTOENGRAVING machine which produces a plastic, zinc, copper, or magnesium HALFTONE plate.

Knocking up (*fin*) The adjustment on one or two edges of a pile of SHEETS so that they can be cut squarely.

Kraft paper (*pap*) Strong brown paper made from sulfate PULP. It is often used for packing books.

L

Lacuna (*typ/rep*) A gap or space in a text where COPY has been lost or damaged.

Laid paper (*pap*) Paper showing the wire marks of the mold or DANDY ROLL used in manufacture.

Laminate (*fin*) To protect paper or cardboard and give it a glossy surface by applying a transparent plastic coating through heat or pressure.

LAN (*com*) see LOCAL AREA NETWORK.

Landscape/horizontal format An image or page format in which the width is greater than the height.

Lap (*rep/pri*) *abb* Overlap, of two colors to avoid registration problems. See also FATTY.

Laser (*com*) The acronym for light amplification by stimulated emission of radiation, meaning an intense, fine beam of highly integrated light, sometimes generated with considerable energy. It is used widely in computer HARDWARE such as OPTICAL DISCS, printers and scanners, and for various commercial printing activities such as platemaking and engraving.

Latent image (*pho*) A photographically recorded image that can be made apparent by chemical processing.

Lateral reverse (*rep*) The TRANSPOSING of an image from left to right, as in a mirror reflection. See also FLOP.

Latin (**1**) The standard alphabet used in most European languages, consisting of the upper- and lower-case characters from A to Z. The exceptions are Greek and Cyrillic (Russian, etc.). Oriental languages, including Arabic and Hebrew, are usually classified as "exotics." (**2** *typ*) A term sometimes given to typefaces derived from letterforms common to western European countries, especially those with heavy, wedge-shaped serifs.

Latitude (*pho*) The range of EXPOSURES that all produce an acceptable image on a given type of film.

Launch (*com*) To open, or start, a SOFTWARE APPLICATION.

Lay edges (*pri*) The two edges of a SHEET which are placed FLUSH with the side and front lay gauges or

marks on a printing machine to make sure that the sheet will be removed properly by the GRIPPERS and have uniform MARGINS when printed.

Layout An outline or sketch which gives the general appearance of the printed page, indicating the relationship between text and illustration.

Lays (*pri*) see GRIPPERS.

LCD/lcd *abb* Liquid crystal display. An electronic method of display commonly seen on calculators, clocks, and computers.

Lead The main story in a newspaper or the opening story.

Leaded (*typ*) Type which is set with spacing, or "leads" between the lines.

Leader (*typ*) A group of dots (usually) or dashes, used to guide the eye across a space to other relevant matter.

Leader line/rule (*typ*) A line on an image, usually keying elements of that image to annotation or a caption.

Leading (*typ*) Space between lines of type, originating from days when strips of lead were placed between lines of type to increase the space. In some computer APPLICATIONS, leading can be specified as: "absolute," meaning the specific value given to spaces between lines of text; "auto," the value given to automatic line spacing by means of a user-definable preference; or "incremental," a value given to line spacing totaling the largest character on the line plus or minus a user-defined value.

Leaf (**1** *pap*) Refers to newly formed SHEETS of paper before they are dried and finished. (**2** *pri*) Each of the folios which result when a sheet of paper is folded. Each side of a leaf is called a page.

Leaf edge (*pri*) The opposite edge to the GRIPPER.

Legend The descriptive MATTER printed below an illustration or map, more often called a CAPTION or key.

Lens flare (*pho*) The diffusion of light that tends to occur in a camera lens if the light source is very strong.

Letterhead(**ing**) Strictly speaking, the heading – a name, address, and telephone number of a business or individual – on

any item of stationery, but sometimes used to describe the item of stationery specifically used for writing letters.

Letterpress (*pri*) The original relief method printing process, whereby the surface of a raised, or relief, image or piece of type is inked and then pressed onto paper or other surface.

Letterset (*pri*) A term deriving from LETTERPRESS and OFFSET, describing a method of offset printing from a relief plate.

Letterspace/letterfit (*typ*) The adjustment of space between type characters from that allocated by the font designer, by kerning or by increasing or decreasing the tracking.

llup *abb* Left-hand page.

Library binding (*fin*) BOOK BINDING strong enough to endure continual handling.

Library of Congress number A reference number given to the American edition of a book and recorded at the Library of Congress. This is common practice, but is not required by law.

Library shot/pic A picture or illustration taken from an existing source, not specially commissioned.

Lift (*pri*) The number of SHEETS of paper that can be cut all together or handled in a single operation.

Lifting (*pri*) see PICKING.

Ligature (*typ*) Two or three type characters tied, or joined together, to make a single type character, as in fi fl ff ffi ffl.

Light face (*typ*) The opposite of BOLD FACE.

Light-fast ink (*typ*) Ink that is not susceptible to fading color when exposed to light over a period.

Light table/box (*rep*) A table or box with a translucent glass top lit from below, giving a color-balanced light suitable for viewing color transparencies and for color-matching transparencies to proofs.

Limp binding (*pri*) A form of binding using a flexible COVER, such as paper, cloth, or leather, and no board stiffener.

Line and halftone (*rep*) A conventional reproduction process in which line and halftone NEGATIVES are combined, printed onto a plate, and etched as a unit.

Line art(**work**) (*rep*) Artwork or camera-ready copy consisting only of black on white, with no intermediate tones and thus not requiring halftone reproduction.

Line board (*pap*) A smoothly finished support suitable for line illustrations and ARTWORK.

Line conversion (*rep*) A photographic process of converting HALFTONE or CONTINUOUS TONE COPY into line images. Middle tones are eliminated to increase contrast.

Line gauge (*typ*) See TYPE SCALE.

Line increment (*typ*) The smallest possible increase in the basic measure between typeset lines.

Line interval (*typ*) The distance between the BASE LINES of following lines of type. When metal type was used, the BODY SIZE dictated the interval.

Line original (*rep*) An original image prepared for line reproduction. See LINE ART.

Line weight (*typ*) The relative thickness of RULES or lines used in illustration.

Linen tester (*rep*) A magnifying glass designed for checking the detail of a HALFTONE DOT pattern.

Lining figures/ numerals (*typ*) A set of numerals aligned at top and bottom. Sometimes called "modern" numerals.

Lining up/lineup table (*rep*) A LIGHT TABLE used for preparing and checking paste-up, FLATS (1), etc.

Linotype Hell A German type foundry and manufacturer of typesetting equipment (such as the Linotronic series imagesetters). The original Linotype machine was the first keyboard-operated composing machine to employ the principle of a "matrix," and cast type in solid lines, or "slugs." It was invented by the German-born American engineer Ottmar Mergenthaler and patented in 1884. The Monotype machine was invented almost simultaneously, in 1885.

Linting (*pri*) The adhesion of loose scraps from the surface of paper to the BLANKET CYLINDER in OFFSET printing. See also PICKING.

Lith film (*rep*) A high contrast and high-quality photographic emulsion used in graphic reproduction.

Lithography (*pri*) A printing process, invented in 1798 by the German Aloys Senefelder, that produces an image from a dampened, flat surface,

using greasy ink, based on the principle of the mutual repulsion of oil and water.

Loading (*pap*) The addition of a substance such as china clay in papermaking to give better opacity and finish.

LOC see LIBRARY OF CONGRESS NUMBER.

Local area network (*com*) A NETWORK of HARDWARE DEVICES confined to a small ("local") area – one room, say – using appropriate connections and SOFTWARE. At its simplest, a LAN may be set up so that several computers have access to a single printer or a centralized HARD DISK.

loc cit *abb* Loco citato, a Latin term for "in the place named," used as a reference in FOOTNOTES.

Log on (*com*) To connect to, or announce your presence on, a NETWORK.

Logo(**type**) Traditionally, any group of type characters (other than ligatures) such as company names or emblems cast together on one metal body. The term is now used to describe any design or symbol, such as a pictogram, for a corporation or organization which forms the centerpiece of its corporate identity.

Long ink (*pri*) Ink mixed to a consistency of flow that can be drawn out in a thread without breaking.

Long letters (*typ*) Type CHARACTERS (1) that extend right across the shank.

Long page (*typ*) A page with type extended by one or two lines to avoid an inconvenient break.

Long S (*typ*) The S used in old forms of printed English, as in ſ.

Look-/see-/show- through (*pri*) The visibility of an image through paper when seen against the light.

Loose leaf (*fin*) A BINDING METHOD that allows the easy removal of individual leaves.

Low key (*pho*) A photographic image given dark tones overall by the lighting or processing methods applied.

Lower case (*typ*) The small letters in a FONT of type.

M

Machine code (*com*) The lowest level of programming language. It is the least like English, but it is the most efficient, as a computer finds it the easiest to understand.

Machine direction (*pap*) The path of paper through a papermaking machine that dictates the GRAIN (1) of the paper.

Machine glazed paper (*pap*) Machine finished paper with a high gloss surface on one side.

Machine-made paper (*pap*) The continuous WEB of paper made on cylinder machines.

Machine proof (*pri*) A final proof made on a machine similar to the one on which it will be printed (if not that actual machine).

Machine sheet (*pri*) A general term for any printed SHEET coming off the press.

Macro (*com*) Literally, macro (deriving from the Greek "makros" = long, large) means large or large-scale, prolonging. Macroscopic means large units as distinct from microscopic, which means small. Thus, when applied to computers, a macro refers to a single COMMAND which contains several other commands – one large unit made up of smaller units. A macro PROGRAM is a small APPLICATION with which you can build or record a sequence of actions into a single keyboard equivalent.

Macron A symbol denoting pronunciation of a long vowel, printed as a horizontal line above the letter.

Macrophotography (*pho*) The photographing of small objects by means of a special lens or lens adapter.

Magenta (M) (*rep/pri*) The special shade of red that is one of the four process colors used in four-color printing, sometimes called process red. Theoretically, magenta contains no blue (CYAN) or yellow.

Magnetic disk (*com*) see DISK.

Magnetic ink characters (*com/typ*) CHARACTERS (1) printed using a magnetized ink which are readable both by humans and by appropriate machines, using a process called MICR (magnetic ink character recognition).

Majuscules (*typ*) An alternative term for CAPITALS.

Make-up (1) The SHEET indicating the placing of the various items on a page. See also LAYOUT. (**2** *rep*) The final preprint assembly, whether it be on paper, film, or on a computer, of all items to be printed.

Making (pap) One whole batch of MACHINE-MADE PAPER.

Making ready (pri) The term describing the process of preparing a printing press before a new run, to establish register, evenness of impression, size, etc.

Manilla (pap) A tough, buff-colored paper used in the manufacture of stationery.

Manuscript (MS/MSS) An author's text submitted for publication..

Marbling (pap) Decorative paper used for binding books, and sometimes the book EDGES. It is done by dipping the SHEET in a bath of colors floating on a surface of gum. The colors do not mix but can be combined into patterns with the use of a comb.

Margins The blank areas of a printed page which surround text or illustrations.

Marked proof (typ) A proof that has any necessary corrections marked on it before it is given to the author.

Mark-up (1 typ/rep/pri) To specify, to anyone in the reproduction process, every detail of a job that the person may require to carry out the job properly. (**2**) The actual item produced to put (1) into effect.

Mask (rep/com) A material used to block out part of an image in photomechanical reproduction, photography, illustration, or layout. On a computer, many applications provide a masking feature which enables you to apply a mask to all or selected parts of an image.

Masking (1 pho/rep) Blocking out part of an image with opaque material to prevent reproduction or to allow for alterations. (**2** rep) A technical method of adjusting the values of color and tone in photomechanical reproduction.

Master cylinder (pri) The cylinder of a printing press that transfers ink from reservoir to plate.

Master plate (pri) The plate containing the image for OFFSET printing.

Master proof A marked proof with client's, editor's, and author's comments combined.

Masthead Details about a PUBLISHER printed in the editorial or contents page of a newspaper or periodical.

Mathematical signs/ symbols Type symbols used as a shorthand for mathematical concepts and processes, i.e. + (add), ÷ (divide), √ (radical, or square root).

Mat(rix) (1 typ) Traditionally, the name for the copper mold from which hot-metal type was cast; the term was later applied to the photographic negative on phototypesetting machines from which type characters are generated. (**2** pri) The impression in papier-mâché taken from a page of type for stereotyping and the stereotyper's FLONG after molding.

Matt art (pap) A clay-coated printing paper with a dull finish.

Matter (typ/rep/pri) Traditionally, MANUSCRIPT or COPY to be printed, or type that has been set.

Mean line (typ) The imaginary line showing the top of the X-HEIGHT of lower-case letters.

Measure (typ) The length of a typeset line, used to indicate the width of a text column, usually measured in PICAS or POINTS, and sometimes in inches or millimeters.

Mechanical (rep) A term for CAMERA-READY COPY or ARTWORK. See also PHOTOMECHANICAL (2).

Mechanical binding (fin) BINDING METHOD securing leaves through punched or drilled holes by means of a metal or plastic device, for permanent or LOOSE LEAF binding.

Mechanical pulp (pap) Untreated paper pulp used as the basis of NEWSPRINT and low-quality papers.

Mechanical tints (rep) The term used to describe a tint, usually flat color, consisting of a line or dot pattern that can be laid down during conventional reproduction or by applying a percentage tint to a selection in some computer graphics APPLICATIONS.

Medallion (fin) An illustration printed on paper, pasted to the front of the CASE of a book.

Media (1) A collective noun used to describe any information or communications medium such as television, radio, newspapers, etc. (**2** com) A collective noun generally

used to describe the actual items on which computer data is stored, such as a floppy, hard, or optical disks, as distinct from the devices in which they are used.

Medium (1) A synonym for a catchline. (**2**) The substance which binds the pigment of paint or ink, also called the "vehicle." Printing ink medium is usually linseed oil. (**3** pap) A standard size of printing paper, 18 x 23in. (**4** typ) A weight of typeface halfway between light and bold, often being the roman version. (**5** pri) Alternative name for a BEN DAY print.

Megabit (Mbit) (com) 1,024 KILOBITS, or 1,048,576 BITS.

Megabyte (M, Mbyte, MB, Mb, meg) (com) A unit of measurement representing 1,048,576 BYTES (1,024 KILOBYTES, or roughly 175,000 words), which is used to describe the amount of MEMORY or STORAGE a computer or DISK may have. Strictly speaking, "mega" means one million (although it derives simply from the Greek word megas = great), but because computers use a BINARY SYSTEM (pairs of numbers), each number is doubled: 2; 4; 8; 16; 32; 64; 128; 256; 512; 1,024, and so on.

Megahertz (MHz) (com) One million cycles, or occurrences, or instructions, per second, generally used to describe the speed of a computer's CENTRAL PROCESSING UNIT, or its "CLOCK SPEED."

Memory (com) The faculty of a computer to recall data and remember it, as distinct from storing the data, for which media such as disks are used. Some computers have two types of memory: RAM, which memorizes the activities that take place on screen until they are written to disk, and which only exists as long as the computer is switched on; and ROM, which is a memory chip that permanently stores data vital to the computer's operation.

Menu (com) A list of COMMANDS available on a computer, depending on the APPLICATION being used.

Metallic ink (pri) A printing ink which produces an effect of gold, silver, copper, or bronze.

Mezzotint (1 pri) An INTAGLIO printing process. (**2** rep) A PHOTOMECHANICAL screen tint used to mimic the effect of a mezzotint engraving.

mf/mtf (*typ*) *abb* More follows/more to follow, marked on COPY being prepared for TYPESETTING.

MF (*pap*) *abb* Machine finished paper.

MG (*pap*) *abb* MACHINE GLAZED PAPER.

MICR *abb* MAGNETIC INK CHARACTER recognition.

Mid(dle) space (*typ*) In traditional typesetting, a standard word space measuring one quarter of an EM.

MIDI (*com*) *abb* Musical instrument digital interface. A communication standard used by computers to control musical sound.

Mill brand (*pap*) The TRADEMARK and brand name of the manufacturer.

Mill ream (*pap*) A bulk quantity of handmade or MOLDMADE PAPER (472 SHEETS).

Millboards (*pap*) Strong gray or black boards of good quality used for the COVERS of a book.

Minuscules (*typ*) An alternative term for LOWER CASE letters.

Mock up The rough visualization of a publication or packaging design showing size, color, type, etc.

Modem (*com*) *abb* Modulator-demulator. A device for transferring DATA from one computer to another across telephone lines, using appropriate SOFTWARE.

Moiré (*rep*) An aberration occurring in HALFTONE reproduction when two or more colors are printed, giving a halftone image an appearance rather like that of watered silk. This is caused by two or more DOT screens being positioned at the wrong angles or, sometimes, by the re-screening of an image to which a halftone screen has already been applied. The angle at which screens should be positioned depends upon the number of colors being printed, but the norm for four-color process printing, and thus the default setting for most computer APPLICATIONS that support four-color separation, is: CYAN 105°; MAGENTA 75°; yellow 90°; black 45°.

Mold (*pri*) A flat impressed SHEET made by beating or pressing a FLONG onto a type, for casting a stereo.

Moldmade paper (*pap*) A manufactured, imitation handmade paper.

Monitor (*com*) The screen on which you view what you do on your computer. A monitor may be able to display in color, GRAYSCALE (2), or MONOCHROME, and is either built into the same case as the computer, or is a separate unit. Monitors are available in a variety of sizes from 9in. (229mm) (measured diagonally) to 21in. (534mm) or more. Although most monitors use CATHODE RAY TUBES, some contain liquid crystal displays, particularly portables and laptops. Monitors are variously called "screens," "displays," "VDUs" and "VDTs."

Mono(chrome) (**1**) Any image or reproduction of varying tones made in a single color. (**2** *com*) Of computer MONITORS, the description of those which display PIXELS only as either black or white, as distinct from GRAYSCALE monitors, which display pixels in a range of grays.

Monogram A design formed from the INITIALS of a name.

Monograph A publication dealing with a single person or subject.

Monotype (**1**) A type foundry and manufacturer of typesetting equipment. The original Monotype process, invented in 1885 by Tolbert Lanston of Ohio (only a year after the invention of the Linotype machine), employed a keyboard-operated composing machine to cast type as individual letters, using large numbers of matrices. (**2**) The process of making a painting on glass or metal and then taking an IMPRESSION on paper. Only one impression can be taken.

Montage Assembling portions of several drawings or photographs to form a single ORIGINAL.

Mordant (*fin*) An adhesive for fixing gold leaf. It is also any fluid used to etch lines on a printing plate.

Morocco (*fin*) Tanned goatskin which is finished by glazing or polishing and used in BOOKBINDING.

Motherboard (*com*) see BOARD.

Mottling (*pri*) An uneven IMPRESSION, especially in flat areas. It is usually caused by too much pressure or unsuitable paper or ink.

Mounting board (*pap*) A heavy board used for mounting photographs or ARTWORK.

Mouse (*com*) The mechanical device which is used to navigate the pointer on a MONITOR screen, thus enabling DATA to be entered into a computer.

Movable type (*typ*) The principle of the original method of typesetting in which single pieces of type were used rather than slugs (whole lines cast as one piece).

MS, MSS *abb* MANUSCRIPT(S).

Mull (*fin*) Coarse variety of muslin which forms the first lining of a CASE-BOUND book. Also known as scrim.

Multimedia (*com*) The activity of integrating text, graphics, sound, and video for presentations and INTERACTIVE publishing works, and the APPLICATIONS that enable you to do this with a computer.

Multiple exposure (*pho*) In photography, stages of the same subject or separate images superimposed to form one image in EXPOSURE or PROCESSING.

Multiple flats (*pri*) FLATS used in printing successive pages where it is required that some elements of the design are matched from page to page.

Multiring binder (*fin*) BINDING METHOD using a number of closely spaced rings to secure leaves.

Multitasking (*com*) The facility to run two or more APPLICATIONS at the same time, when the CENTRAL PROCESSING UNIT will appear to work on them simultaneously by switching very rapidly from one to the other (sometimes called "time-slicing").

Mump (*typ*) A typesetter's term, originally referring to HOT METAL MATS, but still used today with reference to digitized FONTS, meaning to move or copy fonts from one establishment to another (usually unauthorized). Probably derives from the old Dutch word "mompen," meaning "to cheat."

Munsell color system A system of color measurement and notation which defines all colors in terms of hue, value, and CHROMA.

Mutton, mutt (*typ*) A traditional term for an EM QUAD.

N

Nameplate The bold or elaborate printing of the title of a newspaper, as it usually appears at the top of the front page.

Nanosecond (ns) (*com*) A measure of speed, being

one billionth of a second – the fewer ns, the faster.

Naturals see CENTER FOLD.

Neck line (*typ*) The amount of white or leading under a RUNNING HEAD.

Negative (**1** *pho/rep*) A photographic film or paper in which all the dark areas appear light and vice versa. Negatives are used extensively in the reproduction process and are either made direct from originals or from a positive, or produced by an imagesetter. (**2** *com*) Facility (sometimes called "inverting"), of some computer APPLICATIONS, to reverse the screen bit map so that the black PIXELS appear white and vice versa.

Negative leading/line spacing (*typ*) In text, a LINE INTERVAL smaller than the POINT size of the type.

Network (*com*) The interconnection of two or more computers and PERIPHERAL DEVICES, and the HARDWARE and SOFTWARE used to connect them.

Newsprint (*pap*) The paper used for printing newspapers, characteristically absorbent because it is unsized.

Newton rings (*rep*) Patterns occurring when there is interference in the path of light at the contact of two lenses or a convex lens and a plane surface.

Next reading/text matter An instruction to place advertisement COPY next to editorial copy in a publication.

Nibble, nybble (*com*) Half a BYTE (four BITS).

Nipping (*fin*) Pressing a book after sewing, but before FORWARDING. This flattens the BOLTS and expels air from between the SHEETS.

Non-lining figures/ numerals (*typ*) A set of old-style numerals designed with descenders and ascenders (as 1 2 3 4 5 6 7 8 9 0), therefore not of a standard height and alignment, as are lining figures.

Nonpareil (*typ*) The name for an old type size, approximately equal to 6 POINTS. Sometimes used (although increasingly rarely) as an alternative term to indicate spacing.

Not (*pap*) A finish in high-quality RAG PAPERS, which is halfway between rough and HOT-PRESSED.

np *abb* New paragraph. See BLIND P.

O

Object-oriented (*com*) Of graphics APPLICATIONS, those that allow the selection and manipulation of individual, but self-contained, portions of an illustration or design, as distinct from BITMAPPED GRAPHICS which are edited by modifying PIXELS or turning them on or off. An object-oriented application uses mathematical points, based on vectors (information giving both magnitude and direction), to define lines and shapes. Strictly speaking, these points are the "objects" referred to here (as distinct from an illustration, or graphic, as an object) – an object in computer programming is a DATABASE of mathematical formulae. The DATA for each shape is stored in these points, each one a database, which in turn pass information from one to the other on how the paths between them should be described – as straight lines, arcs, or BÉZIER CURVES. This means that the quality of the line between each point is determined entirely by the RESOLUTION of the OUTPUT DEVICE – a line produced by an IMAGESETTER at 2,400dpi will be very much smoother than the same line output on a laser printer at 300dpi.

Oblique stroke (*typ*) see SOLIDUS.

OCR (*typ*) *abb* OPTICAL CHARACTER RECOGNITION.

Octavo A SHEET of paper folded in half three times, to make eighths, or sixteen pages. It also refers to a standard BROADSIDE divided into eight parts.

Off-line (*com*) Work done in relation to a computer or network, but not actually done on the computer or while connected to the network. The opposite of ON-LINE.

Offprint (*pri*) A REPRINT of an article or other part of a publication, produced as a separate item.

Offset lithography (*pri*) A method of lithography, developed separately in the U.S. in the early 1900s by Ira Rubel, Alex Sherwood, and the Harris brothers, in which the image is printed indirectly by "offsetting" it first onto a rubber-covered cylinder, called a "BLANKET," from which the image is printed. It is the most widely used commercial printing process and is sometimes called photolithography.

This book was printed by the offset lithography process.

Offside (*fin*) The part of the CASE which comes at the end of the book.

Old face/old style (*typ*) Type form characterized by diagonal stress and sloped, bracketed SERIFS.

On-line (*com*) Work done on a computer or while connected to a network.

One-and-a-half up ARTWORK prepared at one-and-a-half times the size at which it will eventually be reproduced. It will need to be reduced by one third or to 66 percent, to be the correct size.

Onion skin (*pap*) A thin, translucent paper with a glazed finish used for carbon copies and overlays.

Opacity (*pap*) The term used to describe non-transparency in printing papers.

Opaline (*pap*) A semi-opaque paper, fine and with a highly glazed finish.

Opaquing (*rep*) To paint out unwanted areas in a NEGATIVE (1) with opaque solution before processing the image.

op cit *abb* opere citato, a Latin term meaning "in the work quoted," used as a FOOTNOTE reference.

Operating system (*com*) The SOFTWARE and FIRMWARE that provides the environment within which a computer user operates.

Optical alignment (*typ*) An arrangement of (usually curved or pointed) characters allowing a degree of projection beyond the margin when vertically aligned, to give an overall appearance of alignment between the main vertical strokes. Horizontal optical alignment is normally already designed into a typeface.

Optical character recognition (OCR) (*typ*) A means of inputting copy, without the need to key it in, by using software which, when used with a scanner, converts typescript into editable computer text.

Optical disc/media (*com*) A medium for storing digitized DATA by means of minute pits (the size of which represents a 1 or a 0) imbedded into the disc. They are "read" by an optical pickup using a LASER which is reflected off the disc's surface by a shiny metallic layer. Usually referred to as CDs (compact discs), optical discs are widely used for audio and video recording and computer data storage, and are capable of holding huge amounts of data. CDs are more resilient to damage than magnetic media, but are also much slower.

Optical/optically even spacing (*typ*) The adjustment of letterspaces between CHARACTERS (1) to give an even appearance to a line of type.

Original (*pri*) Any MATTER or image intended for reproduction.

Ornament (*typ*) Decorative elements used with type MATTER such as FLOWERS, BORDERS, etc. Also called DINGBATS.

Orphan (*typ*) A short line, usually the last line of a paragraph, that falls at the top or bottom of a page or column.

Orthochromatic (*pho/rep*) Refers to photographic materials sensitive to green and yellow as well as blue light.

Out of register (*pri*) see REGISTER.

Outline font (*com*) A TYPEFACE formed from an outline which can be scaled or rotated to any size or RESOLUTION. Outline fonts, often called printer fonts or LASER fonts, are generally used for printing by laser printers and IMAGESETTERS, but both POSTSCRIPT and TRUETYPE font outlines are also used for screen display (PostScript outline FONTS require the UTILITY Adobe Type Manager (ATM) to be installed on the computer in order that they can be used for screen rendering). As distinct from BITMAPPED fonts which consist of dots and are used to render PostScript fonts on screen if ATM is not installed on the computer.

Outline letters (*typ*) TYPEFACES in which the letters are formed of outlines rather than solid strokes.

Output device (*com*) Any hardware device capable of displaying or producing data from a computer in a visible form, e.g. a IMAGESETTER, MONITOR, printer, plotter, etc.

Overexposure (*rep*) In conventional reproduction, a fault in platemaking caused when the light source is too close to the VACUUM FRAME.

Overhang cover (*fin*) A book COVER that projects past the trimmed edges of the leaves.

Overmatter (*typ*) The traditional term for typeset matter which will not fit within the space allocated for it.

Overprint (**1** *pri*) To make a second printing, or "pass" (not always in an additional color), on a previously printed sheet. (**2** *pri*) To print two or more colors so that they overlap, thus producing more colors. The opposite of "knockout."

Overs, overruns (*pri*) The term describing printed copies beyond the number ordered. This is normally deliberate to allow for copies that may be ruined during finishing or lost or damaged during shipping.

Oversize (**1**) A term used to describe artwork made at a larger size than that intended for reproduction. (**2** *pap*) A size of paper cut larger than the basic size. (**3** *pri/fin*) A size of book or publication that is larger than the capabilities of all or part of the printing and binding processes and thus may involve some handwork.

Ozalid (*rep*) A brand-name copy made by the DIAZO process and often used to refer to the prepress proofs of an imposed publication.

P

Packing (*pri*) To place paper under a PLATE or BLANKET in printing to guarantee firm contact of surfaces to produce an even quality of print.

Page (**1**) One side of a leaf. (**2** *com*) A contiguous SEGMENT of MEMORY.

Page description language (PDL) (*com*) A type of programming language used to describe image and FONT DATA to a printer so that the printer can construct and print the data to your specifications. POSTSCRIPT is the most widely used PDL.

Page make-up (*rep*) See MAKE-UP.

Page proof (*rep*) A proof of a page that has been paginated. Traditionally, the term refers to the secondary stage in proofing, after galley proofs and before machine proofs, although there may be other stages of proofing both before and after page proofs, such as the "blues" used to check imposition.

Pages to view (*pri*) The number of pages visible on one side of a SHEET that will be, or has been, printed on both sides.

Pagination (*rep*) Strictly speaking, the term given to the numbering of book pages, but also commonly used to describe make-up of material into pages after typesetting and origination.

Pallet (**1**) A wooden storage device on which SHEETS of paper are stacked. (**2** *fin*) A small hand-tool in which letters are placed and heated to stamp the COVER of a book.

Pamphlet A short publication presented unbound and in a soft COVER.

Panchromatic (*pho*) Photographic material which is sensitive to all visible colors and to ultraviolet light.

PANTONE® (*pho*) Pantone, Inc.'s check-standard trademark for color standards, control, and quality requirements. It is a system in which each color bears a description of its formulation (in percentages) for subsequent use by the printer. It is also a system that is used throughout the world, so that colors specified by any designer can be matched exactly by any printer. Computer VDU simulations, supported by some graphics applications, are unlikely to match PANTONE-identified solid color standards, and a current PANTONE color reference manual should always be used to match colors accurately. Pantone, Inc., are extremely vigilant about protecting their system, and conditions for specification and reproduction are very stringent. They will not permit the use of their trademark PMS, the initials of PANTONE MATCHING SYSTEM, and note that in all the references contained in this glossary the word PANTONE appears in capitals – this is another requirement. If you have any doubts about the way in which you want to specify colors – particularly if you are actually reproducing a reference to a PANTONE color – fax the Trademark Control Department at Pantone, Inc., on 201-896-0242.

Paper to paper (*pri*) see FOLD TO PAPER.

Paperback A book with a soft outer COVER made of thick paper.

Paragraph mark (*typ*) A type CHARACTER (1) resembling a reversed P (¶) used to denote the start of a paragraph if text is not indented. See BLIND P.

Parallel (typ) A type CHARACTER (1) in the form of a double vertical bar, used as a reference mark for FOOTNOTES.

Parallel fold (fin) A SHEET (1) folded in half widthwise and then in half again, the second fold parallel to the first.

Parallel interface (com) A computer INTERFACE in which eight BITS (or more) of DATA are transmitted simultaneously in the same direction along a single cable. As distinct from SERIAL INTERFACE.

Parentheses (typ) Strictly speaking, the term refers to a nonessential word, clause, or sentence that is inserted into a text and which can be marked off by brackets, dashes, or commas. However, the term usually describes the pair of rounded brackets ( ) themselves.

Paring (fin) In hand-binding, paring is thinning and chamfering the edges of leather to give a neat turn-in over the boards.

Partition(ing) (com) To divide up a HARD DISK into smaller VOLUMES, each one treated as if it were a separate disk. There are two kinds of partitions – SCSI (real partitions) and FILE partitions, the latter being large files rather than proper mountable volumes.

Pass (pri) The full operational cycle of a printing press, whether it be a single-color press or a four-color press. Subsequent passes of a sheet through a printing press may be required to achieve such things as more colors than the first pass would permit, or to overprint inks.

Paste-up (pri) A layout of a page or pages incorporating all the design elements such as text, illustrations, and rules. A paste-up may be either "rough," in which case, while including all the design elements, it will not be used for final reproduction (except, perhaps, as a guide), or it may be "CAMERA-READY" (also called "MECHANICALS"), in which case it will be photographed to make negatives or positives for reproduction.

Pasting in/on (pri) see TIP IN.

Patent A license granted to a person registering a new invention, object, or process, that protects the inventor's rights.

PE (pri) abb Printer's error. A PROOF CORRECTION MARK showing where an error is the fault of the TYPESETTER, not from editor's or author's COPY.

Peculiars (typ) Type CHARACTERS (1) for non-standard accent-bearing letters used when setting certain foreign languages. Also called special sorts.

Perfect binding (fin) A binding method in which the leaves of a book are trimmed at the back and glued, but not sewn.

Perfecting (pri) see BACK UP (1).

Perfecting press, perfector (pri) A press which prints both sides of the paper at a single PASS. All WEB-OFFSET machines are perfectors.

Perforate (1 pri) "Print" perforation is to make broken slotted rules so that MATTER can be torn off. (2 fin) "Pin-hole" perforation is to punch holes, such as in postage stamps.

Peripheral (**device**) (com) Any item of HARDWARE that is connected to a computer, such as a printer, scanner, or HARD DISK DRIVE.

Photocomposition/ phototypesetting/ filmsetting (typ) Strictly speaking, typesetting produced on photographic paper or film from a film matrix, but now extended to include, by virtue of the output medium being photographically based, computer typesetting produced on an imagesetter.

Photodirect (pri) The description of a method of producing plates for PHOTOLITHOGRAPHY from ORIGINAL ARTWORK without an INTERNEGATIVE being made.

Photoengraving (rep) A PHOTOMECHANICAL method of producing etched line or HALFTONE plates.

Photogravure (pri) An intaglio printing process in which a photomechanically prepared surface holds ink in recessed cells. Widely used for long runs such as magazines.

Photolithography (pri) A method of lithographic printing in which the image is transferred to the plate photographically and printed on a lithographic printing machine. This is sometimes known as OFFSET.

Photomechanical (1 pri) A method of making printing plates that involves photographic techniques.

(**2**) The full version of the term "MECHANICAL."

Photomechanical transfer (rep) A method of photographically transferring images onto paper, film, or metal litho plates. An image produced by this method is commonly called a PMT. Also called diffusion, or chemical transfer, or "velox."

Photomicrography (pho) A way of photographing minute objects using a combination of camera and microscope.

Photomontage (pho) The use of images from different photographs combined to produce a new, composite image.

Photo-opaque (rep) A general term for opaque solutions used to paint out parts of process NEGATIVES.

Photopolymer plates (pri) A light-sensitive polymer or plastic used either as a coating for LITHO plates or as a relief printing plate in its own right for LETTERPRESS or FLEXO, in which case it may have the non-image areas developed away by a solution of alcohol.

Photosensitive (pho) A material treated chemically to become light-sensitive.

Phototypesetting (typ) see PHOTOCOMPOSITION.

Pi characters (typ) see SPECIAL SORTS.

Pica (typ) A unit of typographic measurement, one pica consists of 12 points, and, in true typesetting values, one inch comprises 6.0225 picas or 72.27 points. However, computer applications use the PostScript value of exactly six picas, or 72 points, to the inch.

Picking (pri) Lifting of small scraps of the paper surface in printing, caused by tacky ink or poor-quality paper.

Pictogram/pictograph A sign in the form of a picture showing a simplified image of the object symbolized.

Pin register (rep) In conventional reproduction, a method of securing overlays to keep them in REGISTER.

Pinhole (rep) An unexposed speck on a photographic NEGATIVE, sometimes caused by dust on a lens or film.

Pixel (com) abb Picture element. An individual dot of light on your MONITOR which contributes to forming an image. The more pixels there are per inch, the higher the resolution of your monitor. In its simplest form (MONOCHROME), one pixel corresponds to a single BIT in RAM: 0 = off, or white, and 1 = on, or black. On color or GRAYSCALE monitors, one pixel may correspond to several bits; i.e., an 8-bit pixel can be displayed in any of 256 colors (the total number of different configurations that can be achieved by eight 0s and 1s).

Pixel depth (*com*) A term used to describe the number of colors or grays a single PIXEL can display. This is determined by the number of BITS used to display a pixel. Thus 1-bit equals 1 color (black), 4-bits (any permutation of four 1s and 0s, i.e. 0011 or 1001) equals 16 colors or grays, and so on, up to 24-bits which can produce 16.7 million combinations of twenty-four 0s and 1s, thus 16.7 million colors.

Pixelation (*com*) A term used to describe the effect of an image that has been broken up into square blocks, resembling PIXELS, to give it a "digitized" look.

Planographic (*pri*) Any method of printing from a flat surface, as in LITHOGRAPHY.

Plastic comb/coil binding (*fin*) Mechanical BINDING METHOD using a plastic SPINE with ringed teeth to secure leaves.

Plate (**1** *pri*) A sheet of metal (usually), plastic, or paper from which an image is printed (or transferred, in offset litho, to a blanket and then printed). (**2**) Strictly speaking, a book illustration printed separately from the text and then tipped or bound into the book, but sometimes erroneously used to describe a full-page illustration printed in a book. (**3** *pho*) A size of photographic film, a whole plate measuring 6½ x 8½in. and a half plate measuring 4 x 6½in.

Plate cylinder (*pri*) On a printing press, the cylinder that supports the inked plate.

Platen press (*pri*) A printing press in which a flat plate, or platen, is lowered and pressed against a horizontal FORME.

Plugging (*pri*) A condition in platemaking when COPY is marked or damaged and DOT areas have filled in.

Ply (*pap*) A measurement of the thickness of board stock, deriving from the number of layers in the composition of a SHEET.

PMT (*rep*) abb PHOTOMECHANICAL TRANSFER.

Pocket envelope (*pap*) An envelope with the flap opening on the shorter of its dimensions.

Point (*typ*) Standard unit of type size. In the British-American system, it is 0.013837in, or about 72 to the inch. The Continental (DIDOT) point is calculated differently.

Pointer (*com*) A general term that refers to any of the many shapes of marker on a MONITOR which identifies the current screen location of the MOUSE, the current position in a piece of text, or that the computer is undertaking a particular activity. Typical pointer shapes are the arrow pointer, vertical bar, I-beam, crossbar, or crosshair. Sometimes called a "cursor."

Point of sale The term for display equipment and advertising matter placed in a sales area close to the commodity it concerns.

Polarizing filter (*pho*) A FILTER used in photography which eliminates reflections from water and glass and which will also adjust color balance.

Polaroid (*pho*) A brand-name method of self-processing photographic materials and the equipment in which they are used. These products are used extensively by professional photographers as a means of instantly assessing composition and lighting prior to the actual exposure of a shot.

Port (*com*) Sockets in a computer, or PERIPHERAL DEVICE, into which other devices are plugged.

Portrait/upright Description of an image or page in a vertical format.

Positive (**1** *pho/rep*) An image made photographically on paper or film, usually derived from a NEGATIVE. (**2** *rep*) A photographic color TRANSPARENCY or film with a positive image, used in platemaking.

Posterize To divide a continuous tone image into a predefined or arbitrary number of flat tones.

Postlims SEE END MATTER.

PostScript (*com*) Adobe Systems Inc.'s PAGE DESCRIPTION LANGUAGE (PDL) for image output to LASER printers and high-resolution IMAGESETTERS.

Pothook (*typ*) The sharply curved terminal of a CHARACTER (1), particularly notable in ITALIC TYPEFACES, as: *h*

p, pp abb Page, pages.

Preface An author's statement in the PRELIMS of a book.

Preferences (*com*) An option in many APPLICATIONS to enable or disable features of the application (such as the unit of measurement) and to modify the PROGRAM default settings. Preferences can be modified for a single DOCUMENT or, sometimes, all documents – if none are open when you make the modifications.

Prelims, preliminary matter The pages of a book preceding the main text, usually consisting of the half title, title, preface, and contents.

Pre-make-ready (*pri*) The checking and preparation of printing plates before they are made ready on the press.

Preprint (**1** *rep*) Any MATTER printed separately and pasted to CAMERA READY ART. (**2** *pri*) A SHEET, or sheets, printed in advance of a publication to form a loose INSET in bound copies.

Presentation visual Material prepared as a sample of the proposed appearance of a printed work. Also called a finished rough, it may consist of drawings, typeset COPY, photographically produced prints, or a combination of such elements.

Press proof (*rep*) The last PROOF to be read before giving authorization for printing.

Press run (*pri*) In the printing of a publication, the total number of copies produced in one printing.

Primary colors Pure colors from which theoretically, although not in practice, all other colors can be mixed. In printing they are the so-called "subtractive" pigment primaries: cyan, magenta, and yellow. The primary colors of light, or "additive" primaries, are red, green, and blue.

Print origination (*rep*) In printing, all preparatory work completed prior to proofing.

Print run (*pri*) The number of copies required from a printer and the process of printing the copies.

Print to paper (*pri*) An instruction to print a quantity according to the supply of paper available without fixing the number of copies required.

Printer (pri) The film or plate of a single color produced for four-color process printing.

Printer's ornament (typ) see ORNAMENT.

Printer's reader (typ) see READER.

Printing down frame (rep) see VACUUM FRAME.

Printing processes The generic processes are INTAGLIO (e.g. GRAVURE), PLANOGRAPHIC (e.g. LITHOGRAPHY), RELIEF (e.g. LETTERPRESS), and stencil (e.g. SCREEN PRINTING).

Printmaking (pri) A term referring to printing processes used in making fine art print editions.

Printout (com) A general term for the record of information made by a printing device attached to a computer.

Process camera (rep) A specially designed graphics art camera used in conventional PHOTOMECHANICAL reproduction techniques.

Process colors (rep) see CYAN, MAGENTA, yellow.

Process inks (pri) Printer's inks in the PROCESS COLORS.

Process white An opaque white gouache for correction and MASKING (2) of ARTWORK intended for reproduction.

Program (com) A set of coded instructions that controls the operation of a computer.

Progressive proofs (rep) PROOFS used in color printing to show all colors both separately and in combination.

Promotion Presentation and advertising intended to encourage the production and marketing of a product.

Proof (typ/rep/pri) A representation on paper, taken from a laser printer, imagesetter, inked plate, stone, screen, block, or type, in order to check the progress and accuracy of the work. Also called a "pull."

Proof correction marks (typ) A standard set of signs and symbols commonly understood by all those involved in preparing copy for publication. Text proof correction marks vary from country to country, but color correction signs are more or less internationally recognized.

Proofreader (typ) A person who reads proofs for corrections and marks

them accordingly.

Proofing press (rep) A press, sometimes hand-operated, usually smaller than that used in the full PRINT RUN, on which COPY is proofed.

Protocol (com) A set of mutually agreed rules that HARDWARE and SOFTWARE must observe in order to communicate with one another.

Prove (typ/rep/pri) An alternative term for proofing.

Publisher The company or individual responsible for the distribution and marketing of published works.

Publisher's ream (pap) A bulk quantity of paper consisting of 516 sheets, being more than the standard 500 sheets of a ream (20 quires) to allow for wastage.

Pull (typ/rep/pri) see PROOF.

Pull out (pri) see FOLDOUT.

Pull-out section (pri) Pages of a periodical that can be detached all together and kept as a separate entity.

Pulling (pri) see PICKING.

Pulp (pap) The basic material used in papermaking, broken down chemically or mechanically.

Punch register (rep) A device used in close REGISTER work, requiring holes punched in COPY, film, or plate so they can be assembled on register pins.

Put down/up (typ) An instruction to the typesetter to change CHARACTERS (1) to LOWER CASE (down) or CAPS (up).

Put to bed (pri) The state of printing plates when they are secured to the press ready to print.

Q

QA abb Query author, used as a mark on COPY being edited.

Quad (**1** typ) In conventional typesetting, a space whose width is normally that of its height, thus "to quad," or "quadding," is to fill out a line with quad spaces. (**2** pap) Four times the normal paper size 35 x 45in. (890 x 1143mm).

Quadding (typ) See QUAD (1).

Quarter-bound (fin) A case binding in which the back is covered in one material and the sides in another, e.g. leather back with cloth sides.

Quarto (pap) A piece of

paper folded in half twice, making quarters or eight pages.

Quire (**1** pap) 25 sheets of paper (formerly 24). (**2** fin) Four sheets folded once to form eight leaves, or 16 pages. (**3** fin) A collection of unbound leaves, one within the other.

Quires, quire stock (fin) The SHEETS of a book which are folded, but not yet bound. See FOLDED AND GATHERED.

Quotes, quotation marks (typ) Inverted commas and apostrophes, either single (' ') or double (" "), used before and after a word or phrase to indicate that it is a quotation, title of something, jargon or slang, etc.

qv abb Quod vide, a Latin term meaning "which see," used to accompany a cross-referenced term.

R

® The symbol denoting a REGISTERED DESIGN.

R&D abb Research and development.

RA paper sizes (pap) The designation of untrimmed paper sizes in the ISO A series of INTERNATIONAL PAPER SIZES.

Rag paper (pap) High-quality writing paper made from rag PULP.

Ragged left/right (typ) Typeset COPY in which the lines of type are not aligned at left/right. See UNJUSTIFIED.

RAM (com) abb Random access MEMORY. The working space instantly available to you when you use a computer. When an APPLICATION is launched or a DOCUMENT is opened, it is loaded into RAM and stored there while being worked with. However, an item only stays in RAM for as long as a computer is switched on, or until it is written, or "saved," to DISK. Size of memory is important, since not only do some graphics applications require substantial memory to operate, some tasks may demand even more.

Raised capital (typ) see COCKED-UP INITIAL.

Raised point/dot (typ) A period printed at half the height of CAPITALS rather than on the BASE LINE (1).

Ranged left/right (typ) A style of typesetting in which lines of unequal length line up on either the left or right of a column of text so that they are vertically flush with each other, leaving the opposite ends of the lines uneven or "ragged."

Ranging figures (*typ*)
see LINING FIGURES.

Raster (*com*) The method of displaying (and of creating) images used on video screens, and thus MONITORS. The screen image is made up of a pattern of several hundred parallel lines created by an electron beam "raking" the screen from top to bottom at a speed of about one sixtieth of a second ("raster" comes from the Latin word "rastrum," meaning "rake"). An image is created by the varying intensity of brightness of the beam at successive points along the raster. The speed at which a complete screen image, or frame, is created is called the "frame" or "refresh" rate. See also RIP (1).

Raster image processor (*com*) see RIP (1).

Reader (*typ*) A person who reads and corrects the printer's PROOFS against the ORIGINAL MANUSCRIPT.

Read/write head (*com*) The part of a DISK DRIVE that extracts (reads) DATA from, and deposits (writes) data to, a disk. One read/write head is positioned above each side of every disk platter (a hard drive may consist of several platters). These move, on rails, over the surface of the platter while the platter rotates at speed.

Real time (*com*) The term used to describe the actual time in which events occur, thus on a computer, an event that corresponds to reality. For example, at its very simplest, a character appearing on screen the moment that it is typed, is said to be real-time, as is a video sequence that corresponds to actual clock time.

Ream (*pap*) A standard quantity of paper, usually 500 sheets, although an extra number may be allowed for wastage.

Reciprocity law failure (*pho*) An exception to mathematical law in photographic processing. A short exposure under a bright light does not produce the same result as a long exposure in a dim light, although mathematically it should. The effect produced varies with film types, but on color film, a color caste may occur, so only the exposure range that the film was designed for should be used.

Record (*com*) A set of related fields in a DATABASE which makes up an individual entry.

Recto The right-hand page of a book, or the front of a leaf.

Reducer (*pho/rep*) A chemical which acts upon a photographic image to reduce its density.

Reel fed (*pri*) see WEB-FED.

Reference marks (*typ*) Typographic term describing symbols used in text to refer to footnotes, e.g. an asterisk (*) or dagger (†).

Reflection copy (*rep*) Any flat item which is reproduced by photographic means, using light reflected from its surface. As distinct from a transparency, or slide, original.

Register (*pri*) The correct positioning of one color on top of another or of the pages on one side of a sheet relative to the other (called "backing up") during printing. When a color or page is incorrectly positioned, it said to be "out-of-register." As distinct from "fit."

Register marks (*rep/pri*) The marks used on artwork, film, and printing plates, which are superimposed during printing to make sure that the work is in register. Many computer applications automatically generate register marks outside of the page area.

Register ribbon (*fin*) The ribbon fastened at the back of a book as a book-mark.

Registered design A design officially registered by a PATENT office, to give some protection against plagiarism.

Relief printing (*pri*) The method of printing from a raised surface, as in LETTERPRESS printing.

Relief stamping (*fin*) see DIE STAMPING.

Reportage (*pho*) A style of photojournalism conveying information through graphic images.

Reprint (*pri*) The second or subsequent printing of a publication.

Reproduction copy (*rep*) see CAMERA READY.

Reproduction proof/ repro (*rep*) High-quality PROOFS on art paper, which can be used as CAMERA-READY ART.

Resin coated paper (*pap*) Paper for photographic printing in which the sensitized surface is strengthened with a layer of polyethylene.

Resolution (*rep*) The degree of precision – the quality, definition, or clarity – with which an image is represented or displayed, such as by a scanner, MONITOR screen, printer, or other output DEVICE.

Resolving power (*pho*) The capacity of a photographic lens or EMULSION to record fineness of detail.

Rest in proportion/pro see RIP (2).

Reticulation (*pho*) A variously desirable or undesirable aberration in photographic processing where the clustering of molecules in a film emulsion causes a disrupted, "crazed" pattern. This happens as a result of temperature changes in processing.

Retouching (*rep*) Altering or correcting an image, artwork, or film by hand to make modifications or remove imperfections. Scanned images are usually retouched electronically using appropriate software.

Retree (*pap*) A term referring to a batch of paper that is of substandard quality.

Retroussage (*pri*) The term given to flicking a soft rag lightly over a wiped INTAGLIO PLATE, to draw out the ink slightly and give a softer line.

Reversal film (*pho*) Film emulsion that produces a positive image, as in color transparencies.

Reverse b to w (*rep*) abb Reverse black to white. Instruction to REVERSE OUT an image or type.

Reverse indent (*typ*) see HANGING INDENT.

Reverse l to r (*rep*) abb Reverse left to right. An instruction to the printer to reverse an image laterally. See: LATERAL REVERSE; FLOP.

Reverse out (*rep*) To reverse the tones of an image or type so that it appears white (or another color) in a black or colored background. Also called "drop out," "save out."

Reverse P (*typ*) see BLIND P; PARAGRAPH MARK.

Reverse reading (*rep*) See WRONG READING.

Revise (*typ/rep*) A PROOF which incorporates corrections or revisions marked on an earlier proof.

Rider roller (*pri*) Printing press cylinder that rotates under the force of another cylinder.

Right-angle/chopper fold (*fin*) The standard method of folding a SECTION (1). A SHEET is folded in half, then halved again at right angles to the first fold.

Right reading (*rep*) Description of negative or positive film on which the text, if any, can be read as normal, i.e. from left to right, and in which the photographic emulsion is on the underside. Opposite of WRONG READING.

RIP (**1** *com*) *abb* RASTER image processor, a device that converts DATA generated by a PAGE DESCRIPTION LANGUAGE, such as POSTSCRIPT, into a form which can be output by a high-resolution IMAGESETTER for use in commercial printing. (**2** *rep*) *abb* Rest in pro(portion), an instruction to reproduce an image or ARTWORK, giving only one dimension – the rest to be reduced or enlarged in proportion.

Rivers (*typ*) An aberration in typeset text, in which a series of word spaces form a linked or continuous stream of white space down a page. Often caused by badly justified type.

Roll stand (*pri*) A stand supporting the WEB of a WEB-FED printing press.

Roll-up (*pri*) A check of the first IMPRESSIONS taken while a printing plate is being inked.

ROM (*com*) *abb* Read only MEMORY. Memory which can only be read from, and not written to. ROM is where the "FIRMWARE" part (meaning SOFTWARE that's permanently built in and cannot be changed) of the computer's OPERATING SYSTEM is kept. The DATA stored in ROM can only be updated by changing the ROM CHIP, which is why the constantly changing part of the operating system is provided as DISK-based software. As distinct from the memory stored in RAM, which is lost when power to the computer is switched off.

Roman (*typ*) The standard characters of a font in which the characters are upright, as distinct from ITALIC.

Roman numerals (*typ*) A system of numerical notation based on the symbols I (one), V (five), X (10), L (50), C (100), D (500), and M (1000), used in combinations to represent any number.

ROP (**1** *pri*) *abb* RUN OF PRESS (**2** *pri*) *abb* RUN OF PAPER, see PRINT TO PAPER.

Rotary press (*pri*) A REEL or WEB-FED newspaper press which uses a cylindrical printing surface.

The papers are delivered folded and counted, ready to be dispatched.

Rotogravure (*pri*) INTAGLIO printing performed on a ROTARY PRESS.

Rough A sketch showing a proposed design. Also called a "scamp."

Rough draft An initial stage of a MANUSCRIPT or text, which will be subsequently edited or rewritten.

Round and back (*fin*) Refers to a concave appearance at the FOREDGE of a book and a convex back with a projecting SHOULDER.

Rub-ons A colloquial term for DRY TRANSFER LETTERING.

Rule (*typ*) A line. The term derives from the Latin "regula" meaning "straight stick" and was used to describe the metal strips, of type height, in various widths, lengths, and styles, which were used by traditional typesetters for printing lines.

Run (*pri*) The number of impressions taken from a PLATE at one time.

Run-in heading (*pri*) A HEADING leading into text starting in the same line, as distinct from a heading placed above text.

Run-of-paper (**1** *pri*) see PRINT TO PAPER. (**2**) The position of advertising matter in a newspaper or periodical which gives no display advantages.

Run of press (*pri*) In newspaper and similar work, color printing carried out at the same time as the main run, rather than supplied to the newspaper as a preprinted item.

Run on (**1** *pri*) Sheets printed in addition to the specified quantity. (**2** *typ*) An instruction that two paragraphs are to be set as one as indicated.

Run ragged (*typ*) see RAGGED RIGHT.

Run through work (*pri*) The printing of even, parallel lines across a SHEET using a machine designed for the purpose.

Runaround (*typ*) Text that fits around a shape such as an illustration.

Runners (*typ*) Numbers placed in the MARGIN of a text to form references for identifying particular lines.

Running head (*typ*) The line of type which repeats a chapter HEADING, etc., at the top of a page.

Running text (*typ*) The main BODY of a text which runs from page to page, although it may be broken up by illustrations or other

matter.

S

Saddleback book (*fin*) A book with INSET leaves, secured by stitching.

Saddle-stitch/wire (*fin*) A method of securing pages in a brochure by stitching them, while they are opened over a saddle-shaped support, through the back with wire staples. Also called "wire-stitch."

Sans serif (*typ*) Description of a generic type style without SERIFS and usually without stroke contrast.

Satin finish (*pap*) A smoothly finished paper with a sheen to the surface.

Save (*com*) To transfer, or "write," from RAM to DISK – in other words, making sure that your work is preserved by saving it.

Save out see REVERSE OUT.

sc, s caps (*typ*) *abb* SMALL CAPS.

Scale drawing An illustration, such as a map or technical illustration, which represents an object and its parts in correct proportion to the actual size.

Scaling, scaling up (*rep*) To determine the degree of enlargement or reduction required to obtain the desired reproduction size of an image.

Scamp A ROUGH sketch showing the basic idea for an advertisement or design.

Scanner (*rep/com*) An electronic device which converts ARTWORK and TRANSPARENCIES into digital form so that they can be manipulated on a computer and/or output to separated film. A scanner may be a relatively simple "desktop" flatbed type which is really only suitable, in design terms, for scanning line art, halftones FOR POSITION ONLY, and text input (using an OPTICAL CHARACTER RECOGNITION application). Alternatively, a scanner may be a very sophisticated reprographic device used for high-quality color separation, in which the original image is rotated on a cylinder at a very high speed while a laser beam analyzes its properties before sending the signal to a computer for digitizing and output as a file or as film.

Scatter proofs (*rep*) A PROOF of illustrations in which all the images are positioned at random and as closely packed as possible, without reference to their final page position. This is done in order to cut proofing costs, particularly when large numbers of illustrations are involved, such as in illustrated book work.

Score (*fin*) To make a crease in paper or card so that it will not be damaged by folding.

Scratch (**1** *com*) A term describing DISK space that you may not need for normal computer use, but which you have set aside by creating a PARTITION, in case an APPLICATION requests for temporary STORAGE. Scratch space is used extensively by image-editing and paint applications (these applications automatically create their own partitions). (**2**) Any space set aside for experimenting with ideas, techniques, etc. Commonly called a "scratch pad."

Scratch comma (*typ*) A comma in the form of a short, oblique line.

Screen (**1** *rep*) See HALFTONE SCREEN. (**2** *com*) See MONITOR.

Screen angle (*rep*) A term referring to the angle at which HALFTONE SCREENS of images printing in two or more colors are positioned, to minimize undesirable dot patterns (MOIRÉ) when they are printed.

Screen clash (*rep*) A disruptive pattern in an image produced when two or more HALFTONE SCREENS have been positioned at incorrect angles. See MOIRÉ.

Screen printing (*pri*) A printing process whereby ink is forced through a fine mesh stretched across a frame. The image is formed by means of a hand-cut or photographically generated stencil, which is bonded to the screen. Commercially, screen printing is generally used for printing onto difficult surfaces, for display work and for small print runs.

Screen ruling (*rep*) The grid on a CONTACT or HALFTONE SCREEN.

Scribing (*pri*) A method of altering or correcting an image on film or metal plate by scratching the surface.

Script (*typ*) A TYPEFACE designed to imitate handwriting.

SCSI (*com*) (pronounced skuzzy) A computer industry standard for

interconnecting PERIPHERAL DEVICES such as HARD DISK DRIVES and SCANNERS.

Scumming (*pri*) A condition when the non-printing areas of a PRINTING PLATE attract ink and transfer it to paper.

Second cover The page area on the inside of the front COVER of a publication.

Secondary colors Colors obtained when two PRIMARY COLORS are mixed.

Section (**1** *fin*) A sheet folded to form four or more pages of a book. (**2**) A division of a publication, either smaller than a chapter or consisting of more than one chapter. (**3**) A group of pages, numbered in sequence.

Section mark (*typ*) A type CHARACTER (§) used variously as a reference mark or to identify the beginning of a new SECTION.

Section-sewn book (*fin*) A book in which SECTIONS (1) are sewn together with threads after gathering.

Sector (*com*) A segment of a track on a DISK, containing space for 512 consecutive BYTES of DATA, and being the smallest contiguous space in which data can be stored.

See-through (*pap*) see LOOK-THROUGH.

Segment (*com*) A portion of an APPLICATION. An application may be made up of several segments, not all of which need to be in RAM at the same time.

Self cover (*fin*) A book COVER of the same paper stock as the LEAVES.

Self ends (*fin*) Endpapers formed from the first leaf of the first section and the last leaf of the last SECTION of a book, as distinct from endpapers that are tipped in, or "separate ends."

Separation (*rep*) see COLOR SEPARATION.

Separation artwork (*rep*) ARTWORK in which a separate layer is created for each color to be printed, as distinct from full-color artwork which requires the colors to be separated before printing.

Sepia toning (*pho*) A method of changing black-and-white photographic prints to sepia (brown) tones with chemical bleach and dye.

Serial interface (*com*) A computer INTERFACE which transmits DATA BITS sequentially, one at a time, in the same direction along a single wire or channel inside a cable. As distinct from a PARALLEL INTERFACE.

Serif (*typ*) The small terminal counterstrokes at the end of the main stroke of a type character.

Serigraphy (*pri*) An alternative term for SILKSCREEN process.

Service bureau (*com*) A company that provides general computer services from DISK conversion to color scanning. The main use of a bureau by designers is for high resolution IMAGESETTING – typesetting to bromide or film from your disk.

Set (*typ*) In traditional type design, the width of an individual character. The width, or set, of the widest character (an em) is measured in points and subdivided into units, the set of each other character being a multiple of these units. Not to be confused with "character set" – the full set of characters in a font.

Set and hold (*typ*) An instruction to the printer to prepare MATTER in readiness for future use.

Set close (*typ*) Describes type set with the minimum of space between the words and no extra space between sentences.

Set off (**1** *pri*) The accidental transfer of ink from a printed sheet onto the back of the next sheet. (**2** *pri*) In LITHOGRAPHY it refers to an impression taken from a KEY outline of a design which is powdered with a non-greasy dye while the ink is damp, then placed on the stone or plate and passed through the press.

Set solid (*typ*) Refers to type set without leading (line spaces).

Sewn book (*fin*) Any book, the SECTIONS (1) of which have been sewn together with thread.

Sexto, 6to (*fin*) A SHEET trimmed or folded to one sixth its basic size.

Shaded letter (**1** *typ*) see SHADOW FONT. (**2** *typ*) A letterform filled with hatched lines rather than solid tone.

Shadow font (*typ*) Letterforms given a three-dimensional appearance by heavy shadows beside the main strokes.

Shareware (*com*) The term describing SOFTWARE that is freely available through user groups, bulletin boards, etc., and which you pay for only if you decide to continue using it. Unlike public-domain software, shareware is protected by COPYRIGHT (not to be confused with "copy protected" – shareware, by its nature, is never copy-protected).

Sharpness (*pho*) A characteristic of a photographic image relating to its degree of clarity or FOCUS.

Sheet (*pap*) A single piece of paper, as distinct from paper on a roll ("WEB").

Sheet-fed (*pri*) A term describing sheets which are fed into a printing press one-by-one, as distinct from being "WEB-FED" (on a roll).

Sheet proof (*pri*) see IMPOSED PROOF.

Sheet stock (*fin*) Printed sheets which are not yet folded or bound, as distinct from QUIRE STOCK.

Sheeter (*pri*) A device that cuts SHEETS from a WEB in a WEB-FED printing press.

Sheetwise (*pri*) Printing the pages of a SECTION (1) by printing first one side, then the other of a SHEET.

Sheetwork (*pri*) A term describing printing work involving printing on both sides of a SHEET.

Shelfback (*fin*) see SPINE.

Short and (*typ*) see AMPERSAND.

Short ink (*pri*) Printing ink with a heavy texture that does not flow easily.

Short page (*typ*) A page with text shorter than usual length, adjusted to improve the LAYOUT or accommodate a break.

Shoulder The projection down each side of a book's SPINE, obtained by ROUNDING AND BACKING.

Shoulder notes (*typ*) The marginal notes at the top outer corners of a paragraph.

Show-through (*pap*) See LOOK-THROUGH.

Shrink wrapping (*fin*) Thin, transparent plastic film used in packaging. It is sealed tight around an object by heat action.

Shutter (*pho*) The mechanism of a camera that allows light to pass through from lens to film.

Side heading (*typ*) A subheading set FLUSH LEFT in the text.

Side notes (*typ*) Notes in the FOREDGE MARGIN or occasionally in the GUTTER outside the normal type area.

Side-stab/stitch (*fin*) A method of securing the SECTIONS (1) of a book, with wires passed through close to the BACK.

Signature (**1** *fin*) The consecutive number, letter, or other mark at the tail of each section in a book, which serves as a

guide for binding. (**2** *fin*) A numbered section prior to binding.

Silhouette halftone (*rep*) A HALFTONE image in which background tones have been reduced or eliminated to emphasize the outline of an object.

Silkscreen printing (*pri*) SCREEN PRINTING using a screen made of silk, the traditional method still often used in printing fine art editions.

Single-color press (*pri*) A printing press that has the facility to print only one color at a time, requiring separate runs for prints of more than one color.

Single lens reflex (*pho*) A rollfilm camera in which the image seen in the viewfinder and that recorded on the film are transmitted through the same lens.

Single printing (*pri*) Printing a SHEET on both sides by the WORK AND TUMBLE or WORK AND TURN methods.

Sinkage (*typ*) see CHAPTER DROP.

Sixteen mo, 16mo (*fin*) A SHEET folded or trimmed to one sixteenth its basic size.

Sixteen sheet (*pap*) A standard poster size measuring 120 x 80in. (3050 x 2030mm).

Size (*pap*) A gelatinous solution used to coat paper, to glaze or seal the surface and render the paper less porous. Size may be based on glue, CASEIN starch, or a similar substance.

Skew(ing) (*com*) In some APPLICATIONS, a feature enabling you to slant an item, such as a picture or word.

Slab serifs (*typ*) square serifs of almost the same thickness as the uprights used in most "Egyptian" TYPEFACES.

Slash (*typ*) see SOLIDUS.

Slip case (*fin*) An open-sided CASE to hold one or more books, with their SPINES showing.

Slip page/proof (*typ*) A GALLEY PROOF containing MATTER for one page.

Slip sheeting see INTERLEAVED.

Slit (*pri*) A cut made on the printing press by a rotary knife between IMPRESSION CYLINDER and delivery.

Sloped roman (*typ*) A term describing an ITALIC version of a font that is an optically or digitally distorted version of the ROMAN design, as distinct from being a separate, specially designed italic.

Slur (*pri*) In printing, the

"skidding," or smudged, appearance of an image, an aberration caused by excessive movement between PLATE and paper during IMPRESSION.

Small capitals (*typ*) Capital letters which are smaller than the standard size, usually being about the size of the X-HEIGHT. Traditionally, small caps were a specially designed and cut FONT, rather than just being a smaller size of type. However, on computers, small caps are generated by scaling a single outline printer font, resulting in small caps that are lighter in weight than the capitals and lower case. More fonts are becoming available which have a specially designed version for providing small caps, giving a much more even "color" to text setting.

Soft (**1** *pho*) Description of photographic paper which produces an image of low tonal contrast. (**2** *pho*) A term used to describe an image of low tonal contrast.

Soft copy (**1** *com*) A copy of a file or document supplied on a disk, as distinct from a "hard" copy of the file or document as a printout on paper. (**2** *com*) Text matter appearing on a computer monitor. (**3** *typ*) Typeset copy used for checking a text before CAMERA-READY ART is produced.

Soft cover (*fin*) A book COVER which is neither a CASE nor a SELF COVER. See also PAPERBACK.

Soft dot (*rep*) A HALFTONE DOT on film that is less dense at the edge than at the center and is thus easier to etch for correction purposes.

Soft focus (*pho*) A photographic effect in which the image is slightly diffused to soften the lines and edges of a shape without distorting the true FOCUS. There are different ways of achieving the effect, such as with a specially made filter or shooting through a glass plate smeared with petroleum jelly.

Software (*com*) The term used to describe specially written collections of data, called PROGRAMS, that make it possible for a computer or any other item of computer-related HARDWARE to perform its tasks.

Solarization (**1** *pho*) A method of creating a photographic image which is part positive, part negative, by exposing the film or paper to light during processing. (**2** com) A facility of some computer image-editing applications to simulate digitally.

Solidus (typ) A diagonal type CHARACTER (1) in the form of an oblique stroke, used as a fraction slash (/).

Solus position The position of an advertisement on a page where there is no other advertising MATTER.

Sort (**1** typ) A single CHARACTER (1) of type.(**2** com) A feature provided by some APPLICATIONS to arrange DATA in any chosen order.

Space (typ) An invisible, graded unit for spacing out a line of text.

Special sort (typ) Type CHARACTERS (1) not normally included in a FONT, or character set, such as fractions, musical notations, etc. Also called "peculiars" or "pi characters".

Specification, spec (typ/rep/pri) A detailed description of the components, characteristics, and procedures of a particular job, product, or activity.

Specimen page (typ/rep) A PROOF of a page as an example of a proposed style of design, paper quality, printing, etc.

Spectral sensitivity (pho) The relative sensitivity of a photographic material to different wavelengths of light.

SPH (pri) abb SHEETS per hour.

Spine (fin) The center of the CASE of a book, which runs down the BACK when it is cased in.

Spiral binder (fin) A spiral wire holding the leaves of a book together.

Splayed M (typ) A term for the CHARACTER M when the outer strokes are sloped.

Split boards (pap) Boards used for LIBRARY BINDING. A thick and thin board are pasted together, leaving a split about 1.5in (37.5mm) wide for inserting END PAPERS and tapes.

Split dash/rule (typ) A rule used as a traditional decoration. A split rule is one that is thick at its center and tapered toward the ends, and which is split at the center by a BULLET, STAR, or other ORNAMENT.

Split duct working (pri) A printing technique in which two colors can be printed in one pass on a single-color press by confining the inks to only those ducts that supply ink

to the desired printing tracks.

Spoils, spoilage (pri) Badly printed SHEETS which are discarded before delivery of a job.

Spotting (pho/rep) A term describing the retouching of photographic prints or film to eliminate unwanted spots, blemishes, or pinholes.

Spread SEE DOUBLE SPREAD.

Sprinkled edges (fin) Book edges colored with a brush full of liquid ink or with an AIRBRUSH. Used as decoration for books and also to hide the discoloration of cheap paper used for PAPERBACK books.

Squares (fin) The portion of the inside of a CASE which projects beyond the cut edges of a book.

Square back book (fin) A binding, either limp or cased, that has a square, or flat, spine – as distinct from ROUNDED AND BACKED.

Square serif (typ) see SLAB SERIF.

Squared-up halftone (rep) A HALFTONE image that has been trimmed ("cropped") to a square or rectangular shape.

SRA paper sizes (pap) The designation of untrimmed paper for bled work in the series of INTERNATIONAL PAPER SIZES.

S/S (rep) abb Same size. An instruction to reproduce an item at its original size.

Standing type/matter (typ/rep/pri) Any type matter, film or otherwise, that is held for reprinting if required.

Star (typ) A typographical ORNAMENT.

Starburst filter (pho) A photographic effect of radiating lines from a highlight, provided by a filter that diffuses light from a strong, concentrated source.

Stem (typ) The most distinctive vertical stroke, or the one closest to vertical, in a type CHARACTER (1). Originally the downward stroke of a pen in calligraphy.

Step and repeat To produce multiple copies of an image at different sizes in defined increments.

Step index (fin) An INDEX GUIDE in a book in which steps are cut down the FOREDGES of the page to provide a reference guide to the contents.

Stereo(type) (pri) A duplicate relief printing plate cast in metal, plastic, or rubber from a matrix or

mold.

Stet (typ) A Latin word meaning "let it stand." It is used when marking up copy and correcting PROOFS to cancel a previous instruction or correction.

Stiff leaves (fin) END PAPERS attached by glue to the full width of the first and last leaves of a book.

Stock (**1** pri) The metal part of a printing roller, covered with composition rubber. (**2** pri) The printer's term for paper, etc., to be used for printing.

Stop out (rep) A chemical treatment for printing plates that removes any unwanted COPY or marks.

Storage (com) The term used to describe DATA that is preserved for future use or modification, as distinct from MEMORY, in which data is merely "in transit."

Straight matter (typ) A BODY (2) of text without break for HEADINGS, illustrations, etc.

Strap (typ) A subheading that appears above the main HEADLINE of a newspaper or magazine story.

Strawboard (pap) A board traditionally made from straw, and now from pulp or waste. Used principally for making the covers of cased books. Cheaper and more prone to warping than a mill or binder's board.

Stress (typ) The apparent direction of a letterform, given emphasis by the heaviest part of a curved stroke.

Strike through (**1** pri) The discoloration on the reverse side of a sheet caused by ink soaking through a printed sheet. (**2** typ) The term describing type set with a horizontal rule passing through its center.

Stripping (**1** rep) Assembling two or more images to produce a composite for making final film in photomechanical reproduction. (**2** typ) To insert a typeset correction in film or on camera-ready art. (**3** fin) To glue a strip of cloth or paper to the back of a paperback book or pad as a reinforcement.

Stripping up as one (rep) Assembling two or more images to combine them into a single image for PHOTOMECHANICAL reproduction.

Subhead(ing) (typ) Any heading at the subdivisions of a chapter.

Subject (rep) The term used to describe any

single image which is to be reproduced or originated.

Subscript (*typ*) see INFERIOR CHARACTER.

Subtractive colors (*rep/pri*) The primary colors used in printing – cyan, magenta, and yellow – as distinct from the additive colors used in color monitors.

Subsidiaries see END MATTER.

Suction feed (*pri*) Mechanical paper feeding device using air suction to pass paper into a press or machine.

Supercalendered paper (*pap*) Smooth-surfaced paper produced by rolling it between metal CALENDERS or rollers.

Superior figure/letter (*typ*) The term used to describe figures or letters that are smaller than text size, the top of which is aligned with the cap height of the text as in (²), as distinct from superscript, which appears above the cap height (²).

Superscript (*typ*) see SUPERIOR FIGURE.

Supplement Material added to a publication separately or included in a REPRINT.

Surprinting (*pri*) see OVERPRINT.

Swash characters (*typ*) An old face italic type style with calligraphic flourishes.

Swatch (*rep/pri*) A sample of a color or paper.

Swell (*fin*) Extra bulking at the back of a book caused by the way the SECTIONS (1) have been sewn together.

Swelled dash/rule (*typ*) A RULE which prints as a thick line in the center, tapering at both ends.

Symbol (*typ*) A letter, figure, or drawn sign that represents or identifies an object, process, or activity, although not necessarily pictorially.

Synchronous communication (*com*) A communications PROTOCOL by which DATA is transmitted, in chunks, between rigid timing signals. As distinct from ASYNCHRONOUS communication.

Synopsis A condensed version of the thesis and contents of a proposed book or other item for publication, giving a clear breakdown of the likely or actual progression of the text.

System (*com*) A complete set of connected things, organized to achieve an objective.

T

Tab delimit (*com*) To separate DATA elements such as RECORDS or FIELDS by using the Tab key.

Tab index (*fin*) An index guide similar to a step index, except that the reference guides, or tabs, project from the pages of the book instead of being cut into them.

Tablet (*com*) see DIGITIZER.

Tabloid (*pri*) A page that is half the size of a BROADSHEET.

Tabular work (*typ*) Type MATTER set in COLUMNS (1).

Tabulate, tabulating (*typ*) To arrange text or figures in the form of a columnar table, according to fixed measures.

Tack (*pri*) The adhesive quality of a medium such as printing ink, and of adhesives and adhesive tape.

Tail The bottom edge of a book.

Tail margin The white area at the bottom of a page between the image and trimmed area, also called a FOOT MARGIN.

Tail piece A design, or graphic, at the end of a section, chapter, or book.

Take back (*typ*) An instruction, marked on a PROOF, to take back CHARACTERS, words, or lines to the preceding line, COLUMN, or page.

Take in (*typ*) An instruction, marked on a PROOF, to include extra COPY supplied.

Take over (*typ*) An instruction, marked on a PROOF, to take over CHARACTERS, words, or lines to the following line, COLUMN, or page.

Tear sheet An image, feature, or advertisement torn from a publication and filed as reference material.

Telephoto lens (*pho*) A camera lens designed to focus on distant objects since it gives a larger image than standard types of lenses.

Template (1) A shape, or sheet with cutout shapes, used as a drawing aid. (**2** *com*) A document or page created with page, paragraph, and text formats to be used as a basis for repeated use in other documents.

Text (1 *com*) Information presented as readable characters. (**2** *typ*) Typeset matter forming the main body of a publication.

Text chain (*com*) A set of linked text boxes, with text flowing from one to another.

Text type/matter (*typ*) Any TYPEFACE of a suitable

size for printing a body of text, usually in a range of 8pt to 14pt.

Thermography (*pri*) A printing process that emulates die stamping, in which sheets are printed with a sticky ink or varnish and then dusted with a fine, pigmented powder which forms a raised surface when fused to the paper by heat.

Thick (*typ*) The term sometimes used to describe a word space measuring one-third of an EM.

Thin (*typ*) The term sometimes used to describe a word space measuring one-fifth of an EM.

Thirty two mo, 32mo (*fin*) A SHEET cut or folded to one thirty-second of its basic size.

Thirty-two sheet (*pap*) A poster size measuring 120 x 160in. (3040 x 4060mm).

Threadless binding (*fin*) see PERFECT BINDING.

Throw out (*fin*) see FOLD OUT.

Thumb index (*fin*) An INDEX GUIDE in a book in which steps are cut down the FOREDGES of the page to provide a reference guide to the contents.

Tied letter (*typ*) see LIGATURE.

TIFF (*com*) *abb* Tagged image file format. A standard and popular graphics FILE FORMAT used for scanned, high-resolution, BITMAPPED images. The TIFF format can be used for black-and-white, GRAYSCALE, and color images which have been generated on different computer platforms.

Tint (1) The effect of the admixture of white to a solid color. (**2** *rep*) The effect achieved by breaking up a solid color into dots and allowing white paper to show through. Tints are specified in percentages of the solid color.

Tip in/on (*pri/fin*) A page or image printed as a single page and inserted separately into a book and secured by pasting one edge.

Tissues see LAYOUTS.

Title page The page, normally a right-hand page, at the front of a book which bears the title, name(s) of the author(s), the publisher, and any other relevant information.

Title sheet/section (*pri*) The first printed SHEET or SECTION (1) of a publication.

Title verso, T/V The VERSO (back) of the title

page of a book, usually containing copyright information.

Titling (*typ*) A HEADLINE type, always in CAPITALS.

Tonal value The relative densities of tones in an image. See also COLOR VALUE.

Tone line process (*rep*) A technique of producing line art from a continuous tone original by combining a negative and positive film image. Not to be confused with combination line and halftone.

Tone separation (*rep*) see POSTERIZE.

Tool (*com*) A feature of most graphics APPLICATIONS, consisting of a device (tool) which, when selected, turns the pointer into a shape representing that tool, which you then use to perform the designated task; i.e., you use a box tool for creating boxes.

Tooling (*fin*) A method of impressing decorations and lettering onto the covers of books by hand.

Tooth (*pap*) The surface quality of paper that enables it to hold a painting, drawing, or printing medium.

Track (**1** *pri*) The printing line from the front edge of a PLATE to the back. Items imposed in track will all be subject to the same inking adjustments on press. (**2** *com*) The term describing the concentric "rings" circumscribing a platter, in which DATA is stored. Each track is divided into SECTORS. (**3** *typ/com*) A term describing the adjustment of space between the CHARACTERS (1) in a selected piece of text. As distinct from KERNING, which only involves pairs of characters.

Trademark A word or symbol (™) identifying a product or service and linking it to its maker or supplier.

Tranny (*pho*) abb TRANSPARENCY.

Transfer lettering Lettering and other designs that are transferred to artwork by releasing them from the back of a plastic sheet by rubbing the front of the sheet.

Transparency (*pho*) A term normally used in reference to a color transparency, but applicable to any photographically developed image on transparent film – or even any image on a transparent base, whether

photographic or not.

Transpose (*typ/rep*) To swap the positions of any two items of text, or two images, either by design, or because they are wrongly ordered.

Trapping (*rep*) The slight overlap of two colors to eliminate gaps that may occur between them due to the normal fluctuations of registration during printing.

Trim marks (*rep/pri*) Marks on original artwork, film, or a printed sheet which act as a guide for trimming the sheet during finishing or as register marks during printing.

trs abb TRANSPOSE.

TrueType (*com*) Apple Computer's OUTLINE FONT format produced as an alternative to POSTSCRIPT. A single TrueType file is used both for printing and for screen rendering – unlike PostScript fonts, which require a screen font file as well as the printer font file.

Tungsten film (*pho*) Photographic color film intended for use in artificial light created by tungsten bulbs.

Turned commas (*typ*) see INVERTED COMMAS.

Turned-over cover The COVER of a book with flaps turned inside at the FOREDGE.

Twelve mo, 12mo (*fin*) A SHEET folded or cut to one twelfth its basic size.

Twenty-four-/24-bit color (*com*) The allocation of 24 BITS OF MEMORY to each PIXEL, giving a possible screen display of 16.7 million colors (a row of 24 bits can be written in 16.7 million different combinations of 0s and 1s).

Twice up ARTWORK prepared at twice the size at which it will be reproduced. Artwork that is drawn twice up will need to be reduced by one half, or 50 percent, to print at its intended size.

Twin-wire paper (*pap*) A machine manufactured paper with a smooth finish on both sides.

Two revolution press (*pri*) A printing press with a cylinder rotating twice for each IMPRESSION without interruption for inking of the plate.

Two up, three up (*pri*) Printing method in which more than one image, or a multiple of the same image, is printed on one side of a SHEET by one process.

Type area (*typ*) The area of a page designed to

contain the main body of text, thus creating margins.

Typeface (*typ*) The term describing a type design, including variations on that design such as italic and bold, but excluding all the other related designs, as distinct from TYPE FAMILY.

Type family (*typ*) A term describing all the variations related to a basic type design, such as Goudy Old Style, Goudy Catalogue, Goudy Handtooled, etc., as distinct from a TYPEFACE.

Type mark up (*typ*) see MARK-UP.

Type page (*typ*) see TYPE AREA.

Type scale/gauge (*typ*) A rule marked with a scale of line measurements in varying increments of point size.

Type series (*typ*) The identification of a typeface by a series number, i.e. Univers 55.

Type specimen sheet (*typ*) A printed sample of a font showing the full character set.

Type to type (*pri*) see FOLD TO PRINT.

Typescript (*typ*) A typed MANUSCRIPT.

Typesetting (**1**) The process of converting text into a recognized font and producing it in a form suitable for printing. A person whose job it is to set type is known as a "compositor," or "comp." (**2**) The text item produced by (1).

Typo (*typ*) abb Typographic error. An error occuring during typesetting, such as the wrong font or size, as distinct from a literal, such as a spelling mistake, which may also be an error in a MANUSCRIPT.

Typographer (**1**) A person whose occupation is typography. (**2**) See COMPOSITOR.

Typography The art and arrangement of type.

U

uc/lc (*typ*) abb UPPER CASE/LOWER CASE.

Ultraviolet (*rep*) Lightwaves beyond the visible portion of violet waves in the electromagnetic spectrum, which can be absorbed by some PHOTOSENSITIVE materials.

Uncoated book paper (*pap*) Paper used in printing books, catalogues, etc, in a range of finishes including ANTIQUE (rough) and SUPERCALENDERED (smooth).

Under-color removal

(UCR) (rep) The technique of removing unwanted color from scanned color separations either to reduce the amount of ink or because the colors cancel each other out, such as removing the MAGENTA and yellow dots when there is enough black and CYAN to cover. UCR can reduce TRAPPING problems in printing.

Unit system (typ) A system of type design in which character widths conform to unit measurements associated with the set of the character.

Universal Copyright Convention An international assembly that, in 1952, agreed protection for the originator of an "intellectual work" – a text, photograph, illustration, etc. – to prevent the use of that work without · permission from its creator or copyright owner. The work must carry the copyright mark ©, the name of the owner of the copyright, and the date of its first publication.

Universal Product Code An agreed coding system for product identification.

Unjustified (typ) Lines of type which do not align with both left and right margins, as does justified type. Unjustified type may be ranged left or right, or it may be centered. The appearance of unjustified type is also called "free line fall."

Unsewn binding (fin) see PERFECT BINDING.

Unsharp masking (rep/com) The technique of enhancing the details in a scanned image by exaggerating the density of PIXELS at the edges of a color change (the image is first blurred, hence the term "unsharp").

Upload (com) To send data to a distant computer. Opposite of DOWNLOAD.

Upper case (typ) The CAPITAL letters of a type font.

Upstroke (typ) The finer stroke in a type CHARACTER (1), originally the downward stroke of a pen in CALLIGRAPHY.

User interface (com) see GUI; INTERFACE.

Utility (com) A PROGRAM that enhances or supports the use of a computer generally, or APPLICATIONS specifically. Typical utilities are BACK-UP PROGRAMS, font management programs, file-imaging programs, defragmentation programs, file recovery programs, etc.

UV (rep) abb ULTRAVIOLET.

V

Vacuum frame (rep) A frame used during conventional reproduction to keep an ORIGINAL stable while a copy of it is made.

Value (rep) The tonal measure of a color relative to a scale running from black to white. Where the dark to light value of a color is determined by the degree, or intensity, of luminance it is called "brightness."

Vandyke print (rep) A photocopy print, producing the image as a dark brown print, either negative or positive.

Varnish (prn) A transparent solution mixed with ink or printed over ink to produce a glossy surface finish.

VDU/VDT (com) abb Visual display unit/visual display terminal. A device for displaying information forming the INPUT or OUTPUT of a computer system. See also MONITOR.

Verso The left-hand page of a book or, more precisely, the other side of a leaf from a recto (right-hand page). From the Latin "verso" = turned (leaf).

Vertical page A page in which the COPY is RIGHT READING when the page is held in a vertical position.

vide A Latin term meaning "see," used as a reference in FOOTNOTES.

Video A Latin term meaning "I see," now used in reference to all television-based products.

View camera (pho) A camera in which the image to be photographed is viewed on a ground glass screen behind the film plane at the back of the camera.

Vignette (rep) Strictly speaking, any image without a defined border, but also used to describe a halftone image in which the tones gradually fade out into the background, an effect produced by etching away the dots at the edges of the image.

Virtual (com) Computer jargon for "imaginary" or "conceptual," or something that seems as though it exists, but really it doesn't – or at least it does, but only until the SOFTWARE that created it doesn't! So "virtual reality" is an imagined reality, indistinguishable from real life provided the environment that created it is in operation. "Virtual memory" is a technique of making MEMORY seem larger than it really is by using whatever memory space, other than in its own RAM, that may be available elsewhere for holding data, such as on a HARD DISK, and loading it into main memory in such a way that it appears as if it were in main memory all the time.

Virus (com) A computer PROGRAM that is deliberately written to alter the normal operation of a computer. These virus programs are spread from computer to computer across NETWORKS or when DISKS are copied in one and used in another. Viruses may infect some FILES, but not others (say, APPLICATIONS, but not DOCUMENTS), and they manifest themselves in different ways, sometimes by CRASHING the computer, or by simply beeping, displaying a message, or causing strange behavior such as bouncing the pointer around the screen or altering font styles. Although very few viruses cause malicious damage, some may create serious problems. In any event, all computers should have virus protection software installed.

Visual A mock-up of the proposed appearance of a design or LAYOUT presented as a rough drawing, or if more highly finished, as a PRESENTATION VISUAL.

viz abb Videlicet, a Latin term meaning "namely," and used when citing a reference in FOOTNOTES.

Volume (com) A DEVICE or a PARTITION where DATA is stored.

W

Walk off (prn) The deterioration of the image on a printing plate, occurring during printing.

Wallet envelope (pap) An envelope with a rectangular flap.

Wallet fold (fin) see GATEFOLD.

Washout (rep) The rinsing, cleaning, and drying of NEGATIVES, film plates, etc., during processing.

Wash-up (prn) Cleaning ink from the printing press.

Watercolor printing (prn) Printing process using water-based inks and relatively porous paper so that colors are absorbed and can be mixed by overlapping the layers printed.

Watermark (pap) A

distinctive design
incorporated in paper
during manufacture.
Web (*pap*) Paper made in
a roll on a cylinder, or
"Fourdrinier," machine.
Web-fed (*pri*) Presses on
which paper is fed from a
reel as distinct from sheet-
fed printing presses.
Web (off)set (*pri*) Reel-fed
offset litho printing. The
three main systems are:
"blanket to blanket" when
two plates and two blanket
cylinders on each unit print
and perfect the web; three-
cylinder systems in which
plate blanket and
impression cylinders print
one side of the paper only;
and satellite or planetary
systems in which two,
three, or four plate and
blanket cylinders are
arranged around a
common impression
cylinder printing one side
of the web in as many
colors as there are plate
cylinders.
Weight (*typ*) The degree
of boldness of a TYPEFACE.
Wet on wet (*pri*) A term
describing the process of
printing on multicolor
presses, with each
successive ink color being
printed on the sheet before
the previous ink color has
time to dry.
Wet stripping (*rep*) The
stripping away of a film
base when the image has
been processed, but while
the film is still wet.
wf (*typ*) *abb* Wrong font, a
mark used in PROOF
correction where a
CHARACTER (1) of the wrong
TYPEFACE has been printed.
White line (*typ*) A space
between lines of type
equivalent to the type size,
including leading.
Whiteprint (*rep*) A
reproduction process in
which copies are
produced at the same size
as the ORIGINAL by direct
contact, the image being
formed by a light-sensitive
dye. The original for this
process must be on
transparent or translucent
material.
Wide-angle lens (*pho*) A
camera lens giving an
unusually wide angle of
view without distortion.
See also FISH-EYE LENS.
Widow (*typ*) Strictly
speaking, a short line at the
end of a paragraph that
falls at the top of a column
or page, but the term is
often used to describe a
single word at the end of
any paragraph.
Wild copy (*typ*) Typeset
words that are separate
from the main body of text
and that are to be used as

part of a chart or diagram,
or as annotation to an
illustration.
WIMP(S) (*com*) *abb*
WINDOWS, ICON, MOUSE (or
MENUS) and pointer – the
acronym for a graphical
user interface (GUI).
Window (*com*) An area on
the screen that displays the
contents of a DISK, folder, or
DOCUMENT. Windows can
be opened or closed,
moved around the DESKTOP,
and you can sometimes
change their size or
"scroll" through them.
Wire side (*pap*) The side
of paper which has been
carried on the wire mesh
of a manufacturing
machine and is highly
marked by the wire.
Wire stitch/stab (*fin*)
One of a line of wire
staples passed through the
back of a printed SECTION
(1) used as a method of
binding.
Woodfree/freesheet
(*pap*) Paper made from
chemical PULP containing
no wood fiber.
Word break (*typ*) see
HYPHENATE.
Word processor (**1** *com*)
A computer APPLICATION that
provides text editing
features such as spelling
checkers, indexing,
sorting, etc. (**2**) A
computer dedicated to
achieving (1).
**Work and tumble/turn/
twist** (*pri*) Work that is
printed entirely (and on
both sides of a sheet) from
one plate either: by
changing the gripper edge
(tumble); without changing
the gripper edge (turn); or
by turning the sheet at
right angles (twist).
Working (*pri*) A single
operation performed by a
printing machine, e.g.
embossing, inking.
WORM (*com*) *abb* Write
once read many, a large-
capacity DATA STORAGE
DEVICE utilizing OPTICAL
DISCS onto which data can
be written only once and
which can then never be
erased.
Wove paper (*pap*) Paper
with an smooth, even, and
fine "woven" surface,
rather than the parallel line
pattern of laid sheets.
Wraparound plate (*pri*) A
curved printing plate that
wraps around the cylinder
of a ROTARY PRESS.
**Wrap round/
wraparound** (*pri*) A
printed SECTION (1) of 4 or 8
pages folded around a full-
sized section when work is
gathered.
Wrappering (**1** *fin*) A
paper cover glued or
stitched to the spine of a

publication. (**2** *pri/fin*) Extra
leaves wrapped around a
section to make it up to the
required number of pages.
(**3** *pri/fin*) Illustration pages
wrapped around a section
of text only pages.
Write-protect (*com*) To
protect a DISK from erasure,
accidental or otherwise, or
from contamination by
VIRUSES, by preventing any
DATA from being written to
it or deleted from it,
although the contents can
still be read.
Wrong reading (*rep*)
Description of negative or
positive film on which the
text, if any, is read in
reverse, i.e. from right to
left, and in which the
photographic emulsion is
on the underside. Opposite
of RIGHT READING.
WYSIWYG (*com*)
(pronounced wizzywig) An
acronym for "what you see
is what you get," referring
to the accuracy of on-
screen rendering relative
to printed output.

X

x-height (*typ*) The height,
or "mean-line," of a LOWER
CASE letter, without
ASCENDERS or DESCENDERS.
Xerography (*rep*) A dry
copying process in which
electrostatically charged
powder is bonded to
paper.

Y

Yapp binding (*fin*) A
BOOKBINDING method in
which a limp COVER
projects over the edges of
the book's leaves. The
term derives from the
name of the London
bookseller who, in around
1860, first used such
binding.

Z

Zigzag book (*fin*) A book
made up of a continuous
strip of paper folded in an
ACCORDION FOLD. If secured
at the back, only one side
of the sheet is printed. If it
is printed on both sides,
the book must be left
unstitched.

Foreign language accents

Albanian	Lithuanian
â ç ë	ą č ę ė š ū ų ž
Czech	Norwegian
á č ď é ě í ň ó ř š ť ú ů ý ž	å æ ø
Danish	Polish
å æ ø	ą ć ę ł ń ó ś ź ż
Dutch	Portuguese
æ é è ê ë ó ò ô ij	á à â ã ç é è ê í ì ó ò ô õ ú ù
Esperanto	Romauntsch
ĉ ĝ ĵ ŝ ŭ (h)	ö ü
Estonian	Rumanian
ä ö õ š ü ž	à â ă è ì î ş ţ ù
Finnish	Scottish Gaelic
ä å ö	à é è ì ó ò ù
French	Serbo-Croatian
à â ç é è ë î ï ô œ ù û ü	č ć đ š ž
Friesian	Slovak
ä ê û	á ä č ď é í ľ ň ó ô ŕ š ť ú ý ž
German	Slovenian
ä ö ü ß	č š ž
Hungarian	Spanish
á é í ó ö ő ú ü ű	á é í ñ ó ú ü
Icelandic	Swedish
á æ ð é í ó ö œ þ ú ý	å ä ö
Italian	Turkish
à é è í ì î ó ò ú ù	â ç ğ ı î ö ş ü û İ
Latvian	Welsh
ā č ē ġ ī ķ ļ ņ ō ŗ š ū ž	ä â ë ê î ï ö ô ŵ ÿ ŷ

Greek and Roman numerals

Arabic	Roman	Greek	Arabic	Roman	Greek
1	I	α	20	XX	κ
2	II	β	30	XXX	λ
3	III	γ	40	XL	μ
4	IV	δ	50	L	ν
5	V	ε	60	LX	ξ
6	VI	f	70	LXX	ο
7	VII	ζ	80	LXXX	π
8	VIII	η	90	XC	ϙ
9	IX	ϑ	100	C	ρ
10	X	ι	200	CC	σ
11	XI	ια	300	CCC	τ
12	XII	ιβ	400	CD or CCCC	υ
13	XIII	ιγ	500	D	φ
14	XIV	ιδ	600	DC	χ
15	XV	ιε	700	DCC	ψ
16	XVI	ι	800	DCCC	ω
17	XVII	ιζ	900	CM	
18	XVIII	ιη	1000	M	
19	XIX	ιθ	2000	MM	

Greek alphabet

Αα	Alpha	Ηη	Eta	Νν	Nu	Ττ	Tau
Ββ	Beta	Θθ	Theta	Ξξ	Xi or Si	Υυ	Upsilon
Γγ	Gamma	Ιι	Iota	Οο	Omicron	Φφ	Phi
Δδ	Delta	Κκ	Kappa	Ππ	Pi	Χχ	Chi
Εε	Epsilon	Λλ	Lambda	Ρρ	Rho	Ψψ	Psi
Ζζ	Zeta	Μμ	Mu	Σσς	Sigma	Ωω	Omega

Mathematical symbols

Parenthesis	(	Equal or parallel	⊯	Less than	<
Bracket	[	Between	⟊	Greater than	>
Brace	{	Infinity	∞	Not less than	≮
Angle bracket, colloquially "Bra"	⟨	Varies as, proportional to	∝	Not greater than	≯
Angle bracket, colloquially "Ker"	⟩	Radical sign	√	Equivalent to or greater than	≳
Open bracket	⟦	Plus (Add)	+	Equivalent to or less than	≲
Factorial sign	!	Minus (Subtract)	−	Much less than	≪
Decimal point	·	Multiply	×	Much greater than	≫
Prime	′	Divide	÷	Not much less than	⋘̸
Double prime	″	Plus or minus	±	Not much greater than	⋙̸
Triple prime	‴	Equal to	=	Less than or greater than	≶
Quadruple prime	⁗	Is not equal to	≠	Greater than or less than	≷
Degree	°	Approximately equal to	≈	Less than or equal to	≦
Because or since	∵	Approximately equal to	≑	Less than or equal to	≤
Therefore, hence	∴	Approximately equal to	≏	Not less than nor equal to	≨̸
Sign of proportion	:	Approximately equal to	≃	Not greater than nor equal to	≩̸
Sign of proportion	::	Difference between	∼	Equiangular geometry	≧̲
Divided by, solidus	/	1 Is not equivalent to 2 Is not asymptotic to	≁		
Modulus, used thus	|x|			Approaches or tends to the limit	→
Parallel to	‖				
Congruent to	≡	Is approximately asymptotic to	≈		

Mutually implies	↔	Contains as subset	⊇	Digamma function	F
Implies	⊃	There exists	∃	Integral	∫
Is implied by	⊂	Gamma function	Γ	Contour integral	∮
Contained as subset within	⊆	Partial differentiation	∂		

Conversion factors

To convert	To	Multiply by
Inches	Centimeters	2.54
Centimeters	Inches	0.3937
Feet	Centimeters	30.4800613
Centimeters	Feet	0.0328
Yards	Meters	0.914
Meters	Yards	1.094
Miles	Meters	1609.3
Meters	Miles	0.000621
Square inches	Square centimeters	6.45162581
Square centimeters	Square inches	0.155
Square feet	Square meters	0.093
Square meters	Square feet	10.764
Square yards	Square meters	0.836
Square meters	Square yards	1.196
Cubic inches	Cubic centimeters	16.39
Cubic centimeters	Cubic inches	0.061
Cubic feet	Liters	28.3
Liters	Cubic feet	0.0353
Cubic feet	Gallons (imperial)	6.24
Gallons (imperial)	Cubic feet	0.1602
Cubic feet	Gallons (US)	5.1959
Gallons (US)	Cubic feet	0.1924
Gallons (imperial)	Gallons (US)	1.20095
Gallons (US)	Gallons (imperial)	0.83267
Gallons(US)	Liters	3.785306
Liters	Gallons (US)	0.264179
Gallons (imperial)	Liters	4.546
Liters	Gallons (imperial)	0.22
Cubic feet	Cubic meter	0.028317
Cubic meter	Cubic feet	35.31467
Cubic yards	Cubic meters	0.7645549
Cubic meters	Cubic yards	1.307951
Acres	Hectares	0.404686
Hectares	Acres	2.471054
Square miles	Square kilometers	2.58999
Square kilometers	Square miles	0.3861022
Pounds (avoirdupois)	Kilograms	0 4536
Kilograms	Pounds (avoirdupois)	2.2046
Ounces (avoirdupois)	Grams	28.35
Grams	Ounces (avoirdupois)	0.0352
Grains	Grams	0.065
Grams	Grains	15.432
Hundredweight (short)	Kilograms	45.359237
Kilograms	Hundredweight (short)	0.02204623
British fl.oz.	US fl.oz.	0.961
US fl.oz.	British fl.oz.	1.04058

To convert	To	Multiply by
US fl.oz.	ml	29.57270
ml	US fl.oz.	0.033815
British fl.oz.	ml	30.7728
ml	British fl.oz.	0.0325
Hundredweight (long)	Kilograms	50.8
Kilograms	Hundredweight (long)	0.01968
Tons	Kilograms	1016.0
Kilograms	Tons	0.000984
Hundredweight (long)	Pounds (avoirdupois)	112.0
Pounds (avoirdupois)	Hundredweight (long)	0.00893
Hundredweight (short)	Pounds (avoirdupois)	100.0
Pounds (avoirdupois)	Hundredweight (short)	0.01
Pounds (avoirdupois)	Tons (long)	2240.0
Tons (long)	Pounds (avoirdupois)	0.000446
Pounds (avoirdupois)	Tons (short)	2000.0
Tons (short)	Pounds (avoirdupois)	0.0005
Tons (metric)	Tons (short)	1.102
Tons (short)	Tons (metric)	0.90718
Lb/inch^2	Gm/cm^2	70.307
Gm/cm^2	Lb/inch^2	0.014223
Lb/inch^2	Kg/cm^2	0.070307
Kg/cm^2	Lb/inch^2	14.223533
Lb/feet^2	Kg/m^2	4.883
Kg/m^2	Lb/feet^2	0.205
Horsepower	Force de cheval	1.014
Force de cheval	Horsepower	0.9861
Horsepower	Watts	746.0
Watts	Horsepower	0.00134
Watts	Kg m/sec	0.1
Kg m/sec	Watts	10.0

I US lb. = 1 British lb. (avoirdupois)   I US yd. = 1 British yd.

To convert Fahrenheit to Centigrade:
Deduct 32, multiply by 5, divide by 9

To convert Centigrade to Fahrenheit:
Multiply by 9, divide by 5, add 32

Mathematical formulae

To find the circumference of a circle:	**To find the diameter of a circle:**	**To find the radius of a circle:**
Multiply its diameter by 3.1416	Multiply its circumference by 0.3183	Multiply its circumference by 0.1592
Or divide its diameter by 0.3183	Or divide its circumference by 3.1416	Or divide its circumference by 6.2832

Metric Setting Style

millimeter	mm	degrees Kelvin	°K	vapor density	v.d.
centimeter	cm	alternating current	a.c.	kilometers per hour	km h^{-1} or km/h
gram	g	atomic weight	at.wt		
meter	m	molecular weight	mol.wt		
kilogram	kg	freezing point	f.p.	square meter	m^2
second	s	melting point	m.p.	square centimeter	cm^2
hour	h	ultraviolet	u.v.	gram per square meter	g/m^2
degrees centigrade	°C	vapor pressure	v.p.		

Reference marks

The following marks are available on most fonts, and if more than six are required, they should be doubled-up—two asterisks, two daggers, etc.

Asterisk	*	Dagger	†	Double dagger	‡
Section mark	§	Paragraph mark	¶	Parallel	‖

Metric prefixes

		Symbol				
mega	means a million times	M	centi	means a hundred part of	c
kilo	means a thousand times	k	milli	means a thousandth part of	m
hecto	means a hundred times	h	micro	means a millionth part of	u
deca	means ten times	da	deci	means a tenth part of	d

Computer storage measurements

Although "kilo" means one thousand, computers use a binary system of measurement and instruction, so each number is doubled: 2; 4; 8; 16; 32; 64; 128; 256; 512; 1,024, etc.

8 bits = 1 byte

1,024 bytes = 1 kilobyte (K)

1,024 kilobytes = 1 megabyte (Mb) (1,048,576 bytes)

1,024 megabytes = 1 gigabyte (gig) (1,073,741,824 bytes)

Offset litho printing — problem identifer

Problem	Causes
Binding Image prints very weakly despite looking strong on the plate.	1 Excess gum on the plate may be preventing the image from accepting ink. 2 The ink rollers may be glazed, thus preventing ink from reaching the plate.
Broken images Parts of the image are not printing, or there are fingerprints on the plate.	1 Tape or opaquing solution may be obscuring part of the image on the film. 2 The vacuum frame glass may be dirty. 3 The plate may be underexposed, causing the image to break up after a few impressions.
Dot gain Colors appear stronger on printing.	1 Halftone dots on the film may have become larger during printing, or during exposure or development of the film or plate, or on contact duplication of the film. 2 Excess ink on the plate
Ghosting Weak ink on certain areas.	1 Heavy area elsewhere is not leaving enough ink for affected area.
Halation Copy appears enlarged at the edges; shadows on the type or the dot spreads.	1 Overexposure of the plate exaggerating poor stripping. 2 Poor plate contact during exposure.
Hickies Small areas of unwanted solid color surrounded by a halo.	Specks of dirt on the plate or blanket cylinder.
Picking Fibers of paper lifting, leaving white specks.	1 Poorly sized paper. 2 Ink too sticky. 3 Suction caused by the blanket cylinder.
Plugging Dirty printed image, with dots filling in.	1 Fresh developer contaminated by old developer on the plate sponge. 2 Flecks of dried developer or gum on the plate.
Scumming Ink printing on the non-image areas.	1 Improper sensitization of the plate. 2 Dirty dampening rollers.
Slur Image appears to have "skidded."	Movement of paper or plate on the press.

Envelopes

US sizes	ISO C series	mm	inches
9 x 12in	C0	917 x 1297	36.00 x 51.20
12 x 15^1/$_2$ in	C1	648 x 917	25.60 x 36.00
15 x 18in	C2	458 x 648	18.00 x 25.60
17 x 22in	C3	324 x 458	12.80 x 18.00
22 x 27in	C4	229 x 324	9.00 x 12.80
	C5	162 x 229	6.40 x 9.00
	C6	114 x 162	4.50 x 6.40
	C7	81 x 114	3.20 x 4.50
	DL	110 x 220	4.33 x 8.66
	C7/6	81 x 162	3.19 x 6.38

Paper usage formulae

To calculate the number of sheets of paper required to print a book (excluding covers):

$$\frac{\text{Number of copies to be printed x Number of pages in book}}{\text{Number of pages printing on both sides of sheet}} = \text{Number of sheets required}$$

To calculate the number of copies obtainable from a given quantity of paper:

$$\frac{\text{Number of sheets x Number of pages printing on both sides of sheet}}{\text{Number of pages in book}} = \text{Number of copies}$$

Paper weight, thickness, and bulk

Weight
Under the standard system, paper weight is expressed in pounds per ream (500 sheets) calculated on the basic size for that grade. For example, if 25 x 38inch is the basic size for book paper, it is called 70-pound paper because 500 sheets of this grade weigh 70 pounds. However, paper is usually priced on a 1,000-sheet basis.

Under the metric system, paper weight is expressed in kilograms per 1,000 sheets (or per 100 boards). This can be calculated by using the following formula:

$$\frac{\text{g /m}^2 \text{ x width (cm) x length (cm)}}{1,000} = \text{kg per 1,000 sheets}$$

Thickness and bulk
Thickness (sometimes referred to as caliper) is measured in thousandths and millionths of an inch (or millimeters under the metric system). However, in book production, where the thickness of the book is determined by the bulk of the paper, the formula is expressed differently. Bulk for book papers is calculated according to the number of pages per inch (or millimeter) of the given basic weight. Therefore, the bulk of a 50-pound book paper can range from 310 to 800 pages per inch.

Weights of book papers per 1,000 sheets

Basis (lb)	50	60	70	80	100	120
8^1/$_2$ x 11	9.5	11.8	13.5	15.7	19.7	23.6
17^1/$_2$ x 22^1/$_2$	41	50	58	65	83	99
19 x 25	50	60	70	80	100	120
23 x 29	70	84	98	112	140	169
23 x 35	85	102	119	136	169	203
24 x 36	90	110	128	146	182	218
25 x 35	100	120	140	160	200	240
35 x 45	166	198	232	256	332	398
36 x 48	182	218	254	292	364	436
38 x 50	200	240	280	320	400	480
*metric (gsm)	74	89	104	118	148	178

American paper sizes (untrimmed)

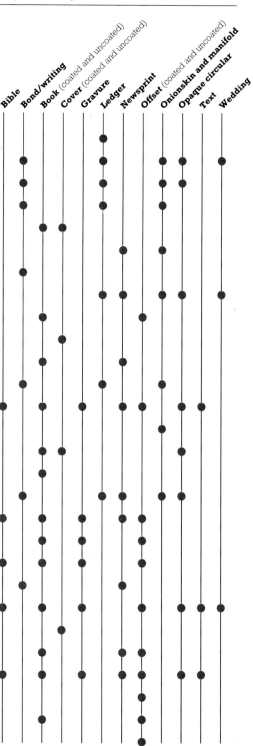

inches	mm	Bible	Bond/writing	Book (coated and uncoated)	Cover (coated and uncoated)	Gravure	Ledger	Newsprint	Offset (coated and uncoated)	Onionskin and manifold	Opaque circular	Text	Wedding
16 x 21	406.2 x 533.4					•							
17 x 22	431.8 x 558.8		•			•			•	•			•
17 x 28	431.8 x 711.2		•			•				•			
19 x 24	482.6 x 609.6		•			•			•				
20 x 26	508.0 x 660.4			•	•								
21 x 32	533.4 x 812.8						•		•				
22 x 24	558.8 x 609.6		•										
22 x 34	558.8 x 863.6						•	•	•	•			•
22½ x 35	571.5 x 889.0		•					•					
23 x 35	584.2 x 889.0				•								
24 x 36	609.6 x 914.4			•				•					
24 x 38	609.6 x 965.2		•			•			•				
25 x 38	635.0 x 965.2	•		•		•			•	•		•	
26 x 34	660.4 x 863.6								•				
26 x 40	660.4 x 1016.0			•	•								
26 x 48	660.4 x 1219.2			•									
28 x 34	711.2 x 863.6			•		•			•	•			
28 x 42	711.2 x 1066.8	•		•		•		•	•				
28 x 44	711.2 x 1117.6			•		•			•				
32 x 44	812.8 x 1117.6	•		•		•			•				
34 x 44	863.6 x 1117.6		•				•						
35 x 45	889.0 x 1143.0	•	•	•		•		•		•	•		•
35 x 46	889.0 x 1168.4				•								
36 x 48	914.4 x 1219.2						•	•					
38 x 50	965.2 x 1270.0	•		•		•		•		•		•	
38 x 52	965.2 x 1320.8							•					
41 x 54	1041.4 x 1371.6			•				•					
44 x 64	1117.6 x 1625.6							•					

British paper sizes (untrimmed)

Sizes of Printing Papers

	inches				mm		
Foolscap	17	x	13 ½		432	x	343
Double Foolscap	27	x	17		686	x	432
Crown	20	x	15		508	x	381
Double Crown	30	x	20		762	x	508
Quad Crown	40	x	30		1016	x	762
Double Quad Crown	60	x	40		1524	x	1016
Post	19 ¼	x	15 ½		489	x	394
Double Post	31½	x	19 ½		800	x	495
Double Large Post	33	x	21		838	x	533
Sheet and ½ Post	23 ½	x	19 ½		597	x	495
Demy	22 ½	x	17 ½		572	x	445
Double Demy	35	x	22 ½		889	x	572
Quad Demy	45	x	35		1143	x	889
Music Demy	20	x	15 ½		508	x	394
Medium	23	x	18		584	x	457
Royal	25	x	20		635	x	508
Super Royal	27 ½	x	20 ½		699	x	521
Elephant	28	x	23		711	x	584
Imperial	30	x	22		762	x	559

ISO A series (untrimmed)

The "A" series system of sizing paper was first adopted in Germany in 1922 where it is still referred to as "DIN A." The sizes were calculated in such a way that each size is made by dividing the size immediately above into two equal parts. The sizes are all the same geometrically as they are made using the same diagonal. The basic size (AO) is one square meter in area It is important to remember that the "A" series sizes refer to the trimmed sheet. The untrimmed sizes are known as "RA." About 26 countries have now officially adopted the "A" system, and it is likely that this system will gradually replace the wide range of paper sizes still used in Great Britain and the USA "B" sizes are used when intermediate sizes are required between two adjacent "A" sizes. Unlike the metricated "A" series of paper sizes, British and American systems refer to the untrimmed size. In Britain sizes are usually referred to by name, but as this can lead to confusion, both the name and the size should be given in any specification.

	inches	mm		inches	mm
A0	33.11 x 46.81	841x 1189	A6	4.13 x 5.83	105 x 148
A1	23.39 x 33.11	594 x 841	A7	2.91 x 4.13	74 x 105
A2	16.54 x 23.39	420 x 594	A8	2.05 x 2.91	52 x 74
A3	11.69 x 16.54	297 x 420	A9	1.46 x 2.05	37 x 52
A4	8.27 x 11.69	210 x 297	A10	1.02 x 1.46	26 x 37
A5	5.83 x 8.27	148 x 210			

	inches	mm		inches	mm
RA0	33.86 x 48.03	860 x 1220	SRA0	38.58 x 50.39	980 x 1280
RA1	25.02 x 33.86	610 x 860	SRA1	25.20 x 35.43	640 x 900
RA2	16.93 x 24.02	430 x 610	SRA2	17.72 x 25 20	450 x 640

ISO B series (untrimmed)

	inches	mm		inches	mm
B0	39.37 x 55.67	1000 x 1414	B6	4.92 x 6.93	125 x 176
B1	27.83 x 39.37	707 x 1000	B7	3.46 x 4.92	88 x 125
B2	19.68 x 27.83	500 x 707	B8	2.44 x 3.46	62 x 88
B3	13.90 x 19.68	353 x 500	B9	1.73 x 2.44	44 x 62
B4	9.84 x 13.90	250 x 353	B10	1.22 x 1.73	31 x 44
B5	6.93 x 9.84	176 x 250